D1548101

A MARITIME KILL WEB FORCE IN THE MAKING

DETERRENCE AND WARFIGHTING IN THE XXIST CENTURY

By Robbin F. Laird

&

Edward Timperlake

This book is dedicated to Ed Timperlake's only Uncle Edward Thomas Conkling KIA on Iwo Jima, to Ed's father the late James E. Timperlake, to James's Navy wife Joan who together were "plank owners" putting into Commission the USS Henry Clay SSBN-625, to Ed's Squadron mates of VMFA-321, the Hell's Angles, and to Ed's brother former Navy surgeon Dr. Roger Timperlake MD USN and with recognition that in the Timperlake family, pride, sacrifice and service runs deep to the sea services and to Bruce Laird, the brother of Robbin Laird, whose sense of humor and perspectives on life allowed for coping with the insanity of the global COVID-19 pandemic.

CONTENTS

THE PERSPECTIVE OF
VICE ADMIRAL DEWOLFE MILLER (RET.),
FORMER COMMANDER NAVAL AIR FORCES

I first met Dr. Robbin Laird and Ed Timperlake in the summer of 2016 when I was the Director of Air Warfare (OPNAV N-98) on the staff of the Chief of Naval Operations. Robbin and Ed previously interviewed Navy Flag Officers who occupied the N-98 office, and I was next in line.

The interview was fascinating - unlike any I had previously experienced. They didn't just ask questions and have me respond. Instead, we engaged in a fulsome discussion about various aspects of warfare. The 30-minute interview turned into an hour and a half exploration on a myriad of topics ranging from platforms and sensors (kill web) to the need for more advanced training, to how we operate and integrate with other services and allies. To be honest, it was invigorating and stimulating, if not mentally taxing. In short, they made me think. This was the start of an ongoing professional relationship that was sustained throughout my Naval career and continues today.

As I pen this forward for Robbin and Ed's book "A Maritime Kill Web Force in the Making: Deterrence and Warfighting in the 21st Century," the USS CARL VINSON Carrier Strike Group just returned from deployment with the first iteration of the "Airwing of the Future" embarked. Specifically, this was the first naval deployment involving the fifth generation F-35C with the highly versatile CMV-22B aircraft onboard a large deck nuclear powered aircraft carrier. These new capabilities joined an already formidable airwing that included the proven capabilities of the E-2D, FA-18E/F/G and both MH-60R and MH-60S helicopters. Of note, the Navy will begin incorporating unmanned capability with the MQ-25 Stingray in a few years as the next evolutionary step for the future airwing.

In many ways, CARL VINSON's deployment to the South China Sea reflects several of the concepts that are discussed in depth in this book. CARL VINSON's airwing was one of the first to benefit from high-end training conducted in Fallon, NV (Chapter 2: The Integratable Air Wing). They were supported by Maritime Patrol Reconnaissance Force (MPRF) assets (Chapter 6: An ISR-Empowered Force), interacted with other Strike Groups - both foreign and U.S. - in a distributed fashion (Chapter 3: Distributed Maritime Ops and Basing Architecture), and conducted bilateral training exercises with allies, including Australia (Chapter 7: Kill Web "Matesmanship"). The fact that USS CARL VINSON is the 3rd oldest aircraft carrier in the U.S. Navy's active inventory and that her weapon system (the airwing) was the most formidable ever, testifies to the versatility and relevance of the large deck nuclear powered aircraft carrier. In Chapter 5, they explore the carrier and kill web task forces to a greater extent, focusing on the FORD Class aircraft carrier which will defend freedom, project power, and continue to support advanced weapons systems (many of which have not yet been designed or developed) for the next 100 years. To that end, the authors couldn't have timed the release of their book any better as USS GERALD R. FORD (CVN78) is expected to commence workups and conduct overseas operations with allies and partners later this year.

By design, the U.S. Navy's forward-deployed operations are shaped in direct support of national security; as such, it's important to remember that the adversary always gets a vote. Today, Russia is threatening Ukraine, China continues to evolve and expand her fleet at a blistering pace, Iran and North Korea remain troublesome, and the threat of terrorism endures. They tackle these challenges head on, providing keen insight on how Naval Forces should respond (Chapter 8: It's not my father's Second Fleet).

Ultimately, peer threats are what drives change and inspires clarity in the way the Navy mans, trains, and equips its forces to defend freedom and deter aggression on a global scale. Those steps require bold decisions by many leaders at many levels, and the concepts and ideas covered in this book will challenge our leaders and decision makers to think, much like the authors challenged me several years ago. In that way, "The Emergence of the Maritime Kell Web Force: Deterrence and Warfighting in the 21st Century" encourages all of us to open up our "thought aperture" and to reflect on the difficult task in front of us, to develop a more networked and integrated Navy that is prepared to fight and win against any future threat, any day.

Enjoy the read.

THE PERSPECTIVE OF
VICE ADMIRAL TIM BARRETT, AO CSC (RET.),
FORMER CHIEF OF NAVY, AUSTRALIA

The maritime battlespace is not what it used to be. This has never been clearer than in the Indo-Pacific region – Australia's part of the world. Changing geo-strategic circumstances, rising nation state ambitions, challenges to political institutions, have all created vast uncertainty in the region. This is occurring within an era of staggering escalation in technological advancement.

But the issue is a global one. The tenets that have driven maritime strategic thinking in the post-Cold War era have been largely rendered obsolete.

The new environment is fast paced, connected, distributed, and relies on more than just having common equipment in the fleet. It requires a new way of thinking about how force is applied and where capability focus needs to be.

As strategic threats develop more rapidly, operational maneuver will need to be more agile to deliver the required tactical outcomes across the warfare spectrum. A commander's success will rely on their ability to better exploit all capability available to them, regardless of who owns it, through technologically enabled systems. Understanding the kill web and thinking differently about how force is applied is key. This publication explains why.

The transition of U.S. forces to this kind of thinking is underway as is clearly shown in the authors discussions with key leaders across the services. Whilst technology has enabled a more agile approach, it is only the means to an end. Strategic thinking needs to be skillfully applied to ensure the full extent of available capability is connected to maximise each part of the kill web. The collection and sharing of trusted information, by and within all assets available to the force, to inform agile and timely decisions is vital. The integration of sensors and shooter at a force level is necessary.

Whilst the U.S. military retains its pre-eminent role in this transformation, Australia too has demonstrated a similar kind of thinking in its recent capability development and acquisition approaches. The emphasis has been on connectivity, accelerated tactical decision making, as well as common equipment, that allows integration of systems within single services, across services and into allied services in a deliberate and disciplined manner. This is essential because the future of combat is to bring trusted and verifiable assets to the fight to enhance the commander's ability to use the full strength of the distributed force when required. This publication provides a timely reminder of why the transformation of today's force is so necessary.

PREFACE

We have worked together for several years. During that time, we have traveled together and visited several U.S. Air Force, U.S. Navy, U.S. Army, and U.S. Marine Corps bases and conducted a wide-ranging set of interviews with the operational forces. We have been impressed with the fighting forces and their innovations. We have written this book around those discussions, visits, and interviews.

This is not a book designed to provide a comprehensive forecast of the future of the fleet or writing a future Jane's fighting ships. But it is a book which focuses on the transition in the fleet, and the relevant joint and coalition forces to blue water maneuver warfare. With the Marines and the Navy shifting from a primary or significant focus on the Middle Eastern land wars, the focus has shifted significantly to blue water operations or blue water expeditionary operations. The U.S. Navy never turned its back on these operations during the land wars, but the fleet was redirected to focus on support for the land wars as a primary mission. This was a political choice made by the nation's political and strategic leadership. Stability operations in faraway lands trumped a focus on the priority defense of the nation against the rising authoritarian "great" powers.

But the return to maneuver warfare, although drawing upon historical legacies, notably from World War II and the Cold War, is unfolding in a new digital age. The focus on the high-end fight against competitors, the return of the great power competition, and the importance of being able to fight across the spectrum of warfare is unfolding in a new phase of technological development.

And many of these developments are unfolding before us now. Notable examples are the Osprey and fifth-generation aircraft. The U.S. forces are the only military operating a high-speed assault aircraft for their

Marines, Air Force and Navy. The U.S. and its allies are flying a common Intelligence, Surveillance and Reconnaissance (ISR), Command and Control (C^2) combat aircraft, the F-35; and the global F-35 enterprise is already having a significant combat and deterrent impact. We wrote about these impacts in our 2013 book, *Rebuilding American Military Power in the Pacific.*

F-35 as Allied Pacific Lynchpin

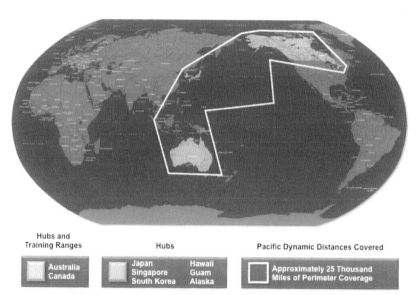

We crafted this graphic in 2012-2013 to project the potential impact of shaping an F-35 enterprise operating in the Pacific. We are still waiting for Canada, but we are now seeing a growth in the sea-based version of F-35s in the case of Japan, and South Korea.

We are focused on the fighting forces and their innovation. Over the past two decades we have interviewed together and separately hundreds of U.S. and allied servicemen and woman, and political and military leaders. Notably, with a focus on the return of great power competition we have focused on those who are charged with the fight tonight and who are driving operational changes for the fighting force. The drive for change is often slowed by excessive bureaucracy from Washington and on crafting and debating long-range force design concepts to show that any new

Administration has a bright new idea and a new departure point. But these are often based on briefing charts more than operational experience or knowledge of how our allies fight and are prepared to fight. Briefing charts do kill but the primary fatalities are thought and discussion about practical ways ahead, rather than enhancing the capability to kill adversaries. When we refer to the fighting Navy it is about those who work in the fleet, deploy into conflict situations, work with allies and are rethinking how to win tomorrow's fight with the evolution of the force we have enhanced by what can be introduced in a timely manner.

It is about the combat effect to be delivered in the mid-term which is at the heart of our book. The template being created for a maritime distributed force—or what we prefer to call an integrated distributed force, provides a solid foundation for the way ahead. Such a template will be able to incorporate new technologies such as new weapons, and autonomous systems within an agile fleet that will be then able to make decisions at the tactical edge within the context of broader mission command C^2.

We are not seeking to write a comprehensive narrative about the future fleet; we are focused on how the fighting U.S. Navy is shaping its future in combat redesign in the next few years. And in so doing, we focus upon the warfighting centers at the heart of prepping the force, as well as how the kill web focus is at the heart of reimaging how the amphibious fleet and the large deck carrier will work together in the years ahead. The arrival of fifth generation air combat capabilities is part of generating a payload revolution to empower a distributed but integratable force.

We have done many interviews in support of the book and spent several months with the Norfolk commands and the North Carolina-based Marines to discuss with them how they were reshaping the force. We thank all of those who have given their time and insights in the process of researching and writing this book.

If you are looking for a book written by armchair strategists or cubical commandos, this book is not for you. We talk with the warfighters and discuss ways to think about the way ahead with the force we have which is being reshaped by near to midterm capabilities. This is not a book about the fleet in 2050, for at the end of the day how well did strategists forecast 2020 from the perspective of 2019?

The book is written in part to try to close the significant gap between discussions inside the Beltway about the way ahead for the force as compared to the perspective of the warriors who both have to fight tonight and evolve the force towards one with greater relevance and capability. Our former boss, Secretary Mike Wynne, often made the point that we have 80% of our force in 20 years right now: how to make that force more lethal going forward with new capabilities evolving into the force? If you have to fight tonight, the future is not all that abstract as it is for armchair thinkers and cubical commandos.

This book builds on several books published earlier which focus on specific aspects of the geopolitical environment, and on combat transitions underway. This book can be read in the context of a wider range of work pursued over the past thirty years. We have published four books in the past few years which focus on the geopolitical transitions and can be read as background to this book, and which provide further detail on reshaping the force to operate in the evolving full spectrum crisis management environment.

The first was published in 2013 and is entitled, *Rebuilding American Military Power in the Pacific: A 21st Century Strategy*. The second was published in 2020 and entitled, *The Return of Direct Defense in Europe: Meeting the Challenge of XXIst Century Authoritarian Powers*. The third focused on Australian defense and was published in 2021 and was entitled *Joint by Design: The Evolution of Australian Defence Strategy*. The fourth focused on the training dimension of crafting an integrated distributed force and was published in 2021 and entitled, *Training for the High-End Fight: The Strategic Shift of the 2020s*. In addition, there is a companion book to this one published earlier this year which focused in detail on the various phases of USMC transformation since 2007 and provides a more detailed look at the USMC side of the dynamics of change working with the U.S. Navy.

We discuss the role of nuclear weapons briefly in this book but have dealt with this issue much more comprehensively, including in several published books on nuclear issues in the past. These books include, *France, the Soviet Union, and the Nuclear Weapons Issue*; *The Future of Deterrence: NATO Nuclear Forces after INF*; *The Soviet Union and Strategic Arms*; and *The Soviet Union, the West and the Nuclear Arms Race*.

As mentioned earlier, we conducted several interviews during our research for the book. We have provided footnotes in some cases for those interviews, but, of course, in the case of quotations from other sources we have clearly footnoted those. We would like to thank all of those at various Naval and Marine Corps commands as well as our allies in Australia and Europe who have provided insights throughout our book-writing process.

CHAPTER ONE:
THE COMING OF THE KILL WEB FORCE

As the U.S. Navy returns to a priority focus on maneuver warfare at sea, it is doing so in a new strategic context, and with a new approach to reshaping the combat force. The new strategic context is provided by the rise of the 21st century authoritarian powers. The force structure response to the challenge of dealing with authoritarian military powers is to reshape the force to work across the extended battlespace with an integratable force, both to enhance lethality and survivability of the overall force, and to augment the capability to be present in areas of interest. This reshaping effort can be characterized as building out an integrated, distributed force enabled by interactive kill webs. The kill web has arrived along with the enhanced focus on configuring a distributed force which is integratable.

Operating and Prevailing in the Extended Battlespace
The Offensive-Defensive Enterprise Operating As a Kill Web

Strategic Direction
Senior Commanders Adjust Force Packages in a Dynamic Response as Operations Evolve and Outcomes and Effects are Identified

Distributed C2
Empowering the force operating at the key choke points or the critical nodes of attack or defense

21st Century Con-Ops

ISR Reach and Assessment
A Continuous Process Delivered by Connected Platforms Operating in the Battlespace

Distributed Strike
Multi-Domain Strike Capabilities Deployed by Ground, Air, Space and Maritime Forces

Secure Information Parsimony
"The right information delivered to the right person, at the right time and at the right place."

Conceptualizing the extended battlespace within which the integrated distributed force operates. Credit: *Second Line of Defense.*

The kill web paradigm is laying down the template for building out the future force. New technologies coming to the fleet, such as maritime autonomous systems, the weapons revolution, decision making aided by artificial intelligence, and new material technologies will build out the capabilities to have a more effective integrated distributed force. But it is not just about technology. It is about working new training and exercise approaches as well as shaping new ways to share data, make decisions and carry out operations in an extended battlespace with allies as well. Such force integration capabilities at the tactical edge will enable the kind of crisis management and combat capabilities needed to deal with the challenges in the new strategic environment.

What is the Kill Web?

We first discussed the kill web in terms of a spider web concept. And we did that in a 2013 interview with Rear Adm. Moran when he was head of N-98 in Op Nav. We raised that point in our discussion with him about the USS Gerald R. Ford. He described the new carrier as operating much more flexibly than a traditional carrier, and one which can become a central piece in a combat spider web, rather than operating at the center of a concentrated carrier task force. According to Moran: "The Ford will be very flexible and can support force concentration or distribution. And it can operate as a flagship for a distributed force as well and tailored to the mission set. When combined with the potential of the F-35, FORD will be able to handle information and communications at a level much greater than the Nimitz class carriers.

"People will be able to share information across nations, and this is crucial. We call it maritime domain awareness, but now you've included the air space, that's part of that maritime domain."[1]

We continued that discussion later with Rear Adm. Manazir both when he was at N-98 and N-9 in Op Nav. In our 2016 interview with Rear Adm. Manazir, we discussed the kill web approach as a way to shape more

---

1   "The USS Ford in the U.S. Navy's Future: Enabling the Distributed Force," *Second Line of Defense* (May 15, 2013), https://sldinfo.com/2013/05/ the-uss-ford-in-the-u-s-navys-future-enabling-the-distributed-force/.

effective integration of forces and convergence of efforts. The kill chain is a linear concept which is about connecting assets to deliver fire power; the kill web is about distributed operations and the ability of force packages or modular task forces to deliver force dominance in a specific area of interest. It is about building integration from the ground up so that forces can work seamlessly together through multiple networks, operating at the point of interest.

In that interview, he highlighted the key significance of evolving C^2 capabilities to deliver a kill web capability. "The hierarchical CAOC is an artifact of nearly 16 years of ground war where we had complete air superiority; however, as we build the kill web, we need to be able to make decisions much more rapidly. As such, C^2 is ubiquitous across the kill web. Where is information being processed? Where is knowledge being gained? Where is the human in the loop? Where can core C^2 decisions best be made and what will they look like in the fluid battlespace?

"The key task is to create decision superiority. But what is the best way to achieve that in the fluid battlespace we will continue to operate in? What equipment and what systems allow me to ensure decision superiority?

"We are creating a force for distributed fleet operations. When we say distributed, we mean a fleet that is widely separated geographically, capable of extended reach. Importantly, if we have a network that shares vast amounts of information and creates decision superiority in various places, but then gets severed, we still need to be able to fight independently without those networks. This requires significant and persistent training with new technologies but also informs us about the types of technologies we need to develop and acquire in the future.

"Additionally, we need to have mission orders in place so that our fleet can operate effectively even when networks are disrupted during combat; able to operate in a modular-force approach with decisions being made at the right level of operations for combat success."-

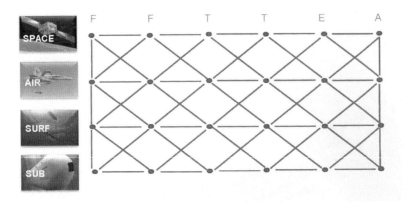

In a presentation to the Williams Foundation, Canberra, Australia on March 22, 2018, Rear Admiral Manazir then retried, provided his graphic representation of how to understand the kill web.

In the graphic provided by Rear Admiral (Retired) Manazir in the Williams Foundation 2018 seminar, he took the sequence of find, fix, track, target, engage and assess and highlighted how those functions were now exercised in a distributed integrated manner by the various platforms operating within a task force. This task force can be understood either organized organically or scalable and aggregable and operating as flexible modular task forces. With the distribution of sensors and strike throughout the battlespace, the force operates as a strike and sensing grids to gain combat dominance.

In some ways, the difference can be seen as a shift from a linear kill chain to a distributed kill web. The difference in focus was highlighted in a discussion in 2020 with Cmdr. Peter "Two Times" Salvaggio, the head of the new Maritime Intelligence Surveillance and Reconnaissance (MISR) program at the Navy's Naval Air Warfare Development Center, at Air Station Fallon, Nevada. "We need a paradigm shift: The Navy needs to focus on the left side of the kill chain." The kill chain is described as find, fix, target, engage and assess. Kill chain is to find, fix, track, target, engage and assess. For the U.S. Navy, the weight of effort has been upon target and engage. As "Two Times" puts it "But if you cannot find, fix or track something, you never get to target."

There is another challenge as well: in a crisis, knowing what to hit and what to avoid is crucial to crisis management. This clearly requires the kind of ISR management skills to inform the appropriate decision makers as well. The ISR piece is particularly challenging as one operates across a multi-domain battlespace to be able to identify the best ISR information, even if it is not contained within the ISR assets within your organic task force. And the training side of this is very challenging. That challenge might be put this way: How does one build the skills in the Navy to do what you want to do with regard to managed ISR data and deliver it in the correct but timely manner and how to get the command level to understand the absolute centrality of having such skill sets?

Here we are entering the domain of the kill web. The focus is upon how force packages are configured, and how they are empowered to leverage ISR and fire capabilities at the point of interest, and to both contribute to and leverage capabilities resident in other force packages available to deliver the desired combat or crisis management effect.

Kill webs rely on networks, wave forms, connectivity, distributed C^2, and platforms which can leverage all of the former. Platforms are the time-space entities which enable the force; integrability allows a distributed force to deliver the desired combat effect. The kill web is about networks of sensors that can provide assessment data for shooters operating over an extended battle space. The kill web provides enhanced resilience and more capability to respond deliberately as needed. It also allows for target assessments being coupled with evolving risk assessments in terms of deterrence risks and consequences.

The kill web is a collection of sensors with C^2, able to reach into those cascading sensor networks. Software technologies are key parts of the way ahead to allow for switching across secure domains to provide for a secure operational web. The U.S. Air Force and the U.S. Navy are working to shape a big blue blanket, 21st century style, in terms of interactive webs over the operational areas. In World War II, the U.S. Navy shaped what became called the big blue blanket of ships to cover the Pacific operations.

Obviously, this is beyond the ken of current realities in terms of ship numbers but by shaping a connected set of U.S. and allied forces, a C^2/ISR set of webs can deliver wider coverage than simply the number of ship hulls afloat.

Notably, in conflict with nuclear powers, target assessment and discrimination are critical. With the inevitable nuclear and conventional blending of targets in any large-scale conflict, it will be crucial to be able to provide a risk assessment of which targets are priority ones, but which ones might trigger actions one does not wish to see happen. It is not just a question of the speed to kill; it is the speed to kill the right target, at the right time and the right place.

The linkage among kill webs, tactical decision making at the edge, and software upgradeability, was highlighted in a discussion with a young navy officer who is a software guru and who works in support of the P-8 at Jacksonville. In a 2020 discussion at Jax Navy with Lt. Sean Lavelle, the officer discussed how the new kill web approach affected software development and acquisition, in his perspective.

"I've been digging more into your work and am getting a lot of ideas. The more I think about it, the more I think software-defined tactics are the key to quickly adding capabilities to different assets that are supposed to work together. It's kill chain vs. kill web for acquisitions.

"In the kill chain, you devise a new weapon for a shooter, then figure out the sensor you need for the ISR node, then you figure out the network that makes the most sense to transmit data, then you write the pro forma comms. After that, you must try to sequence all the capabilities so that they arrive roughly at the same time with the network infrastructure coming before there's real capability.

"Then when you add a sensor or a weapon, you have to teach the opposite unit what that brings to the table and how they can maximize it. The synergies are probably really hard to think through and even harder for most individuals to become experts. All of that adds so much time to acquisitions/incorporation, and you end up buying weapons and sensors much slower than the pace of what is technologically possible.

"In the kill web, you buy whatever improves your capability as a sensor or a shooter. Period. If there isn't a pro forma network to transmit info right away, it's okay. Just write an application that knows all the available assets from a basic datalink, has some basic modeling assumptions, and can give the task force a good, ad hoc plan that gets to a local maximum solution.

"We actually just did this for a new classified ASW weapon. Twenty hours of software development solved the entire coordination problem for a completely new concept and optimized the sensor/shooter team. It lets the sensor act as a cloud processing node for the team, even if the human in the aircraft isn't really an expert in what the shooter brings to the table. That speeds up everything. It would have taken at least two years to wait for a prime contractor-built software update solution."

In some ways, the kill web approach recalls an earlier emphasis on network-centric warfare, but it is significantly more than that. The presence force can be designed to operate effectively organically because the presence force can now be enabled by organic ISR and C^2 systems operating at the tactical edge. But the design of the presence force is such that it is inherently scalable so that reachback to complimentary or supplementary force elements can augment the lethality and survivability of the presence force. It is about designing and operating presence forces as modular task forces with aggregability built into the design of the force, the training of the force and the concepts of operations for the force.

The evolution of 21st century weapon technology is breaking down the barriers between offensive and defensive systems. Is missile defense about providing defense or is it about enabling global reach, for offense or defense? Likewise, the new 5th generation aircraft have been largely not understood because they are inherently multi-domain systems, which can be used for forward defense or forward offensive operations. Indeed, an inherent characteristic of many new multi-domain systems is that they are really about presence and putting a grid over an operational area, and therefore they can be used to support strike or defense within an integrated approach.

In the 20th Century, surge was built upon the notion of signaling. One would put in a particular combat capability – a Carrier Battle Group, Amphibious Ready Group, or Air Expeditionary Wing – to put down your marker and to warn a potential adversary that you were there and ready to be taken seriously. If one needed to, additional forces would be sent in to escalate and build up force. With the new multi-domain systems – 5th generation aircraft and Aegis for example – the key is presence and integration able to support strike or defense in a single operational presence capability. Now the adversary cannot be certain that you are simply putting down a marker. The strategic thrust of integrating modern systems is to create a grid that can operate in an area as a seamless whole, able to strike or defend simultaneously.

The strategic context and thrust of the kill web focus is upon force distribution, scalability and integratability for a modular combat force. This is very different from network centric warfare for it is about shaping new concepts of operations, new ways to build multi-domain force packages and those forces are operating in a very different strategic context within which Cebrowski was living in. In a discussion during a visit to Australia in 2017 with our colleague Air Vice Marshal (Retired) John Blackburn, he recalled his dealings with Admiral Cebrowski, who pioneered the concept of network-centric warfare. "Let me go back to the difference between the two – NCW and the kill web. I was head of strategic policy at the time (in the Australian MoD) and we worked with Admiral Cebrowski after he launched the NCW discussion. He told us, "NCW is an idea which we are just getting out there. If 40% of what I'm saying ever comes true, that'll be a fantastic result, because it's an idea. The reality is, we're never going to be totally network-connected. It's not going to happen. It's like saying you're going to have unlimited bandwidth, and everybody can connect without the adversary disrupting those networks. You've got to start with the idea. You've got to get people talking about it and to get the language out there into the debate."

"Where we're at now is moving to the next stage, of applying a bit of thrust with building this integrated force and not just talking about it and getting a focus on a new phase of how to integrate a distributed force through kill web capabilities and training.

"We're able to exchange situational awareness at such a rate now that you can have a broad understanding and knowledge of what tools you actually have in the combat space. A lot of the cultural barriers between services are greatly diminished, if not erased. Because it goes to the larger understanding of what the kill web is. Some might say that the kill web is just an extension of the network-centric warfare from Cebrowski, and all those others. But we are certainly more capable to deliver integratability in this day and age. And the key is to get some of the old cultural barriers, and perceptions out of the way, to work the kind of integratability which we need to deliver in the contested battlespace against peer competitors."

Another way to look at the kill web versus the kill chain was suggested by the well-respected warfighter and analyst, U.S. Air Force Col. (Retired) Robert "Juice" Newton, in a 2021 meeting with him. In his view, the role of kill web thinking is a key part of reworking how to prepare the force for new phases of combat engagement. For the kill chain, the focus is upon kinetic kill with a sense of permanence about it. In kill webs, one is focused on engagement density, and shaping the kind of combat effects which enable escalation control.

There is another analogy which captures what a kill web enabled force can do with regard to combat learning as well. As Blackburn underscored, the C^2 and ISR technologies we now have enables smaller, and denser modular force packages to distribute and to operate both independently and interdependently. But a waze analogy also highlights how these modular task forces working independently or interpedently learn during their operations. This is how Brigadier General (Retired) Rob Novotny put it during an interview we conducted with him when he was posted to Air

Combat Command in 2017. "Waze is really a common operating environment that is only good if people put information into it. It's completely agnostic to your platform. It doesn't care if you have a Samsung galaxy, or an iPhone, or a Google phone, it doesn't care. It doesn't care about your data connection. It doesn't care if you're on Verizon, or AT&T, it didn't care if you're on Wi-Fi or cellphone, 4G or LT.

"All that matters is that you participate in the network. As you participate in the network, it becomes greater fidelity, and allows you to make decisions, and sometimes Waze makes decisions for you as far as plotting your route of travel.

"It identifies threats, okay that road's closed, there is a police officer there, there's a car accident, and it will reroute you. It will allow you to push data in. It also pulls data from you. Not only does it have your overall geolocation and speed, but it will actually interact with you as the user, and it will say, "Hey, you're slowing down, that usually means you might be in traffic. Are you in traffic?" You go, "Yes, I am in traffic." Immediately the road turns yellow, or orange, or red, and it will begin to reroute.

"For us, the advanced battle management system (the USAF approach to shaping a kill web) in the future is very similar to Waze. Every single platform is sensor agnostic. I don't care if it's a frigate radar, I don't care if it's a submarine, I don't care if it's overhead, I don't care if it's F35, I don't care if it's fourth generation, I don't care if it's Army MLRS sensor. I don't care if it's commercial. We have ATT radars, we have DirecTV making transmissions, we have weather radars. A Common Operating Picture is generated which then can be leveraged as the task demands."

"And in a system where every platform is a sensor, then when a force package is tasked to do a mission, other users can leverage data generated by the force package participants in the system to do their missions as well. The system will recognize that there is data missing on a potential target. Based on idle time, let's say a sniper pod out a strike Eagle, as the pilot's flying to the tanker, the sniper pod is usually in idle status, it's not doing anything, but now in advanced battle management system says,

"Hey, you have an opportunity, based on your location, and what I know about your system, and the fact that I can communicate, that you can potentially surveil that target." It just commands the sniper pod to go take a look at it."[2]

Another conceptualization of the kill web comes from DARPA and its program of Adapting Cross-Domain Kill Webs. As Dr. Greg Kuperman has put it: "The goal of the Adapting Cross-Domain Kill-Webs (ACK) program is to provide a decision aid for mission commanders to assist them with rapidly identifying and selecting options for tasking – and retasking – assets within and across organizational boundaries. Specifically, ACK will assist users with selecting sensors, effectors, and support elements across military domains (space, air, land, surface, subsurface, and cyber) that span the different military Services to deliver desired effects on targets. Instead of limited, monolithic, pre-defined kill chains, these more disaggregated forces can be used to formulate adaptive "kill webs" based on all of the options available."[3]

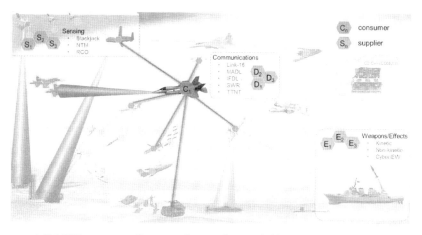

A DARPA conceptualization of cross-domain kill webs. Credit: DARPA

2   Robbin Laird, "Bringing the Future Forward: Accelerating U.S. and Allied Combat Power," *Second Line of Defense* (November 15, 2017), https://sldinfo.com/2017/11/bringing-the-future-forward-accelerating-u-s-and-allied-combat-power/.

3   Dr. Greg Kuperman, "Adapting Cross-Domain Kill Webs," https://www.darpa.mil/program/adapting-cross-domain-kill-webs.

Mission command guides a diversity of modular task forces, which deploy into the areas of interest, and provide engagement density. Sensor networks and C^2 at the tactical edge enable modular task forces to execute their assigned missions and to do assessments and with their inherent ISR capabilities are able to ensure that the mission effect is being achieved.

The late Andrew Marshall, Director of Net Assessment, in a one-page paper introduced what he visualized as a Revolution in Military Affairs (RMA). His brilliant insight is captured by two points: combining information war with precision guided munitions with remote sensors was the foundation for the RMA. Over time the word "information" was captured and essentially bigfooted by all things "cyber." Fortunately, an appreciation is coming back on all aspects of "information" as a key valuable strategic driver with cyber subsumed as just an important and critical tool. With the issue of precision guided munitions, many often looked at the technological necessity of trusted remote sensors at the point of interest enabling the kill web.

At the strategic level, rather than the experience of the land wars where central control drilled down to the battalion level and geographic control, the focus is upon understanding the interactive multi-domain combat effects of distributed forces, With the deployment of multiple modular task forces to the point of strategic or tactical interest, the kill webs may reshape the entire battlespace. The centralized command, in turn, is focused on leveraging those evolving effects to shape combat or crisis management outcomes at the broader escalation management strategic level.

Looking Back and Looking Forward

The kill web approach enables a force to operate in a distributed manner, and to be integratable to deliver the desired combat effect. Integratability is the key focus, not interoperability. Interoperability can facilitate integration for sure, but the focus is upon how shared information from sensor networks can enable a force package to be assembled and to fight as one.

The U.S. Navy has highlighted the importance of shaping a distributed maritime operational capability to prevail in the face of the high-end fight. In a discussion on October 6, 2020, Rear Adm. Meier, Commander Naval Air Forces Atlantic, discussed U.S. Navy thinking about distributed maritime operations with Matthew Danehy, Director of Concepts, Naval Warfare Development Command.

According to Danehy: "Concept is a visualization of future operations that describes how war fighters using, and these are key words, military art and science are expected to employ capabilities in the future and exploit future opportunities. What this is, is a force shaping tool. In other words, we're not just replacing the things we have, we're looking at what the future challenges are going to be, and then how do we need to shape our force to meet those challenges using not just a science, a tool, a platform, but also how we're going to apply the art, how we think, because we think that's a critical piece. So, we came up with DMO. DMO looked at how we envisioned the future fight, and we envisioned it against great power peer competitors.

"This is going to be different than what we've seen in the last so many decades. And we're going to have to operate sea control again, and that's something that…I know we're approaching our 245th anniversary of the United States Navy, but sea control is what the Navy has done; it is one of its primary functions, and DMO is a return to sea control.

"There's many of us that have been in the Navy, but there's not many of us that did sea control, at least practiced it. I was young enough to come in when they were still called the Soviet Union, and we talked and practiced sea control, but then we went into the land campaigns of the last several decades. We didn't think primarily power projection, and that's a different way of providing naval power. We need to return to sea control and DMO gets at that.

"DMO looks at taking a distributed force that exploits integration of capabilities and maneuver in all domains to mass effects at the time and place of our choosing. It's fleet centric. So if you're operating as a fleet, you're operating and maneuvering your forces at the time and place that you were choosing."

Rear Adm. Meier: "Clearly, what is being focused upon is blue water operations. This year we have focused in our various visits on the challenge of reshaping the force to do a variety of blue water operations, this time with the joint and coalition force, not just with the U.S. Navy and its fleet. In many ways, this is drawing upon experiences in World War II but in a new technological age."

As Danehy put it: "Maneuvering your forces, trying to pick a time and place of your choosing to get him at your advantage. Basically, shift the calculus if you will. I think we were successful, and it's worth understanding that because the thinking hasn't changed. The technology and the environment have, but we have to change the way we each provide our force, if you will, to meet that future challenge."

He then added about the World War II experience: "Anytime you fix your force, you're no longer maneuverable and it's a target that's easily taken… I believe, if I remember right, as we were going well in Guadalcanal and Leyte, as we were fighting these larger forces, we got fixed in support of these land operations, and that allowed them to basically take away our maneuver advantage. And that placed our forces at risk."

Rear Adm. Meier commented on the Guadalcanal example. "I'm glad that you brought up Guadalcanal. It really reminds me of one of my favorite World War II history books. That is *Neptune's Inferno* by James Hornfischer… We were really hanging on by a thread around Guadalcanal. We had overextended ourselves and you're absolutely right about the more fixed we were, the more we made it easier, at that time, against a numerically superior adversary."

Rear Adm. Meir then raised the challenge of logistical support to a distributed integrated force. Matthew Danehy: "You think of Guadalcanal and that tremendous fight that the Navy Marine Corps did for six months, to me, in my mind, as I read the book, that was a logistics fight.

"It was a race, who could support those two armies. The first one who was unable to support led to its withdrawal. And that was the Cactus Air Force. It was used during the day to keep resupply ships from coming down, forcing the Japanese to only come at night….That Cactus Air Force, that pounding of the logistics, allowed the Marines to basically outlast an eventual withdraw and produced victory.

"So, when we look at that Pacific fight, logistics is the key. I think as we look at the new concepts and we started to look at logistics, for the last 20-some years, we built a logistic posture that was peacetime and focused, just-in-time efficient. As the wing commander, I knew how many engines were located on what ship and what was available. We had just a correct number of supplies based on demand, which is rearward looking.

"But in the future, it's going to be a different kind of usage. We're going to operate 24 hours, seven offs, we're going to operate a lot more sorties, but our posture is based on a peacetime demand signal. We have to get into more of a push logistics, more algorithms that predict when operations ramp up, the supply system is ramping up prior to that, and start moving those key components forward. We had to get the ability to have these algorithms to accurately predict to say, when I'm about to have the first day of the war and I'm going to launch these long weapons, I don't need to wait until I fire the weapon to call back home to say, send more out here. They should be moving forward, even before I pull the trigger. So, the next day the resupply ship is pulling up, and I'm reloading. That's the kind of mindset we need to be able to do. That's kind of what we're trying to get at operational logistics; is more of a forward looking instead of a rearward peacetime kind of a focus."

Rear Adm. Meier highlighted the logistics support structure challenge. "And that is exactly what the professionals that analyze distributed maritime operations are looking at; it is those strengths of the carrier strike group that we touched on earlier of maneuver. The fact that our carrier strike groups can move 700-plus miles in a 24-hour period, the increasing range and lethality of our ever-advancing air wing and the weapons that those aircraft carry can hold huge areas of the surface at risk. Over the course of a three-day period, it would mean just a staggering volume of a real estate, roughly the entire Pacific AOR over a 72-hour period. But it is that logistics support train that is really a key part that makes that happen."[4]

Escalation Management

A shift to a kill web approach to force building, training and operations is a foundation from which the U.S. and its allies can best leverage the force we have and the upgrade paths to follow. A kill web linked force allows a modest force package – economy of force – to reach back to other combat assets to provide for enhanced options in a crisis or to ramp up the level of conflict if that is being dictated by the situation.

Kill web enabled distributed forces which are inherently integratable provide a strategic direction for both fleet development and for U.S. and allied concepts of operations. Such a trajectory is symmetrical with the evolving strategic environment where peer competition entails both ongoing multi-dimensional conflict and multi-domain warfare to compete across the global domain and to anchor crisis management and escalation control capabilities.

The U.S. military has been focused along with core allies in dealing with counterinsurgencies for two decades, which represents a defining generation of combat experience for the joint, and coalition force. We have an entire generation of military officers with little or no experience in dealing with the direct threat from peer competitors or operating in contested air and maritime space.

---

4   We have a book in process looking at mobile basing as a strategic capability in large part because of meeting the logistics challenge which Rear Admiral Meier identifies. This is why the larger ships, the aircraft carriers and large-deck amphibious ships, will remain key but reimagined as we do in later chapters. They will increasingly play a role of mother ships as logistical support from the sea is not easy and the military sealift command is short of ships and manpower, and will be for the foreseeable future.

With the return of great power conflict and the return of core nuclear questions—with the coming of a second nuclear age—force structures are changing along with concepts of operations as well as the need for relevant and effective crisis management strategies. A strategic shift is underway for the military establishments in the liberal democracies. For the past decade, the military has primarily focused its training and operations dealing with counterinsurgency and stability operations.

Now the need to deal with operations in contested air and sea space from adversaries who can bring significant capability to bear against U.S. and allied forces requires a significant reset of efforts. It is a strategic space in which operations in contested settings is where the military will operate. It is about learning how to deal with the policies and capabilities of peer competitors who are seeking strategic and military advantage against the liberal democracies.

And this challenge is one which will require the civilian leadership to come to terms with the challenge of crisis management in which escalation and de-escalation will have to be mastered as a strategic art form. It is not just about sending off the military to fights thousands of miles away and welcoming them back from time to time. It will be about facing the adversary squarely and forcing his hand and shaping outcomes to the benefit of the liberal democracies against those of the illiberal powers and doing so by using military means as one of the key tool sets.

A key aspect of peer competition with the 21st century authoritarian powers is over what limits should be crossed to manipulate the risk of going to a higher intensity of competition. In the Cold War these limits defined the "system dynamics" of the competition. Shaping them was important, because they were the foundation for winning a war that might erupt, or toward stabilizing a competition in a way that gave advantage to one side or the other. Seen this way Korea, Vietnam, Berlin, etc. were about winning those local wars. But they were more importantly about shaping the global competition between the United States and the Soviet Union.

Quite elaborate rules were worked out for this. It took substantial time during the evolution of the Cold War (to make sure that it was indeed was a cold war from a global conflagration point of view) for this learning curve to develop. Limited wars, like Korea, produced know how about escalation control and dominance.

The problem today is that we are only at the earliest parts of this learning curve for our age. We're in a long-term competition with authoritarian powers, but it's like it was 1949 in terms of our know how for managing this rivalry to our advantage. The problem isn't simply to defend Ukraine and Taiwan; it's to do it in such a way that doesn't lead to crazy escalations or that doesn't scare the daylights at of our allies.

In an interview with Dr. Paul Bracken, the noted nuclear strategist: "It is preferable to use the term "limited war" to describe the nature of conflict between the authoritarian powers and the liberal democracies. "A term was invented in the Cold War which is also quite useful to analyze the contemporary situation, namely, limited war. This term referred to conflict at lower levels and sub-crisis maneuvering. And that is what is going or today in cyber and outer space, to use two examples. But it also applied to higher levels of conflict like limited nuclear war."

"The notion of limited war focuses escalation as a strategy. What is the difference between limited and controlled war? That's a really important question with enormous implications for command and control. Today, for example, limits are determined in a decision-making process whereby the Pentagon goes to the White House and says we'd like to do this operation. The White says yes or no. Left out of this is any discussion of building a command-and-control system for controlled war. This means keeping war controlled even if things go wrong — as they always do. Without an emphasis on controlled war, and not just limited war, I would estimate that the United States will be highly risk averse, that is, the fear of an escalation spiral will drive the United States toward inaction.

"Our language shapes our strategy. An image of war that blows up, that's unlimited, or that you've declined to fight because of your fear that it would become so is where we are. In academic studies and think tanks the focus is overwhelmingly on "1914" spirals, accidental war, entanglement, and inadvertent escalation. If it's going to be controlled or limited, how are you defining that it is limited? Is it limited by geography? Is it limited by the intensity of operations? Is it limited by the additional political issues that you will bring into the dispute?

"These are never specified in discussions that I see of hybrid or gray zone warfare. To use a very sensitive example. In a Taiwan scenario, will the United States Navy and Air Force be allowed to strike targets in China? I see a real danger that this isn't being thought through. If we think it through only in a crisis, we're likely to find a lot of surprises in how the White House and Joint Chiefs of Staff see things differently."

These expressions – hybrid war and gray zone conflict – are treated as if they are self-evident in term of their meaning. Yet they are part of a larger chain of activities and events. We use the term peer competitor but that is a bit confusing as well as these authoritarian regimes do not have the same ethical constraints or objectives as do liberal democratic regimes. This core cultural, political, and ideological conflict who might well escalate a conflict beyond the terms of what we might wish actually to fight.

And that really is the point – escalate and the liberal democracies withdraw and redefine to their disadvantage what the authoritarian powers wish to do. Bracken noted: "That's a good distinction too, because it brings in the fact that for 20 years, we've been fighting an enemy in the Middle East who really can't strike back at the United States or Europe other than with low-level terrorist actions. That will not be the case with Russia, China, and others.

"The challenge is to define limited war, and I would add, controlled war. Is it geographic or Is it the intensity of the operations? How big of a war is it before people start unlocking the nuclear weapons? Every war game I've played has seen China declare that its "no first use" policy is terminated. The China player does this to deter the United States from making precision strikes and cyber-attacks on China. This seriously needs consideration before we get into a real crisis.

"Russia and China' are trying to come in with a level of intensity in escalation which is low enough so that it doesn't trigger a big Pearl Harbor response. And that could go on for a long time and is a very interesting future to explore."

Limited war requires learning about escalation control i.e., about controlled war, which when one uses that term, rather than hybrid war or gray zone conflict, connects limited war to the wider set of questions relating political objectives of the authoritarian powers. Bracken concluded: "I believe using those terms adds to the intellectual chaos in Washington. It prevents us from having a clear policy discussion of what the alternatives for escalation control and management are in any particular crisis. This is a lot more dangerous than mishandling the Afghan exit, or the COVID pandemic."[5]

In today's world, this is what full spectrum crisis management is all about. It is not simply about escalation ladders; it is about the capability to operate tailored task forces within a crisis setting—to dominate and prevail within a diversity of crises which might not be located on what one might consider an escalation ladder.

The nature of the threat facing the liberal democracies was well put by a senior Finnish official: "The timeline for early warning is shorter; the threshold for the use of force is lower." What is unfolding is that capabilities traditionally associated with high-end warfare are being drawn upon for lower threshold conflicts, designed to achieve political effect without firing a shot.

Higher-end capabilities being developed by China are Russia are becoming tools to achieve political-military objectives throughout the diplomatic engagement spectrum. The non-liberal or authoritarian powers are clearly leveraging new military capabilities to support their global

---

5   Robbin Laird, "Gray Zones or Limited War?" *Defense.info* (December 27, 2021), https://defense.info/re-thinking-strategy/2021/12/gray-zones-or-limited-war/.

diplomacy to try to get outcomes and advantages that enhance their position and interests. The systems they are building and deploying are clearly recognized by the Western militaries as requiring a response; less recognized is how the spectrum of conflict is shifting in terms of using higher-end capabilities for normal diplomatic gains.

Shaping a Way Ahead

In a global competition with multiple authoritarian adversaries, presence is crucial and given the global nature of the global coemption with 21st century authoritarian powers, the U.S. will never have the size of presence forces that supported the global stance which it once enjoyed in the 1950s. This means strategic downsizing, shaping objectives within reach for the United States and embracing a coalition focused effort, where allies often lead in defending joint interests.

This means for the United States making strategic and tactical choices to prioritize national defense and a realistic approach to national interests. Fortunately, for the United States, several key allies are in the process of building modern defense forces which are focused on force integration, built around modern C^2 and ISR systems, as is the United States.

This means that global presence will come through collaboration among U.S. and allied presence forces and working ways to extend their capabilities through force operational integration. Force distribution and kill web enablement are crucial for the kind of deterrent forces which the liberal democracies need to engage and manage the challenges of 21st century authoritarian powers.

Or put another way, kill web enabled forces are symmetrical with the kind of global presence and escalation management critical to managing the global competition of the new era into which we have entered.

More effective force distribution is now possible because of the revolution in C^2 and ISR capabilities extant and evolving. A future book will deal with this revolution and the key elements of how new C^2 and ISR is being delivered to the U.S. and allied combat forces.

Force packages or combat clusters are deployed under mission command with enough organic C^2 and ISR to monitor their situations and integrate the platforms that are part of that combat cluster and to operate effectively at a point of interest. Within that combat cluster, the C^2 and ISR systems allow for reachback to non-organic combat assets which are then conjoined operational for a period of time to that combat cluster and becomes part of an expanded modular task force.

With the right kind of security arrangement, and C^2 and ISR capabilities, the presence force, now an expanded modular task force, need not be American to expand the reach and effectiveness of the operational force in the extended battlespace.

Such an approach and capabilities are the essence of what a kill-web enabled force is and how such integratability can close the geographical and combat seams which 21st century authoritarian powers are focused on generating. This allows for the kind of escalation management and control crucial for the competition with the 21st Century authoritarian powers.

It is not about getting to World War III as rapidly as possible or generating nuclear exchanges early in a widening conflict. It is about escalation control and management, and an ability to close seams which adversaries seek to open to gain significant escalation dominance as they expand the reach and range of those 21st century authoritarian powers.

A shift to a kill web approach to force building, training and operations is a foundation from which the U.S. and its allies can best leverage the force we have and the upgrade paths to follow. For this approach to work, there is a clear need for a different kind of C^2 and ISR infrastructure to enable the shift in concepts of operations.

Indeed, when describing C^2 and ISR or various mutations like C^4ISR, the early notions of C^2 and ISR seen in both air-land battle and in joint support to the land wars, tend to be extended into the discussions of the

C^2 and ISR infrastructure for the kill web or for force building of the integrated distributed force.

But the technology associated with C^2 and ISR has changed significantly throughout this thirty-year period, and the technology to shape a very different kind of C^2 and ISR infrastructure is at hand to build enablement for distributed operations. The new C^2 and ISR infrastructure requires rethinking considerably the nature of decision making and the viability of the classic notion of the OODA loop. If the machines are fusing data or doing the OO function, then the DA part of the equation becomes transformed, notably if done in terms of decision making at the tactical edge. The decisions at the edge will drive a reshaping of the information about the battlespace because actors at the tactical edge are recreating the information environment itself.

In effect, chaos theory becomes a key element for an understanding of what C^2 at the tactical edge means in terms of the nature of the fleeting information in a distributed combat space itself. As one C^2 expert put it: "With the new technologies, what you are calling the new C^2 and ISR infrastructure, enables new warfighting approaches which need to be shaped, exercised and executed, and in turn affect how our forces train for the high-end fight."

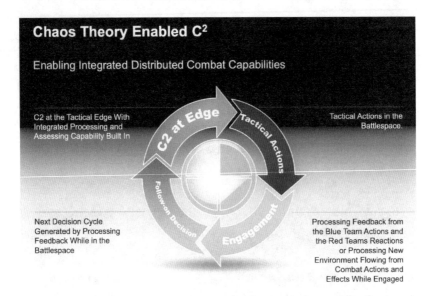

Conceptualizing the evolution of the dynamics and impact of C^2 at the tactical edge. Credit Graphic: *Second Line of Defense.*

This analyst underscored a key difference as well from the earlier phase of network-centric warfare. "I think of net-centric as a hardwired con-ops. I think it's preplanned. You can do it, but there's no adaptability, there's no protection, there's no scalability as far as those architectures were concerned. Now we're going to the next step where we're making networks adaptable and scalable so that you can essentially re-plan on the fly and make decisions differently, in a distributed manner. It's not a preplanned or scripted way of operating anymore."[6]

Notably, as the U.S. Navy works a new template of command and control, they are able to tap into various technological innovations as well underway. In effect, there is a co-evolution of the command shift with the technological dynamics for enabling technologies in the C^2 domain. Industrial expert Mike Twyman, who has worked for many years on the evolving C^2 technologies provided, an assessment of how this co-evolution is underway. According to Twyman in a March 2021 interview: "I love the

---

6   Robbin Laird, "Shaping the C^2/ISR Infrastructure for an Integrated Distributed Force," *Second Line of Defense* (October 19, 2019), https://sldinfo.com/2019/10/shaping-the-c2-isr-infrastructure-for-an-integrated-distributed-force/.

concept of co-evolution because, what you're seeing now with what the Navy's doing is they're leading with ideas. And they're basically developing the plans and the tactics with existing capabilities. They're integrating the F-35. They're integrating the Triton. They're integrating the P-8. They're integrating all these great capabilities and really, in very novel ways, to build this distributed integrated task force. That's going to be what they go to the fight with today but are positioning themselves for what new technologies can enable down the road."

He added: "Co-evolution is a key element of how to understand what is happening in the C^2 domain. There are three streams of activity shaping the way ahead. The first is how the adversaries are working C^2 for themselves and shaping tools for disruption and contesting the C^2 space. Second, there is what our warfighters are doing to shape operational art and innovation. Third, there are the dynamics of change in the C^2 domain globally, such as the emergence of 5G systems. It's really the co-evolution of operational art and technology that leads to new solutions to counter the threat, both today and in the future."

In other words, reworking the command element enabling an integrated distributed force, will be reinforced in the next few years by innovations in the C^2 and ISR (understood as Information, Surveillance and Reconnaissance) technologies. Co-evolution is a key driver of change in combat capability.

And going forward we will look at new platforms quite differently. Rather than discussing generations of platforms, with the information and decision-making infrastructure building out an integrated distributed force, we will look at platforms in terms of what they contribute to the overall capability to such a force, rather than simply becoming autistic injections into the force.

CHAPTER TWO:
THE INTEGRATABLE AIR WING

In 2016, we visited Colorado Springs, Colorado, and met with the commander of the head of the North American Aerospace Defense Command and U.S. Northern Command (NORAD-NORTHCOM), Adm. Bill Gortney. Even though the Administration at the time was not focused on what the next Administration would call the return of great power competition, the Admiral was already focused on the new state of affairs. And in his view his command needed to be reworked to do multi-domain defense against the threats from the Pacific and the Atlantic which he saw as increasingly cross-cutting.

His conception of the threat was very clear—it was multiple nuclear and an air-maritime strike and defense threats facing the country from two sides simultaneously. While the Russians face three nuclear powers in the North Atlantic, the United States and its allies face three nuclear powers in the Pacific. There was no ambiguity in the thinking from Adm. Gortney. He put this in two different but related ways.

On the one hand, according to Adm. Gortney: "The Russians are evolving their long-range aviation and maritime capabilities. They are fielding and employing precision-guided cruise missiles from the air, from ships and from submarines. Their new cruise missiles can be launched from Bears and Blackjacks, and they went from development to testing by use in Syria. It achieved initial operating capability based on a shot from a deployed force. The air and sea-launched cruise missiles can carry conventional or nuclear warheads, and what this means is that a "tactical" weapon can have strategic effect with regard to North America.

"Today, they can launch from their air bases over Russia and reach into North American territory. The challenge is that, when launched, we are catching arrows, but we are not going after the archers. The archers do not have to leave Russia in order to range our homeland.

"And with the augmentation of the firepower of their submarine force, the question of the state of our anti-submarine warfare capabilities is clearly raised in the North Atlantic and the Northern Pacific waters. What this means for NORAD as well is that limiting it to air defense limits our ability to deal with the multi-domain threat."

On the other hand, according to Adm. Gortney: "We can look at the evolving threat as a ten o'clock and a two o'clock fight, because they originate from the ten and two. And the ten o'clock fight is primarily right now an aviation fight. They're moving capability there, but it's nothing like what they have at the two o'clock fight. The two o'clock fight is more of a maritime fight."

In other words, the Russians and the Chinese are very good students of Andy Marshall and his focus on the revolution of military affairs and have added new capabilities for the evolving digital age, in terms of information and cyber warfare capabilities as well.

This is a notional rendering of the 10 and 2'Oclock challenge. It is credited to *Second Line of Defense* and not in any way an official rendering by any agency of the U.S. government. It is meant for illustration purposes only.

For the U.S. Navy in addressing the fight as described by Admiral Gortney, shaping a way ahead for air and sea integration with the ability to tap into relevant ground capabilities or maneuver forces is crucial to the defense of the United States. To do so means that integrated airpower between the Navy and the Air Force becomes increasingly important and with changes such as the modernization of the bomber force and the joint operation of fifth generation aircraft, this also becomes a key strand of shaping a more lethal, and capable force.

With the enhanced priority to maneuver warfare at sea, and with an emphasis on distributed maritime operations as a core enabler for maneuver warfare, the question of how one trains to do so is a key priority. The kill chain has required sequential linear thinking to execute maritime mission operations; the kill web focuses on distributed operations, integratability and third-party targeting.

The kill web is different; and training for it is different as well. And that training is a key part of the further development and modernization of the fleet and its concepts of operations. Operations, training, and development are emerging as an ongoing cycle of innovation driving the fighting navy towards enhanced capabilities to prevail in full spectrum crisis management.

Seen from San Diego

The U.S. Navy is shifting from its training and operational focus on the traditional integrated air wing to building, developing, and deploying the integratable air wing. In a series of meetings with the Navy Air Boss and his staff during 2019 and 2020, Vice Admiral Miller and his team provided guidance with respect to the transition affecting not just Naval Aviation but the entire operational approach of the fleet.

During a 2019 visit to Naval Air Station, North Island, in San Diego, Vice Adm. Miler emphasized that fifth-generation capabilities coming to the carrier is "a catalyst for change: how we fight, how we train, how we maintain and sustain aircraft, how we flight test, and how we man our squadrons (pilots and maintenance personnel). The emphasis is interoperability, networking, distributed forces, and integration."

But several new capabilities are being introduced into the operational force, such as the Triton, P-8s, modernized Super Hornets, the new Hawkeye, the MQ-25 unmanned tanker. These new capabilities are being worked into an evolving Naval strike force to shape new capabilities for the carrier and for the distributed force.

Vice Adm. DeWolfe H. Miller III, commander, Naval Air Forces, inspects a new gunner seat of an MH-60S Sea Hawk, assigned to Helicopter Sea Combat Squadron (HSC) 3 on Naval Air Station North Island, U.S. Navy photo by Mass Communication Specialist 3rd Class Jeffery L. Southerland, October 21, 2019.

The training function is changing dramatically. Capt. Max McCoy, the Chief of Staff for Vice Adm. Miller, joined into the conversation and highlighted what one might call the forcing function of the F-35 and of the F-35 aviators upon the training dynamic. "We are teaching F-35C pilots to be wingmen but training them to think like mission commanders. F-35C provides more situational awareness than ever before and pilots must be able to influence the battlespace both kinetically and non-kinetically. The pilot must interpret cockpit information and determine the best means to ensure mission success either through his own actions or by networking to a distributed force.

"The pilots need to think like mission commanders, in which they are operating in terms of both leveraging and contributing to the networked force. This means that the skill sets being learned are not the classic training, tactics and procedures (TTPs) for a combat pilot but are focused on learning how to empower and leverage an integrated force."

According to Capt. McCoy: "Training can no longer focus solely on T/M/S capabilities. Training has to develop young aviators who appreciate their role within a larger maneuver/combat element. Specifically, how does F-35C complement 4th generation capabilities within the Carrier Air Wing and surface combatants distributed within the Carrier Strike Group? It is no longer about fighting as a section or division of fighter aircraft."

Capt. McCoy then went on to define the way ahead: "We only win if we fight as an interoperable, networked, and distributed force. We are still learning and incorporating 5th generation capability into the Navy. Our efforts must be calculated and measured but push beyond historical comfort zones. We must embrace what is new and redefine what is basic warfighting capability."

Capt. McCoy further explained the challenge of the training reset and how crucial it was to shape the way ahead for maneuver warfare. "This starts with the Fleet Replacement Squadron (FRS) and Air Combat Training Continuum (ACTC) syllabi. We must make integrated training a key component of a pilot's progression from FRS graduate to mission commander. F-35C is an enabler, if and only if, we train our pilots to think well beyond the limits of their cockpit and reach of an individual aircraft's weapons system."

The challenge is to learn how to operate as a distributed force or to operate in modular force packages. This is leading to radical disjunctures from traditional training approaches and thinking. How do you best train your aviators to tap into networks and provide for distributed strike? In shifting from a training focus on traditional TTPs, how do Naval aviator's problem solve differently? How does one reshape effectively the infrastructure to support new training approaches? How do Naval aviators integrate with and maximize their impact for and on the joint or coalition combat force?

Training is now about shaping domain knowledge for the operational force to ensure that "we can be as good as we can be all of the time." According to Vice Adm. Miller and Capt. McCoy: "The ability to reshape training and change culture requires a warfighting community to break from traditional training methods either on the range, at sea and in the simulated environment. There are numerous reasons why we must find a new balance among live, virtual and constructive (LVC) training in a distributed mission training (DMT) construct. Range infrastructure, threat simulation, cost to operate, and security are driving us to search for new training opportunities."

They added: "However, the most important reason is operational readiness—warfighting first. We must be ready and prepared to fight at all times. LVC/DMT is the only way to be good all of the time given a unit's resourcing that includes manpower, aircraft, and flight hour budget. It forces integration among 4th and 5th generation aircraft while also providing the medium to integrate with surface combatants."

Taking a kill web perspective, they added: "Again, in the future, we are all wingmen in the battlespace who must think well beyond the cockpit or bridge of our platforms. LVC/DMT will be the proving ground that unlocks how we think and encourages TTP development that would otherwise be hindered by fiscal constraints and under-resourced or inadequate ranges. It is the bridge that builds cooperation and cohesiveness among communities. LVC/DMT is the common ground that teaches our amazing tacticians how to appreciate a wide range of capabilities that are far more effective in the collective." Since this interview, Rear Admiral McCoy has become head of the Naval Aviation Development Command (NAWDC).

Mike Wallace, Boeing test pilot with Air Test and Evaluation Squadron (VX) 23, utilizes the Manned Flight Simulator at Naval Air Station Patuxent River, Maryland, during the Secure Live Virtual Constructive Advanced Training Environment (SLATE) demonstration. Naval Air Systems Command, Patuxent River, Md., October 6, 2021. Credit: NAVAIR

Seen from NAWDC

We have visited what is now NAWDC three times since 2014. And the thrust of change in terms of focusing on fleet operations within a joint and coalition force is evident. During our 2014 visit, the Commander of NAWDC was Rear Adm. Scott Conn, who at the time of this writing was Vice Adm. Scott Conn, Commander of the Third Fleet. During our most recent visit in 2020 to NAWDC, several of the warfare commanders now at NAWDC underscored how important they saw Vice Adm. Conn's leadership while in command. In retrospect, he was there as the U.S. Navy was starting its shift from the priority focus on support to the ground wars to refocusing on the Russians and Chinese, with Putin's actions in Crimea certainly marking the transition.

The F-35 was looming on the horizon for the U.S. Navy, although the other part of Naval Aviation, the USMC had already embraced the new aircraft and was reworking their concepts of operations to embrace the new capability. The funding shortfalls had led to a significant reduction in readiness and flight hour training which provided a significant challenge for the Navy as well.

Ed Timperlake with Vice Admiral Conn during our
2014 Fallon Visit. Credit: *Second Line of Defense.*

During our 2014 visit, the staff and leadership at Vice Adm. Conn's command were very focused on the challenges of the high-end fight and how to reset training to do a better job to prepare. We asked him during the visit, about how he saw the way ahead and this is what he told us. "First and foremost is to continue to provide trained and ready aircrew to operate forward. In looking to the future, in five years we are going to have JSF in the fleet. In five years, we may have UCAS on our carriers. In five years, the Super Hornet of today is going to be different. In five years, the E-2D capabilities and our networks will have matured. In five years, the threat is going to change, and competitors will have more capability. In working with Naval Aviation Leadership, we are on a journey of discovery with regard to how to best create a training environment that replicates potential adversary's capabilities. Before I leave, I would like to hand my relief a destination to drive to in this regard."

Vice Adm. Conn can look back with pride for he certainly did this. When we next went to NAWDC, the commander was Rear Adm. Harris, who was head of N-98 at the time of this writing, the head of Naval Aviation on the Op Nav staff. When we visited the command in 2017, the full up transition set in motion by Vice Adm. Conn was in clear evidence.

The surface warfare community was now an integrated element within NAWDC and the cooperation with the USAF, and the Air Warfare Training Center had been stepped up. Rear Adm. Harris told us: "We have surface warfare officers here at NAWDC. We work closely with the Surface Warfare training community as well in shaping a more integrative and integrated approach as well."

He added: "With regard to the USAF and integrative training, our HAVOC team works with the USAF Weapons School in the Weapon School Integration phase which runs about a month. If you want to think of it in the college realm, this is a 400-level class. And we're seeing the Growler used differently by the Air Force than we would probably use it in the Navy. That cross-pollination has been extremely useful for both the services."

At the time we were very impressed with the core emphasis on bringing integratability to the surface warfare and aviation communities. Rear Admiral Harris provided further details on what was going on at the time of our 2017 visit. "The SWO boss, Adm. Rowden, has been pretty adamant about the benefits of their Warfighting Development Center, the Surface and Mine Warfighting Development Center. SMWDC has been, in my mind, going full bore at developing three different kinds of warfare instructors, WTIs. They have an ASW/ASUW, an anti-surface and anti-submarine warfare officers. They have an IAMD officer, and they have an expeditionary warfare officer."

Rear Adm. Harris added: "Admiral Rowden talks about distributed lethality and they are getting there rapidly. We are watching young lieutenants share with their bosses in a training environment, specifically during IADC (Integrated Air Defense Course). This is probably not the way we want AEGIS set up, or how we want the ship to be thinking in an automated mode. We may not previously have wanted to go to that next automated step, but we have to because the threat envelope is going to force us into that logic."

An F-18 takeoff from the Naval Air Station Fallon, 2017.
Credit: *Second Line of Defense.*

In 2020, a visit to NAWDC provided an update on the way ahead. The discussion with Rear Adm. Brophy, the CO of NAWDC, started with a simple question: "Obviously, NAWDC is in significant change, and your job seems to be to expand the dialogue between NAWDC and the rest of naval warfighting centers as well as the USAF and the USMC and with allies. How would you describe your job?"

Rear Adm. Brophy provided a very clear answer. "Adm. Miller gave me the following charge when I took command: 'Snap,' when you go there get us in a great power competition mindset. From a wholly integrated perspective, look at what we need to do at NAWDC in order to win the next fight. And to do this, he emphasized that, my job was to pursue holistic training with the Navy and to work with other U.S. warfighting centers and key allies."

During the visit, several key developments stood out. First, there is a re-imaging of the carrier going on associated with the return to blue water operations and rethinking how the carrier works with the fleet to deliver enhanced expeditionary reach that the carrier air wing can support. This has meant a growing working role with the Marines, who in Rear Adm. Brophy's words "have significant experience and expertise with expeditionary operations, and with whom we can collaborate to develop new concepts of operations." Rear Adm. Brophy underscored that there was clearly an enhanced working relationship with MAWTS-1 at Yuma MCAS going on as a result.[7]

Second, this has meant as well that the U.S. Navy and the USAF are establishing new ways to work more effectively together. Notably, with the coming of the B-21 to the force, there is a clear opportunity to integrate the bomber into fleet operations and provide a very flexible and powerful, distributed payload capability for the air-maritime force. But for this to happen, the USAF has to think beyond a traditional bomber role for the B-21 and to train with the joint force from the outset to shape that platform's further development.

Third, the theme of integratability beyond the carrier air wing is a key one being worked at NAWDC. As Rear Adm. Brophy put it: "From a training standpoint, we work from the perspective of 'it is not going to be a carrier strike group that wins the next fight on its own, it's going to be an integrated joint force that wins the next fight. We've really broadened our aperture. Everything we do here now is based off of a single lens: does it move the needle for great power competition or not?"

Fourth, an integrated training center has been built from the ground up to support the integratable air wing to train in the kill web space. After the interview we toured the new facility which consists of two buildings. The first building is a meeting center with areas for working groups to meet at various levels of security within a global teleconferencing framework, as the need demands. This building can allow for scenario generation, assessment of findings and evaluations from the physical test range, or utilization of the simulated test range that is contained in the second building

The second building houses multiple simulators for different platforms being flown by the fleet. As Rear Adm. Brophy put it: "We're going to put

---

7   The intersection of the transformation of the USMC with the evolving U.S. Navy approaches is discussed throughout Robbin Laird, *The USMC Transformation Path* (2022).

in an entire Air Wing's and strike group's worth of simulators." The focus is not only on platform learning, but significantly, working in an integratable environment. Those specific simulators, continued in various rooms in the building, can be linked with outside simulation facilities as well.

As Rear Adm. Brophy put it about the new facilities and their contribution: "The Integrated Training Building will be the future of virtual and constructive training for the majority of naval aviation. Not only will we provide cutting-edge training in Fallon, but fleet concentration areas will be able to train remotely with the Subject Matter Experts (SMEs) at NAWDC in a virtual, constructive environment at any time, day or night."

Fifth, even with the new facility, changes are necessary with the physical ranges to adjust to the high-end training of fifth generation warfare. There are requests in to adjust the ranges to accommodate the kind of targeting challenges which the high-end air arm needs to train for to prevail in the high-end fight.

As Rear Adm. Brophy emphasized: "Fallon is the only United States Navy facility where an entire air wing can conduct comprehensive training while integrating every element of air warfare. While aircraft and weaponry have evolved substantially in the last several decades, the ranges at Fallon have not changed significantly in size since 1962. Our naval aviators use the desert skies to learn critical warfighting skills necessary to defend our nation and preserve our way of life from those who would want to cause us harm. To that end, we are working with the local community, as well as natural and cultural resource experts, to find a way forward together to expand the range."

Sixth, a measure of the change at NAWDC has been the generation of working groups based at NAWDC that reach out to the fleet to devise and implement new ways to operate in the evolving strategic situation. COVID-19 has slowed down this process, but the trajectory is clear. For example, in the first quarter of 2020, NAWDC sponsored work with the other Navy warfighting centers to address the question of fleet wide TTPs to execute maritime strike. The purpose here was to think beyond the classic airwing focus to a wider integratable air wing in support of fleet-wide operations. Clearly, the new infrastructure highlighted above would be a key asset in shaping such new TTPs for the fleet and its integratability into the joint and coalition force.

Seventh, the new MISR or Maritime ISR warfighting center is managing an important new Navy exercise, Resolute Hunter, which is focused on the evolving role of ISR and sensor networks in guiding C² and integrated operations going forward. As Rear Adm. Brophy highlighted: "In the Resolute Hunter exercise, we are really looking hard at the kill web aspect and focusing on utilizing every asset that's out there to ensure that we're the most effective warfighting force we possibly can be."

Rear Adm. Richard Brophy, Commander, Carrier Strike Group 4, aboard the Wasp-class amphibious assault ship USS Kearsarge (LHD 3) Dec. 12, 2021. (U.S. Navy photo by Mass Communication Specialist 3rd Class Jesse Schwab)

Taken together, the work of MISR, the Information Warfare program, Resolute Hunter, and the work with the Marines and the USAF, highlights the challenge and opportunity for shaping a Maritime Squadron Targeting Concept. This is a clear expression that NAWDC and the Navy are focusing on ways to leverage an integratable air wing for the fleet, and for the joint and coalition force. As Rear Adm. Brophy put it: "What exactly do 21st century fires look like from a maritime perspective?"

Eighth, Rear Adm. Brophy underscored how important it was to ensure kill web capabilities and effectiveness. A distributed fleet without integratability delivered by interactive kill webs would weaken the force. It is crucial to ensure that a distributed force has ready access to fires across the joint and coalition force to ensure combat dominance.

Key Building Blocks

NAWDC is a key epicenter of where the current force is becoming more capable and lethal, and the aperture of the integratable air wing has been opened to provide a key venue for the kind of force transformation needed for full spectrum crisis management dominance. There are several key building blocks being put in shape to drive this kind of innovation. In this section, we will address a number of these key building blocks and do so from the perspective of the officers at NAWDC working on shaping these building blocks. There are many such building blocks, but we will focus on four key elements: dynamic targeting; fleet wide TTPs for maneuver warfare; the emergence of the Maritime ISR or MISR officers; and the first re-design of the strike syllabus in two decades.

Dynamic Targeting

With the strategic shift from the land wars to the more fluid battlespace involving peer competitors engaged in full spectrum crisis management with the United States and its allies, one aspect of the change for military forces is how to use lethal force effectively. This comes down in part to how to target dynamically in a fluid political and military situation. And within the dynamics of management of escalation, how does one ensure that one has had the combat effect which provides an effective solution set?

From a strictly military point of view, the strategic shift is from deliberate to dynamic targeting.

As one analyst has put the issue of the shift affecting the maritime domain: "Perhaps the most acute differences that the maritime theater will present are the target sets. Targets that can be categorized as deliberate will now be the exception to the rule. Relatively fixed land targets will yield to highly mobile maritime targets. Therefore, targets may be known but not fixed."[8]

How significant the shift is can be seen in a USAF explanation of the difference between deliberate and dynamic targeting. "Dynamic targeting complements the deliberate planning efforts, as part of an overall operation, but also poses some challenges in the execution of targets designated within the dynamic targeting process. Dynamic targets are identified too late, or not selected for action in time to be included in deliberate targeting."[9]

The assessment adds that: "Dynamic targeting is a term that applies to all targeting that is prosecuted outside of a given day's preplanned air tasking order (ATO) targets (i.e., the unplanned and unanticipated targets). It represents the targeting portion of the "execution" phase of effects-based approach to operations (EBAO). It is essential for commanders and air operations center (AOC) personnel to keep effects-based principles and the JFC's objectives in mind during dynamic targeting and ATO execution.

"It is easy for those caught up in the daily battle rhythm to become too focused on tactical-level details, losing sight of objectives, desired effects, or other aspects of commander's intent. When this happens, execution

---

8   Lt. Cmdr. Mitchell S. McCallister, "The Maritime Dynamic Targeting Gap," *Naval War College Review*, May 4, 2012.

9   https://www.doctrine.af.mil/Portals/61/documents/Annex_3-60/3-60-D16-Target-Dynamic.pdf

can devolve into blind target servicing, unguided by strategy, with little or no anticipation of enemy actions."

But what if dynamic targeting becomes the norm and deliberate targeting the exception? With specific regard to the Pacific, the strategic shift could well generate a significant targeting shift. But how to train, plan, and execute a dynamic targeting approach?

That is a challenge being addressed by the NAWDC team, with Cmdr. Joseph Fraser, head of the Information Warfare Directorate, which has been designated the executive agent for targeting for the United States Navy. NAWDC is an integrated warfighting center, not simply the classic Top Gun venue. With officers from the various elements of Navy warfighting present within NAWDC, as well as enhanced engagement with the other services' warfighting centers, NAWDC makes perfect sense to work the 360-degree dynamic targeting solutions set for an integrated distributed force. Obviously, this is both challenging and a work in progress. But the core point is that Navy has laid the foundation within, and at NAWDC, to shape such a way ahead.

By working a new model of dynamic weapons engagement now, prior to the coming of directed energy weapons to the fleet, it will be possible to determine how to use these new technologies effectively by which platforms, in which situations and in which combat areas within the fluid and extended battlespace. This can also be true with regard to future precision weapons as well and can provide a guide for shaping a future weapons inventory. Which weapons would make a significant difference if added to the fleet to maximize dynamic targeting capabilities against which adversaries and in which situations?

This is an area where expanded work with the other services is clearly crucial. But if the Pacific is taken as a baseline case, then the question of maritime targets, or targets that operate within that domain become crucial challenges to be dealt with. And certainly, these targeting challenges really have little to deal with the legacy targeting solution sets generated in the land wars, and, frankly, the lessons learned will have to be unlearned to some extent.

What this means in blunt terms, is that the U.S. Navy plays a key role in this strategic targeting shift. We are talking about targeting solutions enabled by interactive webs, but not necessarily what passes for joint targeting. The maritime domain is very different from the land or air-space domain. While the U.S. Army and USAF can provide key capabilities to provide for dynamic targeting, the domain knowledge of the U.S. Navy will be a central piece of the puzzle.

And much the same could be said with regard to the other domains, and what the role of the U.S. Navy would be in a dynamic targeting solution set. Much like how words like C^2, ISR and training are being changed fundamentally in terms of their meaning with the building of a kill web integrated distributed force, the term joint also is changing, or will need to change if combat effectiveness is to be realized. There is a tendency to slip into the last twenty years of jointness which has been dominated by the U.S. Army and the land wars. The new strategic and combat environment is dramatically different.

TTPs for the Fleet

The focus is on how to shape fleet-wide maneuver warfare. This is part of the NAWDC-led effort to work TTPs for a force element, not just a single platform, or a platform operating off a single ship, such as Super Hornets working with an aircraft carrier. The reason for this focus is rooted in a shift in how ISR is changing and how new options are becoming available for targeting.

A key element of the new approach is how platforms will interact with one another in distributed strike and defensive operations and enable cuing weapons across a task force. It is about how to leverage weapons capabilities across a task force and shaping an expanded capability and process for empowering third-party targeting.

There is a clear need to expand targeting domain knowledge to include both non-lethal and lethal effects. Cmdr. Fraser put it this way in a 2020 interview: "Nirvana for me is a fully integrated strike squadron capability that does both kinetic and non-kinetic missions to provide a range of options to the commander."

Part of the challenge is putting in place a cadre of officers with the kind of strike domain knowledge, covering both lethal and non-lethal, who are not attached to a particular carrier wing. This would allow for the strengthening of the cadre and the ability to deploy to the operational need, rather than the operating cycle of a particular air wing.

How to shape dynamic targeting knowledge and training, notably in terms of the dynamics of change both in terms of ISR availability and the evolution of the weapons enterprise? How will the fleet be empowered by new ways to build out weapons arsenals and provide for adequate stockpiles for the force? That was the subject of conversation during the July 2020 visit at NAWDC with Capt. Edward Hill, the oldest Captain in the U.S. Navy at sixty years of age. Because he goes back to the Cold War operating Navy, he can bring that experience to the return-to-the-contested environment challenges facing the weapons enterprise.

Clearly, building adequate stockpiles of weapons is crucial. But also important is working a new weapon mix to ensure that one is not forced by necessity to rely on the most expensive weapons, and the ones that will almost always have a stockpiling issue, but to have a much more cost-effective set of options in the weapons mix.

As Capt. Hill put it in a 2020 interview: "We need to get beyond golden bee-bee solution. We need to have a weapons barge come with the battle group that has an affordable weapons mix. We need $50,000 weapons, not just million-dollar weapons. We should have weapons to overwhelm an adversary with Joe's garage weapons and not having to use the golden bee-bees as the only option."

To get to this point raises another key question, namely, how to address the evolving sea denial and sea control challenges reaching out into the

Sea Lines of Communication (SLOCS). What weapons mix do we need in which engagement zone? It is not going to be all about hypersonic weapons. The strategic shift from the land wars highlights the growing role of dynamic targeting in a contested environment. And as new platforms and capabilities come into the force, they can be looked at in terms of how these new capabilities empower a kill web force, rather than simply fitting into the older kill chain approach.

MISR Officers

Frankly, until a visit with the U.S. Navy Air Boss to San Diego in February 2020, we had never heard of Maritime ISR officers. But now NAWDC is training MISR officers, and they have their own warfighting patch as well. The importance of MISR cannot be understated. As Vice Adm. Miller, the Navy's Air Boss at the time of this writing has put it: "The next war will be won or lost by the purple shirts. You need to take MISR seriously because the next fight is an ISR fight."

The MISR Department head, Cmdr. Pete "Two Times" Salvaggio highlighted what he sees as a cultural shift in the U.S. Navy in interviews conducted in 2020. "We need a paradigm shift: The Navy needs to focus on the left side of the kill chain." The kill chain is described as find, fix, target, engage and assess; Kill chain is to find, fix, track, target, engage and assess. For the U.S. Navy, the weight of effort has been upon target and engage. As "Two Times" puts it "But if you cannot find, fix or track something, you never get to target."

There is another challenge as well: in a crisis, knowing what to hit and what to avoid is crucial to crisis management. This clearly requires the kind of ISR management skills to inform the appropriate decision makers as well. The ISR piece is particularly challenging as one operates across a multi-domain battlespace to be able to identify the best ISR information, even if it is not contained within the ISR assets within your organic task force. And the training side of this is very challenging.

The MISR Patch: Credit: U.S. Navy

That challenge might be put this way: How does one build the skills in the Navy to do what you want to do with regard to managed ISR data and deliver it in the correct but timely manner and how to get the command level to understand the absolute centrality of having such skill sets?

"Two Times" identified a number of key parameters of change with the coming of MISR. "We are finally breaking the old mindset; it is only now that the department heads at NAWDC are embracing the new role for ISR in the fight. We are a unique organization at NAWDC for we do not own a platform. We are not all aviators; we have intel specialists, we have cryptographers, pilots, crewmen, etc. Aviators follow a more rapid pace of actions; non-aviators do not have the same pace of working rapidly within chaos. Our goal at MISR is to be comfortable to work in chaos."

Another part of the shift is to get recognition that ISR does not SUPPORT the force; it is an essential element of the combat capability for the force to be able to operate effectively. It is inherent to the force; not external to it. The kill web approach is about breaking the practice of correlating specific sensors with specific weapons; it is about shaping a much broader understanding of how to work sensor networks to deliver the outcome one is seeking.

"Two Times" argued that the training within NAWDC to build MISR officers is not bad, but the big challenge is to work to break down habitual operational patterns of senior commanders, who really are not focused on how the ISR revolution is changing warfighting. How to do a better job of linking up warfare training outside of NAWDC with the fleet?

They have deployed MISR officers on five CSGs to date; and the reaction of the senior officers is that they would never deploy again without this skill set. But it has taken 2-3 months during the deployment to get senior officers to gain appreciation of what a MISR officer can bring to the fight.

The kill web perspective is founded on a core combat platform or combat group understanding what adjacent forces, whether Navy, joint U.S., or coalition, can be leveraged for enhanced reach and combat effectiveness. The traditional carrier strike group (CSG) model focuses on its organic capabilities, and the skills are honed to get complete combat value from the integrated air wing working with the other elements of the carrier task force.

The kill web model is different. The CSG is operating in the extended battlespace. One is able to deliver multiple functionalities from the CSG, but the focus then is upon contribution to the extended fleet or combat force, but not just in terms of what a tightly integrated CSG can provide This means that it is important to understand what the assets outside of the CSG can bring to the fight and, conversely, how carrier-based assets can contribute more broadly to a distributed fleet as well.

And according to "Two Times," this is one of the key foci of what MISR officers are addressing. "That is what we teach; we are an effects focused contributor; not a platform focused effort. There are not enough platforms to go around; not everyone is going to have their own P-8 but they may well need the kind of information which a P-8 like asset can provide. That is where the MISR approach comes in. You do not need to control the platform. Tell me what it is you need to know about, and we will reach out and find a way to get you that information. What critical pieces of information do you need to make the critical decision that you need to make.

We will find a way to get you that information. And we work that entire process." This is why ISR has moved from being Intelligence, Surveillance and Reconnaissance to Information, Surveillance and Reconnaissance.

In effect, the MISR officers are translators to the fleet of shaping requests for information to the kill web rather than to a specific Navy platform. "You can paint our uniforms into many colors. We are doing multi-domain ISR. We are building products for mission execution that get everyone on the same page."

The coming of MISR is a key part of reshaping the force and building out a kill web foundation for the maritime force. But being knowledgeable about ISR assets throughout the joint and coalition force and being able to tap into those either at the level of CSG or numbered fleet levels will be a significant training challenge. And new ways will have to be found to meet those challenges for sure.

Re-Designing the Strike Syllabus

Cmdr. Papaioanu (N-5 Strike Department Head) has been put in charge at NAWDC for a complete revamping of the strike syllabus at NAWDC. As he underscored in a 2020 interview: "This was the first major rewrite of the strike syllabus at Fallon in more than twenty years."

The change was being driven by the shift from the land wars to great power competition and the need to operate in a fluid extended battlespace. As CDR Papaioanu put it: "The level of modern warfare is nothing like we have seen before. We are talking about extraordinarily intense capabilities across a broad spectrum of warfare." How to fight effectively in such conditions? According to Cmdr. Papaioanu: "The key to the modern fight is an ability to integrate an effective force package."

The strike syllabus has been redesigned to work a combat force able to "integrate an effective force package." Clearly, the coming of the F-35 is part of the technological stimulus to such a rethink and redesign. But it is also part of a significant change in how C^2 and ISR is being used to shape the approach to strike as well. As discussed with Cmdr. Fraser, head of the information warfare department, dynamic targeting is a key capability which the fleet needs to be able to deliver. The new strike syllabus is designed in large part to deliver a dynamic targeting capability. According to Cmdr. Papaioanu, the redesign was driven by inputs from the theater commanders with regard to what they wanted from Naval Aviation in the context of the strategic shift to the high-end fight. Based on feedback from the theater commanders, they began the process of reworking the curriculum. He and his team worked closely with COCOM planning staffs in thinking through the redesign.

On a visit to Eglin Air Force Base, we had a chance to discuss with the Grim Reapers (VFA) 101 who had just stood up in the spring of 2012 at Eglin AFB along the USAF and USMC communities already operating form the base. Credit: *Second Line of Defense.*

The fleet is a key enabler of combat flexibility. "We are the 9/11 force for the nation, so we have to be able to be able to operate across a spectrum of conflict, including higher end missions." As he described a key driver of the change has been with regard to the ISR enablement of the fleet. They are focused increasingly on the left side of the kill chain and leveraging ISR assets to be able to do so. In the kill chain focus, the priority emphasis has been upon target and engage with a priority training focus on targeting.

Cmdr. Papaioanu put it this way: "Now we need to focus much more on the find, fix and track functions. And we need to pay more attention on working with ISR assets to work the left side of the kill chain, and we have altered the syllabus to enable training to work the left side of the kill chain more effectively."

In terms of training, the syllabus emphasizes a couple of core changes. First, is the clear focus on mission command. Cmdr. Papaioanu noted: "We take the mission commanders and challenge them to think through how various assets could be used in an ISR enabled strike package? How will they use the range of capabilities available? How can I as a strike commander take advantage of the sensors on a P-8? How do I ensure that I am getting the kind of information from a platform at the time I need it to execute my mission?"

Cmdr. Christopher Papaioanu, left, off-going commanding officer of Strike Fighter Squadron (VFA) 147, and Cmdr. Patrick Corrigan, on-coming commanding officer of VFA-147, salute each other during the squadron's change of command ceremony on the flight deck of the aircraft carrier USS Nimitz (CVN 68), November 16, 2017. Photo by Petty Officer, 2nd Class. Elesia Patten.

And it is very clear, that the shift in training which CDR Papaioanu described is part of a broader change in the training function. Training in the new syllabus is highly interactive with real world evolution of combat capabilities and operations. This generates a continuous learning cycle for training from ops to training to development and back to ops.

The Way Ahead for the CVW

The U.S. Navy over the next decade will reshape its carrier air wing (CVW) with the introduction of a number of new platforms. If one simply lists the initial operating capabilities of each of these new platforms, and looked at their introduction sequentially, the "air wing of the future" would be viewed in additive terms—what has been added and what has been subtracted and the sum of these activities would be the carrier air wing of the future.

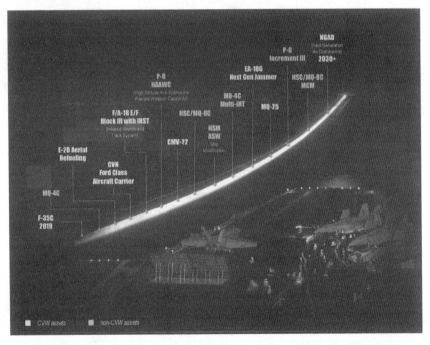

The timeline trajectory for adding platforms to the carrier air wing. But these additions are not simply additive but expanding how the air wing supports the joint and coalition force in terms of kill web integratability. Credit graphic: U.S. Navy

What is underway is a shift from integrating the air wing around relatively modest and sequential modernization efforts for the core platforms to a robust transformation process in which new assets enter the force and create a swirl of transformation opportunities, challenges, and pressures. How might we take this new asset and expand the reach and effectiveness of the carrier strike group? How might it empower maritime, air, and ground forces as we shape a more effective (i.e., a more operationally integrated in terms of effects) force?

What is being set in motion is a new approach where each new platform which comes into the force might be considered at the center of a cluster of changes. The change is not just about integrating a new platform in the flight ops of the carrier. The change is also about how the new platform affects what one can do with adjacent assets in the CSG or how to integrate with adjacent U.S. or allied combat platforms, forces, and capabilities.

Vice Adm. Miller in our interview in February 2020 at his office in North Island, San Diego, provided several examples of how this shift affects the thinking about new platforms coming onboard the carrier deck. One such example is the new unmanned tanker, the MQ-25. The introduction of this new air asset will have an immediate effect in freeing up 4th gen fighters, currently being used for tanking, to return to their strike role. Even more importantly, from a transformation perspective, the MQ-25 will have operational effects as a platform which will extend the reach and range of the CVW.

But MQ-25 will be a stakeholder in the evolving C^2/ISR capabilities empowering the entire combat force, part of what is really 6th generation capabilities, namely enhancing the power to distribute and integrate a force as well as to operate more effectively at the tactical edge. The MQ-25 will entail changes to the legacy air fleet, changes in the con-ops of the entire CVW and trigger further changes regarding how the C^2/ISR dynamic shapes the evolution of the CVW and the joint force.

The systems to be put onto the MQ-25 will be driven by overall changes in the C²/ISR force. These changes are driving significant improvements in size, capability, and integration, so much so that it is the nascent 6th gen. This means that the USN can buy into "6th gen" by making sure that the MQ-25 can leverage the sensor fusion and the integrated communications, navigation, and identification (CNI) systems on the F-35 operating as an integrated force with significant outreach. It is important to realize that an eight-ship formation of an F-35 operating (in the Block IV software configuration) as an integrated man-machine based sensor fusion aircraft can operate together as an eight-ship pack fully integrated through the CNI system, and as such can provide a significant driver of change to the overall combat force.

This affects not only the future of training, but how operations, training, and development affect individual platforms once integrated into the CVW and larger joint force. A key piece in shaping the integratable air wing is building out a new training capability at Fallon and a new set of working relationships with other U.S. and allied training centers. As Vice Admiral Miller put it: "We need to properly train the integratable airwing and we are investing in expanded ranges and new approaches such as Live Virtual Constructive training. I often use the quote that 'your performance in combat never raises to the level of your expectations but rather it falls to the level of your training.' This is why the training piece is so central to the development for the way ahead for the integrable training. It is not just about learning what we have done; but it is working the path to what we can do."

Consider the template of training for carrier air wing integration. On the one hand, the CVW trained at Fallon needs to prepare to go out into the fleet and deliver the capabilities that are available for today's fight. On the other hand, as this template is executed, it is important to shape an evolving vision on how to operate platforms coming to the fleet or how those assets have already been modified by software upgrades.

A software upgradeable fleet, which is at the heart of the 5th gen transition, and which lays down the foundation for 6th generation C^2/ISR provides a key challenge. The F-35 which operated from the last carrier cycle, or flew with the P-8 or Triton, all of these assets might well have new capabilities delivered by the software development cycle. How to make certain that not just the air wing, but the commanders at sea fully understand what has changed? The challenge is to shape the template for training today's fleet; and to ensure that the template being shaped has an open aperture to handle the evolution of the CVW into the evolving integrated and distributed force.

In short, the fleet is in the throes of significant transition as the integratable air wing operates, trains, and further develops and evolves.

CHAPTER THREE:
DISTRIBUTED MARITIME OPS AND
BASING ARCHITECTURE

With the return of the high-end fight, and the challenge of delivering tailored military capabilities to ensure escalation dominance in the maritime domain, a broadened focus on maneuver warfare in the maritime space has emerged. In both theaters which Admiral Gortney highlighted in our interview with him, distributed operations within a wider capability to integrate the force is a key focus of shaping a way ahead for the high-end fight and crisis management.

For North Atlantic defense, Second and Sixth fleets are working with the joint force and allies to shape distributed forces which can integrate to deal with various Russian threats, from the hybrid to the gray zone to high-end warfare. We focus on that in chapter eight. For the Pacific, the defense of the outer islands of Japan through to Guam to Australian defense provides the core defense zone from which power is projected into the areas where the Chinese are pushing out for greater influence and combat effects.

Strategic Geogrpahy

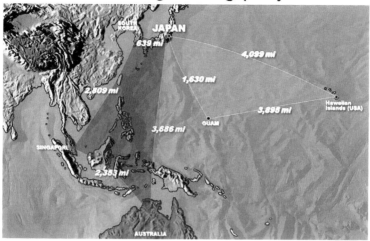

Conceptualizing the strategic triangle of force generation in the Pacific by U.S. forces and the strategic quadrangle of the operation of those forces in the Pacific. Credit: *Second Line of Defense*, 2013.

But distributed operations which can deliver an integrated effect is an art form which requires significant training as well as capabilities to deliver C^2 and relevant information at the tactical edge. But they also provide for connectivity among the pieces on the chessboard to provide for the kind of escalation management crisis for crisis resolution. With the development of flexible multi-mission platforms, there is an ability to flex between offensive and defensive operations within the distributed battlespace. It is clearly challenging to operate such a force, delegate decision making at the tactical edge, but still be able to ensure effective strategic decision-making.

The strategic thrust of integrating modern systems is to create a grid that can operate in an area as a seamless whole, able to strike or defend simultaneously. This is enabled by the evolution of C^2 and ISR systems. By shaping an evolving ISR-enabled C^2 system inextricably intertwined with platforms and assets, which provide for kill web integratable forces, an attack and defense enterprise can operate to deter aggressors and adversaries, or to conduct successful military operations.

The Intersection of DMO with a Basing Architecture

A key element for shaping such a force, able to operate throughout a chess-board on the geo-political space, highlights the need to join the flexibility of seabasing with various other forms of flexible basing which can enable the joint and coalition force. Distributed maritime operations or DMO is part of a larger effort, one in which the joint forces are working force mobility and basing flexibility to intersect with DMO to deliver a much more lethal, and survivable force. It is also one that is agile and can operate at the point of impact within a crisis environment.

The USMC has been for a very long time the core joint force specialist with regard to force mobility. The build out of their aviation capabilities over the past two decades, even while being tasked with Middle East land war duties, has put in place key assets which allow for force mobility. The Osprey has brought speed and range to the assault force. The F-35B has brought a sensor rich, C^2, strike aircraft to naval aviation by the Marines paving the way. The coming of the CH-53K adds another key capability to enable the expeditionary force able to be sustained over from the sea to the sea.[10]

The USAF has certainly gotten the point, and innovations like Rapid Raptor, which is designed to allow for force dispersion in times of crisis is clearly a case in point. We first heard of Rapid Raptor in a discussion in Hawaii with the then head of the Pacific Air Force, General "Hawk" Carlisle, in 2014. He indicated in that discussion that the Rapid Raptor concept was being implemented whereby four F-22s are supported by a C-17 at an airfield different from where they took off. This is a clear indica-tor of the projected trend line. And from discussions with the PACAF staff at the time, it is clear that a major effort is underway to shape the logistics and support approach to allow for the operation of a dispersed air force executing a distributed operational approach throughout the region.

---

10 Laird looks at the USMC transformation process in *The USMC Transformation Path: Preparing for the High-End Fight* (2022).

U.S. Air Force Airmen, assigned to the 517th Airlift Squadron and the 773rd Logistics Readiness Squadron, load cargo on a C-17 Globemaster III while conducting Rapid Raptor training at Joint Base Elmendorf-Richardson, Alaska, March 26, 2015. The training exercised Rapid Raptor capabilities to quickly deploy a package of combat-ready F-22 Raptors and C-17 Globemaster IIIs loaded with supporting personnel and equipment to any forward operating base in the world. (U.S. Air Force photo/Alejandro Pena)

Later discussions at the USMC center of excellence for air-enabled combat training, MAWTS-1 highlighted the recognition which the USAF has for USMC domain knowledge with regard to delivering force mobility. We learned in various visits over the past five years to MAWTS-1, that they were working closely with the Air Warfare Center at Nellis Air Force base regarding expeditionary air operations.

The experience the Marines have had with F-35B, the most expeditionary of all versions of a fifth-generation aircraft, has clearly impacted the reworking of mobile basing as well. For example, in a 2020 discussion at MAWTS-1 with Maj Brian "Flubes" Hansell, MAWTS-1 F-35 Division Head, the expeditionary nature of the USMC and its intersection with and integration with the F-35 was underscored. "The Marine Corps is a force committed to expeditionary operations. When it comes to F-35, we are focused on how best to operate the F-35 in the evolving expeditionary environment, and I think we are pushing the envelope more than other services and other partners in this regard. One of the reasons we are able to do this is because of our organizational culture. If you look at the history of the Marine Corps, that's what we do. We are an expeditionary, forward-leaning service that prides itself in flexibility and adaptability."

The USAF operating from protected land bases—building revetments and working the lost art of rapid runway repair—can provide key elements for providing force to the air-maritime fight that defines both of the threat areas highlighted by Adm. Gortney. And the extant bombers and, even more significantly, the coming of the B-21 will add a very flexible, and scalable force to the distributed seabase chessboard.

Taking off from the USS Wasp in May 2015 during F-35 sea trials. Laird shot this picture while part of a media visit to the ship to witness the sea trials. Credit: *Second Line of Defense.*

An example of the shift in USAF efforts could be seen in the WestPac exercise of January 2020.[11] The exercise had the stated purpose of distributing airpower throughout the operational area and working integratability to shape the desired combat effect. But not overtly noted in the official

11 "18th Wing, Joint Partners Execute First WestPac Rumrunner Exercise," 18th Wing Public Affairs (January 10, 2020), https://www.pacom.mil/Media/News/News-Article-View/Article/2054808/18th-wing-joint-partners-execute-first-westpac-rumrunner-exercise/.

statements was the growing concern and focus on the USAF working with the U.S. Navy and the USMC, and where relevant the U.S. Army to deal with a major threat to its operational basing—the air and maritime strike threat from Russia and China in the Pacific.

Airmen assigned to the 18th Aircraft Maintenance Squadron conduct maintenance on a 44th Fighter Squadron F-15C Eagle during Exercise West-Pacific Rumrunner at Kadena Air Base, Japan, July 31, 2020. The 18th Wing-led exercise was the second of its kind and demonstrated Team Kadena's readiness to operate in contested environments. (U.S. Air Force photo by Staff Sgt. Kristan Campbell)

When the B-21 comes to the force, it will have a significant role in the reworking of the kill web approach to dealing with the air as well as maritime strike threats to USAF operational basing. With the U.S. Navy highlighting a distributed maritime operations approach along with the USAF highlighting its Agile Combat Employment (ACE) approach, a key question is how these will dovetail and shape an effective kill web capability in the Indo-Pacific and European regions.

With the two services clearly focused on ensuring their capabilities to work integrated distributed operations, how do they view the strategic direction they would most like to see from the USMC? What kind of mobile basing and expeditionary operations will be best aligned with where the USAF and the U.S. Navy are shaping their strategic trajectories in their warfighting approaches?

For the U.S. Navy, the evolving approaches to distributed maritime operations involve fighting as a distributed fleet but with integrated combat effects. This involves working on fleet operations which operate over 360-degree space with multi-domain operations and combat effects.

In the next three chapters we address these dynamics of change regarding the amphibious, carrier and maritime patrol forces. But a key part of reworking the seabases as a chessboard force is finding new ways effectively to cross-integrate U.S. and allied maritime assets, such as using aviation assets differently to provide for cross-decking and more effective use of land mass as part of maritime based sea control and sea-denial efforts.

A key cross-decking capability is provided by the Osprey and with the U.S. Navy introducing its version, the CMV-22B, there are expanded capabilities to deliver cross-decking support capabilities to the fleet. In the photo, Laird and Captain Dewon "Chainsaw" Chaney, then the Commander of COMVRMWING (or Fleet Logistics Multi-Mission Wing) at North Island stand in front of the first CMV-22B at the Naval Air Station. June 2020. Credit Photo: U.S. Navy

Mobile basing needs to become a strategic capability, and not just one at the heart of how the USMC operates with in its amphibious mode with the U.S. Navy. This is a subject which deserves greater attention and is the focus of ongoing research by our team and the subject of a forthcoming book.

As the Navy rethinks how to use its aircraft carriers, how to use its amphibious forces and how to use the whole gamut of its surface and subsurface forces to fight as a fleet, an opportunity for change is clear: Why not rework how air assets move across the sea bases to provide the fleet with a wider variety of combat capabilities tailored to specific combat scenarios? Notably, moving helicopters and tiltrotor assets across the fleet provides for a wider variety of options than simply having a set piece of equipment onboard each class of ship. And why not rework the seabases to be bult to further enable the kill web concept of operations?

The mobility of the fleet is a baseline capability which the seabase brings to a more agile combat force. Ships provide for presence, but mobility at sea, with variable degrees of speed and stealth. But added to this are a range of other mobility capabilities which can work effectively with the fleet to expand its reach, range, and lethality. This is certainly part of the wider kill web approach.

The first is the use of land basing either as protected nodes from which air assets, manned or unmanned (for that is what weapons are) can operate as reachback forces to enhance the scalability of a modular at sea task force. We discussed earlier, how the USAF can expand its role in this regard, and in the next section will discuss how the U. S. Army could do so as well.

The second revolves around how the Marines can leverage their expeditionary history and capabilities to operate more effectively with the DMO fleet. One way is to enhance how they can operate off of the amphibious fleet to play an expanded role in sea control and sea denial at sea. Rather than looking at the amphibious fleet as providing greyhound buses to jump off to fight on land, the focus is upon how the amphibious fleet today and redesigned into the future can be part of the wider DMO sea control and sea denial mission sets. We discuss this aspect more fully in the next chapter.

A second way is to enhance their capabilities to operate as crisis management integrated forces, such as marine expeditionary units or marine expeditionary brigades to operate from mobile bases. These capabilities have clearly expanded as they are building out the Osprey-F-35B-CH-53K triad. The focus here is upon having an integrated modular force capability, survivable and lethal enough to fight as an integrated combat force while operating from distributed bases. We discuss this approach more fully later in this chapter.

The third way is what the current Commandant of the USMC has labelled as expeditionary basing. This is the Commandant's version of a wider focus by navies on how to deploy an Inside Force to support the outside force. By the Inside Force, one is referring to a small force operating inside an adversary's weapons engagement zone. The challenge of course is to not have these forces compromise the larger outside force, or to simply put in play chess pieces on the chess board which the adversary can use more effectively than the U.S. forces can. He has referred to these as EABOs, or expeditionary advanced base operations.

Prior to looking at how the USMC is focusing on how it can deliver integrability with the U.S. Navy to expand the basing flexibility for maneuver warfare, both in the littorals and in the blue water, we will look briefly at another partner in leveraging geography to deliver new capabilities, namely, the U.S. Army's missile defense capabilities. For both can deliver, different. but related capabilities to strengthen the survivability and lethality of the fleet notably in Pacific operations where time and distance are key challenges for the operational force.

Re-thinking the Role of ADA in the Maneuver Space

In 2014, we interviewed the first deployed THAAD commander in the Pacific shortly after his unit arrived in Guam. According to the Task Force Talon Commander, Lt. Col. Cochrane, "The mission here is to defend the island of Guam against the North Korean tactical ballistic missile threats. If the strategic deterrent should fail, our task is to intercept North Korean ballistic missiles. We are here to defend the entire island of Guam."

Lt. Col. Cochrane added: "Missile defense is more than just one platform or system. It is a classic case of what you call no platform fights alone. It is a system of systems. We combine Aegis, with THAAD with short-range defense systems, etc. For example, at Hickam Air Force Base in Hawaii, the 94th AAMDC and the 613 AOC coordinate air and missile defense for the Pacific Theater. The Navy and the Air Force all come together and conduct that coordination in terms of how we protect and coordinate our defense so that we are maximizing our capabilities.

"It is not just a single system standing alone or operating independently. It is the inter-dependence and the inter-operability of all these systems to all three of the branches that are actively engaged in missile and air defense. In my unit, we are looking aggressively at how to cross link with Aegis, for example."

Task Force Talon commander Lt. Col. Clyde S. Cochrane III walks U.S. Army Pacific commander Gen. Vincent Brooks to his plane after his visit to the A4 THAAD at Andersen AFB, Guam, on Sunday, Aug. 18, 2013. The A4 THAAD deployed to Guam in April as a part of the 94th AAMDC Task Force Talon Mission. Photo by Angela Kershner, U.S. Army Pacific Public Affairs Office

Lt. Col. Cochrane forecast: "I think you are going to end up seeing more and more emphasis on the continued growth of our cooperative jointness between the Navy (Aegis ships), the Air Force (Defensive Counter Air) and the Army (Air and Missile Defense). It is clear that our operational capabilities are important in and of themselves and as part of strategic messaging to North Korea and to our allies and friends. We tell them, 'We are capable. You threaten this island specifically, we are going to defend this island,' and by doing so we are not only sending a strategic message to North Korea but also to other friends and allies in the area and any potential adversaries."

As the U.S. Navy and the USMC refocus on the Pacific and on blue water maneuver warfare, the U.S. Army could add a significant capability to such warfare. Reimaging how to use ADA in the Pacific could provide a significant contribution to the way ahead for a kill web enabled force. The U.S. and core allies can build out the support facilities throughout the Pacific whereby THAAD and air defense can be supported. THAAD– globally transportable, rapidly deployable capability to intercept and destroy ballistic missiles inside or outside the atmosphere during their final, or terminal, phase of flight. THAAD weight launch vehicle fully loaded 40,000kg=88, 184 lbs. or 44 short tons. The Gross Vehicle Weight Rating (GVWR) of missile battery truck alone is 66,000 lbs.

Now let us rethink how it might be deployed to remote islands as part of a flexible grid. The Marines have already incorporated one key element of an ability to support such an ADA strategy. The MV-22 human capacity is 24 combat-loaded Marines-range approximately 700 miles. The Marines are introducing into the combat force a new CH-53 called the CH-53K which could provide the lift to deliver the ADA weapon to the prepared island. The actual missile battery is 26,000 lbs. and well inside the lift capacity of a CH-53K.

The problem is the mechanics to raise and lower the battery and rearm. A battery lowered from the air on reinforced concrete pads with calibrated launch points may make sense. A separate modular lift device could be put in place to load and reload. Consequently, taking apart modules doesn't appear to be a showstopper, and Marine MV-22s flying in Army ADA troops into any reasonable terrain is absolutely no problem. The weight of TOC and Radar maybe of concern, and it appears that in today's world there may have been little appreciation by Big Army on using MV-22 and CH-53Ks. To be very fair the U.S. Vietnam War Army did get it brilliantly right by setting up firebases in remote areas with helo lift of very heavy guns.

A THAAD island maneuverability concept is the same in principle but with different technology.

With the ability to move a floating airfield as needed inside the potential sanctuary of a 200+ KM protection umbrella of disbursed island bases with ADA batteries, the result would be power projection of the sort needed in Pacific defense.

The island geography around the Pacific Rim is a critical physical reality which such a deployment approach can play to: Japan is an archipelago of 6,852 islands; the Philippine archipelago comprises 7,107 islands, of which only about 2,000 are inhabited; Korea has more than 3,300 islands; Vietnam has 20 Islands--including their claim on Sprats and Parcels cluster; And finally, Republic of China islands provide additional deployment options.

The geography of islands inside the Pacific strategic quadrangle can favor moving a THAAD Battery to various pre-planned island launch pads to protect vital runways and harbors.

When combined with Aegis ships and 7th AF maneuverability, cross-domain synergy is enhanced which can then greatly complicate Chinese and North Korea targeting and thereby enhance deterrence.

In a 2014 visit to the 94th Army Air and Missile Defense Command located at Fort Shafter near Honolulu, Brig. Gen. Daniel Karbler emphasized that the joint force was focused on finding ways to shape enhanced cross domain synergy and cross-linking assets for a kill web defense. One of the participants in the roundtable held at the base during our visit underscored: "The objective is to have the relevant platform to a mission able to draw on deployed sensors within the grid to execute the most effective approach for mission execution. General Hostage (the ACC Commander) has spoken of the combat cloud. That is what we are building here in the Pacific. For example, the contribution of the F-22 may not be in the air-to-air domain but to provide the best sensor available to the relevant task in a mission. The F-35 will add significant new capabilities to the layered approach as well."[12]

The photo shows the participants in the 2014 roundtable on the role of the Army in missile defense in the Pacific and its contributions to the joint force. Credit: *Second Line of Defense.*

The Army's ADA community is truly cutting edge in thinking about an integratable force able to work a very flexible sensor shooter relationship at the heart of a kill web. During our visit to Fort Sill in 2018, the U.S. Army's center of excellence for ADA, we discussed with the senior officers involved in shaping the way ahead regarding ADA in an integrated battlespace. The Air Defense Artillery community is focused upon shaping a more integrated approach to defense with offensive capabilities. A key

---

12 Robbin Laird, "A Key Army Contribution to Pacific Defense: The Evolving Missile Defense Mission," Second Line of Defense (March 11, 2014), https://sldinfo. com/2014/03/a-key-army-contribution-to-pacific-defense-the-evolving-missile-defense-mission/.

driver of change here is working Patriot with THAAD integration via the new Integrated Air and Missile Defense Battle Command System (IBCS).

Here the focus is upon shaping a common operational picture to drive an integrated firing solution set. As IBCS is continued to be tested and refined the ADA branch is also looking at how the military specialties will change as well. With the enhanced integration of THADD with Patriot envisaged under IBCS, there is a planned transition in the military specialties. As one Army officer put it: "So instead of identifying oneself as a Patriot operator or a THAAD operator they will be radar operators or launch operators." And when the Army deploys IBCS, the Army could drive fundamental change in how it transforms and modernizes the force.[13]

As the CO of the Command at the time Brig. Gen. McIntire put it: "This will allow us to componentize acquisition in the future. We can prioritize sensors or weapons and hang them on the network, rather than having to drive stove piped modernization of a particular defensive system. We need to ensure that every requirement we write for a future system is IBCS compliant to drive such a fundamental change." IBCS is clearly a kill web enabler.

The goal for enhanced ground defense capabilities is to empower the joint maneuver force able to operate in the integrated battlespace. The Commanding General captures the forte of the American military as operating as a joint force globally. "The goal is to be able to open up operational space for the maneuver force, whether led by the Air Force or the Army, and to be able to go into the objective area and dominate the adversary. We can debate forever what we think the multi-domain battle means. But at the end of the day, my tactics have to change and my ability to collaborate in the battlespace to enhance joint warfare capabilities with my other service mates."

---

13 https://www.northropgrumman.com/what-we-do/land/
    integrated-battle-command-system-ibcs/.

Basing, Geography and Maneuver Warfare at Sea

What ADA could deliver to the island geography in the Pacific are payloads which could reinforce the ability of the fleet to have greater survival and lethality. As we will argue later in the book, when thinking through a kill web force, payloads are key building blocks for the distributed integrated capability which gives the force the necessary combat power. Those payloads can be found on a variety of sources, from air combat platforms, ships as sea bases, islands, land bases, mobile or expeditionary bases. The kill web mosaic is about having the launch point for key payloads which are appropriate to combat and escalation dominance

In a recent Congressional Research Service note on geography and U.S force structure, a key argument was made along these lines: "The goal of preventing the emergence of regional hegemons in Eurasia is a major reason why the U.S. military is structured with force elements that enable it to deploy from the United States, across broad expanses of ocean and air space, and then conduct sustained, large-scale military operations upon arrival in Eurasia or the waters and airspace surrounding Eurasia. Force elements associated with this objective include, among other things:

- "An Air Force with significant numbers of long-range bombers, long-range surveillance aircraft, and aerial refueling tankers.
- "A Navy with significant numbers of aircraft carriers, nuclear-powered (as opposed to non-nuclear-powered) attack submarines, large surface combatants, large amphibious ships, and underway replenishment ships.
- "Significant numbers of long-range Air Force airlift aircraft and Military Sealift Command sealift ships for transporting ground forces personnel and their equipment and supplies rapidly over long distances.

"Consistent with a goal of being able to conduct sustained, large-scale military operations in Eurasia or the oceans and airspace surrounding Eurasia, the United States also stations significant numbers of forces and supplies in forward locations in Europe, the Persian Gulf, and the Indo-Pacific."[14]

This approach highlights platforms, basing and location. But what we add to this equation is the question of distributed payloads capable of being integrated to deliver the kind of combat and crisis management effects desired. As adversaries have increased their capabilities to attack fixed bases, the United States and its allies have focused on hardening those bases but expanding the role of mobile and flexible basing as well.

No military service has provided greater deep knowledge competence and experience regarding flexible basing than the U.S. Marine Corps. Thus, it is no surprise that a key part of the rethink regarding blue water expeditionary operations and maneuver warfare is seeing greater focus on innovations in terms of the U.S. Navy working with the U.S. Marine Corps.

In a September 2020 visit to MAWTS-1, the USMC's premier weapons training integration facility in the USMC located at MCAS Yuma, we talked with the CO of MAWTS-1, Col Steve Gillette, about the way ahead regarding U.S. Navy-USMC integration. Our interview highlighted the way ahead, and the key role of flexible basing by the USMC in support of core U.S. Navy combat missions.

We started by focusing on ways the Marines might best contribute to the sea control and sea denial mission with the U.S. Navy and allies. Colonel Gillette argued that: "Working through how the USMC can contribute effectively to sea control and sea denial for the joint force is a key challenge. It is the question of how to insert force in the Pacific where a key combat capability is to bring assets to bear on the Pacific chessboard. The long-precision weapons of adversaries are working to expand their reach and shape an opportunity to work multiple ways inside and outside those strike zones to shape the battlespace.

---

14 "Defense Primer: Geography, Strategy and Force Design," *Congressional Research Service*, November 5, 2020.

"What do we need to do in order to bring our assets inside the red rings our adversaries are seeking to place on the Pacific chessboard? How do you bring your chess pieces onto the board in a way that ensures or minimizes both the risk to the force and enhances the probability of a positive outcome for the mission? How do you move assets on the chessboard inside those red rings which allows us to bring capabilities to bear on whatever end state we are trying to achieve?

"For the USMC, as the Commandant has highlighted, it is a question of how we can most effectively contribute to the air-maritime fight. For us, a core competence is mobile basing which clearly will play a key part in our contribution, whether projected from afloat or ashore. What assets need to be on the chess board at the start of any type of escalation? What assets need to be brought to bear and how do you bring them there? I think mobile basing is part of the discussion of how you bring those forces to bear.

U.S. Marine Corps Lt. Col. Steve Gillette, VMFA-121 squadron commander, explains the capabilities of the F-35B Lightning II to Dr. Ng Eng Hen, Singapore minister of defense, at Luke Air Force Base, Ariz., Dec. 10, 2013. (U.S. Air Force photo by Senior Airman Jason Colbert)

"How do you bring forces afloat inside the red rings in a responsible way so that you can bring those pieces to the chess board or have them contribute to the overall crisis management objectives? How do we escalate and de-escalate force to support our political objectives? How do we, either from afloat or ashore, enable the joint force to bring relevant assets to bear on the crisis and then once we establish that force presence, how do we manage it most effectively? How do we train to be able to do that? What integration in the training environment is required to be able to achieve such an outcome in an operational setting in a very timely manner?"

One way to do this is to reshape the current amphibious fleet to provide for sea control and sea denial capabilities. This fleet is changing with the addition of the new America-class ships being a key driver for change. We discuss this more fully in the next chapter, but Colonel Gillette provided insight into the way ahead. "The traditional approach for the amphibious force is to move force to an area of interest. Now we need to look at the entire maritime combat space, and ask how we can contribute to that combat space, and not simply move force from A to B.

"I think the first leap is to think of the amphibious task force, as you call it, to become a key piece on the chess board. As with any piece, they have strengths and weaknesses. Some of the weaknesses are clear, such as the need for a common operational picture, a command-and-control suite to where the assets that provide data feeds to a carrier strike group are also incorporated onto L-Class shipping. We're working on those things right now, in order to bring the situational awareness of those types of ships up to speed with the rest of the Naval fleet.

"There is a significant shift underway. The question we are now posing is: 'What capability do I need, and can I get it from a sister service that already has something that provides the weapons, the C^2 or the ISR that I need? I need to know how to exploit information which benefits either my situational awareness, my offensive or defensive capability of my organic force. But you don't necessarily need to own it in order to benefit from it.

"And I think that when we really start talking about integration, that's probably one of the things that we could realize very quickly is that there are certain assets and data streams that come from the Air Force or the

Navy that make the USMC a more lethal and effective force, and vice versa.

"The key question becomes: 'How do I get the most decisive information into an LHA/LHD? How do I get it into a marine unit so that they can benefit from that information and then act more efficiently or lethally when required?'"

Shaping a Way Ahead for Mobile Basing

The USMC has mobile basing in its DNA. With the strategic shift from the Middle Eastern land wars to full spectrum crisis management, an ability to distribute a force but to do so with capabilities which allow it to be integratable is crucial. For the Marines, this means an ability to operate an integratable force from sea bases, forward operating bases (FOBs) or forward arming and refueling points (FARPs). As the Marines look forward to the decade ahead, they are likely to enhance their capabilities to provide for mobile bases which can empower the joint and coalition force by functioning as a chess piece on the kill web enabled chessboard.

But what is required to do mobile basing? What are the baseline requirements to be successful? A very good place to start to shape answers to these questions is the USMC's center of excellence on warfighting training, MAWTS-1 located at MCAS Yuma. In two 2020 discussions with LtCol Barron, Tactics and Evaluation (ADT&E) Department Head at MAWTS-1, the officer provided several insights with regard to mobile basing. There is a base line requirement for decision makers to determine why a mobile base is being generated and what the tactical or strategic purpose of doing so is. It takes time and effort to create a mobile base, and the mobile base commander will need to operate with mission command with regard to his base to determine how best to operate and for what purpose.

Next it is crucial to determine the projected duration of the particular base which entails the core question of sustainability. How long and for what duration shapes the understanding of what kind of modular force is enabling a mobile base and for what purpose. What is needed? How to get it there? And from what supply depot—afloat or ashore in adjacent areas? What needs to be at the base to provide for organic survivability? What crosslinks via C^2 and ISR will provide for an extended kill web to support the base and its survivability?

No mobile base fights alone. With the evolution of technology, it is possible now to have processing power, and strike capabilities distributed and operated by a smaller logistics footprint force, but how best to configure that base to provide the desired combat effect for the joint or coalition force?

How to better ensure the mobile bases survival and effectiveness during it operational duration?

Operating in a contested environment requires signature control, or an ability to have as small a signature footprint as possible, commensurate with achieving the desired combat effect. Signature management could be seen as a component of survivability.

Finally, it is crucial to have an exit strategy in mind. For how long should the force be at the mobile base? For what purposes? And what needs to be achieved to enable the decision to move from the mobile base?

As the U.S. services work their way ahead in the evolving strategic environment, the USMC core skill set with mobile basing will figure more prominently and become a key part of the Marines working with the joint and coalition force in shaping a more effective way ahead for the integrated distributed force. The Marines have added new capabilities which allow them to enhance their capabilities to work mobile and accretionary basing. For example, the heavy lift element – the CH-53C --which is a bedrock capability for the insertion force, is older, not easily integratable, and is in diminishing numbers. The CH-53K which is to replace it will provide significant capability enhancements for an insertion force operating from afloat or ashore mobile bases but needs to be ramped up in numbers capable of raising the combat level of the current force.

Laird with LtCol Frank, VMX-1, at New River, July 13, 2021,
standing in front of one of the unit's CH-53Ks.

In short, the Marines will fight with the force they have; and as far as near-term modernization, ensuring that digital interoperability is built in and accelerated, full use of what an F-35 wolfpack can bring to the insertion force, and the continuing modernization of the assault force staring with the coming of the CH-53K in sufficient numbers, these are all elements for enhancing mobile basing capabilities moving forward.

Military capabilities are being reshaped to operate in a contested environment involving peer competitors, and there is a clear opportunity to leverage new platforms and systems to shape a military structure more aligned with the new strategic environment. Mobile basing and recrafting combat operational architecture are clearly key parts in shaping military capabilities for the new strategic environment. Mobile basing is an air-maritime-army effort to shape a chessboard of capabilities which can deal with the threats of peer competitors which deploy into the extended battlespace.

As Jim Strock, former Director of the Seabasing Integration Division at the USMC, put it in a recent interview: "Sea control against adversaries that are relying on long-range fires to push our fleet back further is a key challenge. The carriers, the submarines, the DDGs provide significant firepower and can extend sea control in terms of firing solutions. But the expeditionary force based on the interconnected sea bases from which one can project an air and ground integrated force provides a very different but complimentary capability to the largely missile strike force.

'I think what needs to be really brought into the conversation about these new operating environments is how Naval Expeditionary Forces with the current and evolving aviation capabilities can operate across all the warfighting functions, C^2, fires, maneuver, logistics, force, protection, and ISR. How can you leverage their ability to extend sea power ashore in these new operating environments?"[15]

Jim Strock during our interview with him in a
2010 visit to his office at Quantico.

Fortunately for the sea services, such a re-imaging and reinvention is clearly possible, and future acquisitions which drive new connectors, new support elements, and enhanced connectivity could drive significant change in the value and utility of the amphibious fleet as well. In addition, as the fleet is modernized new platform designs can be added to the force

15 Robbin Laird, "Mobile Basing as a Strategic Capability," *Defense.info* (January 18, 2022), https://defense.info/re-thinking-strategy/2022/01/ mobile-basing-as-a-strategic-capability-continuing-the-conversation/.

as well to create moving "islands" from which operations can be staged and sustained.

The ability to operate, sustain, defend, and project power will be re-shaped as new connectors, different ways of using aviation assets, the addition of a core capability like directed energy weapons is added to the fleet, and the potential for the USAF to incorporate seabasing as part of agile combat employment could drive both force redesign and con-ops innovation for force distribution and integration.

The U.S. Army if it is to be of real relevance in the evolving strategic situation in the Pacific, both from the standpoint of U.S. forces and for allied forces can build out its ability to work from seabases as well as to add speed and range to its forces as well. Buying a high-speed helicopter or tiltrotor platform combing with working with a significant national effort to build out the maritime side of basing can provide a significant enhancement to the U.S. Army's role in the Pacific as well.

Autonomous systems can provide significant connectors for the forces at sea, as well as delivering a variety of payloads which can be delivered by air or sea to areas of interest. From this point of view, the future evolution of Unmanned Surface Vessels (USVs), for example, can be considered as contributing seabasing nodes for the extended battlespace.

The U.S. Navy launched Task Force 59 in September 2021 to focus on ways to integrate autonomous system and artificial intelligence with maritime operation in the 5th Fleet area of operations. In the photo, Secretary of Defense Lloyd J. Austin III speaks with Cmdr. Tom McAndrew, Deputy Commodore Task Force 59, Unmanned & Artificial Intelligence (A.I.) Integration in Bahrain, Nov. 21, 2021. MARTAC's Devil Ray USV is seen in the background. Photo by Chad McNeeley, Office of the Secretary of Defense Public Affairs.

The entire Naval strike fleet can be rethought in terms of how it could and should operate as a significantly enhanced seabasing approach is shaped and implemented as well. The new USS Gerald R. Ford, for example, is uniquely suited to take advantage of such a revolution if it were to occur.

There is the question as well as how to use larger seabasing platforms as mother "islands" from which to launch both air and smaller sea platforms to reach into the extended battlespace. Sustainability is enhanced for the forward projected force by having a capability to reach back to the "mother" floating islands as well.

And force distribution enhanced by a robust seabasing enterprise would provide for the kinds of combat clusters or modular task forces which the U.S. and the allies will shape going forward to project the kind of influence and power necessary to engage in the kinds of operations necessary for crisis management and escalation control.

CHAPTER FOUR:
THE EXPEDITIONARY SEA BASING
FORCE IN MANEUVER WARFARE

The U.S. Navy will never have enough ships to dominate as it did in World War II with the strike force that hit Saipan. And with the naval build-up of the Chinese and the Russians, the threat envelope is expanding at the same time.

This means that the U.S. Navy will need to get full value out of the ships they have and to leverage flexible basing options in maritime maneuver warfare, shape enhanced integratability with the USAF and find more effective ways to operate with allies and partners. Shaping an integrated distributed force for maneuver warfare at sea, operating through interactive kill webs, is not a nice transformation to have but a requisite one.

There is no area where better value could be leveraged than making dramatically better use of the amphibious fleet for extended battlespace operations. This requires a re-imaging of what that fleet can deliver to sea control and sea denial as well as Sea Lines of Communication (SLOC) offense and defense.

Fortunately for the sea services, such a re-imaging and reinvention is clearly possible, and future acquisitions which drive new connectors, new support elements, and enhanced connectivity could drive significant change in the value and utility of the amphibious fleet as well. In addition, as the fleet is modernized new platform designs can be added to the force as well. And as we will address later in the book, this entails shaping variant payloads as well to be delivered from a distributed integrated amphibious fleet. As building out the evolving fleet, larger capital ships will be supplemented and completed with a variety of smaller hull forms, both manned and autonomous, but the logistics side of enabling the fleet will grow in importance and enhance the challenges for a sustainable distributed fleet. That is certainly why the larger capital ships – enabled by directed energy weapons as well – will see an enhanced role as mother ships to a larger lego-like cluster of smaller hull forms as well.

The Return to the Sea and Bold Alligator

During the land wars, the USMC leadership understood that they needed to prepare for the return to the sea as a primary domain for the way ahead for USMC combat operations. It is difficult to overstate how dominant the warfighting experience ashore has been for shaping this generation of Marines. But it is also an overstatement that the return to the sea started with call of the current Commandant to enhance naval integration capabilities for the USMC itself. It did not.

That call to return to the sea was crystallized in the launching of the Bold Alligator series of exercises beginning with Bold Alligator 2011. We attended several of the Bold Alligator series exercises and witnessed how the USMC, the U.S. Navy and several allies and partners joined in the relaunch in many ways of the next generation of amphibious warfare being transformed now into expeditionary sea control, sea denial and force insertion. For that relaunch was happening, as the Osprey was joining the fleet.

Bold Alligator 2012 (BA-12) was a training exercise for the expeditionary strike group, and the shaping of a new template for the amphibious task force with the coming of the Osprey and the anticipated arrival of the F-35. The template introduced in BA-12 provided a lay down within which force modernization associated with the F-35B and the VM-22 unfolded. What was evident in that exercise, and the Bold Alligator exercises which followed, was that the amphibious fleet was shifting from using the ships to function largely as a Greyhound bus carrying Marines ashore to becoming a strike force at sea, and from the sea and from the shore back to the sea.

At that 2012 exercise we discussed the effort being generated at the time to lay down a new template with officers involved with that exercise Capt. Sam Howard at the time of the exercise was Special Assistant to the Chief of Staff of U.S. Fleet Forces Command in Norfolk VA and Marine Col Phil Ridderhof, was senior Marine Corps adviser to U.S. Fleet Forces Command in Norfolk, Va. Capt. Howard began his career in destroyer operations and most recently before his Norfolk Assignment was the skipper of the USS Bataan. During his time on Bataan, he participated in the Haiti relief efforts.

Capt. Howard emphasized that one of the opportunities generated by the Bold Alligator exercise was to familiarize other services with the key advantages provided to the joint force by seabasing capabilities. "A seabase is a concept that regrettably is foreign to the other services, at least in real practice; and we were able to certainly demonstrate it in real practice in real-time in the case of Haiti and will be able to expand on the exercise." Howard underscored the importance of the exercise as a combined arms approach and useful to re-shaping military doctrine. "It's a combined arms endeavor, and so getting to that thought process of making it a combined arms thing is certainly very important to us."

Captain Howard during our 2012 interview.
Credit: *Second Line of Defense.*

Col Ridderhof picked up on the combined arms theme introduced and discussed by Capt. Howard. He emphasized that the exercise was built in part around operating at a different level than an Amphibious Ready Group-Marine Expeditionary Unit (ARG-MEU) was capable of operating. "The ARG and the MEU are very important, very capable. When you start getting bigger than the ARG and the MEU an amphibious operation is not simply a quantitative increase. There's a qualitative difference in how you think about organizing the task force.

"The ARG-MEU is built around three core ships and the MEU is of a regimental size, with a battalion landing team, combat logistics, battalion, and the composite squadron. The MEB being used in this exercise is a different animal. One of our challenges in the Marine Corp is how do you describe the MEB? It can be anywhere from 10,000 to 17,000 soldiers, but in general, it is a regimental landing team with at least three battalions, plus a Marine air group size of an aviation combat element and combat logistics regiment-sized support element.

"One of the key things is that to do all six functions of Marine Corp Aviation, to do command and control, is central to the operational capabilities. A MEU has little pieces, but to do the big Marine Corp Aviation Command and Control pieces is a significant jump in capability. You need all of the pieces of Marine aviation, and then all the logistics to sustain that for 30 days plus."[16]

And the large-deck carrier is shifting its approach as part of this operational construct. Col Ridderhof underscored: "Bold Alligator is testing today's capability but because we haven't done this this way. The Combined Force Maritime Component Commander (CFMCC) has typically not been considering the littoral as a whole, going all the way to that objective ashore as his battle space. He's influencing it surely but hasn't been thinking of it all the way there. Just as the ARG MEU would be first on the scene, how does the Carrier Strike group fold into the scalability of the operation?"

---

16 The six functions of Marine Corps Aviation are offensive air support, anti-air warfare, assault support, air reconnaissance, electronic warfare, and control of aircraft and missiles.

Capt. Howard emphasized: "The reality is, all this is in the context of a joint war fighting organization. And among the lessons we will take from this is how to develop further the unique war fighting relationship between the Navy and Marine Corps and how does that best plug into the total force, joint force."

One could note that the current focus on how the Navy and the Marine Corps could integrate more effectively for the peer fight was already being worked in 2012. It just required the nation's political leadership to get caught up with what its real priorities were. Or put simply: the refocus on the strategic shift from the primacy of the land wars to engaging peer competitors was already underway in this Bold Alligator 2012 exercise.

In our interview with BGen Owens, the 2nd MEF Commander, held after that exercise, he highlighted how he saw the exercise effort. "One of the things that was different in this exercise from many previous amphibious large-scale exercises is we executed in what we called a medium threat, anti-access, area denial (A2AD) environment. The threat focus is primarily on the area denial piece, which is closer in, but which is more realistic for the timeframe of the exercise.

"The threat we faced at sea started with submarines, missile patrol boats, fast-attack craft, fast inshore attack craft, and some asymmetric threats with commandeered fishing boats, low slow-flyers, and some tactical air. But of greater concern was coastal defense cruise missiles, initially fixed sites, as well as mobile, and then ultimately, just a threat of additional mobile sites.

"And then, the most ubiquitous threat that we're going to face is mines. In the exercise, we faced a very robust mining capability. We had a wide range of capabilities on the Navy side to help deal with those threats, but we also integrated the MEB in that, particularly our air. These assets were used both in targeting threats to the amphibious taskforce ashore, as well as providing defense of the amphibious taskforce primarily with our aviation asset. But we also involved some of our ground combat elements when they were aboard the ship.

Brigadier General Owens during our interview with him.
Credit: *Second Line of Defense.*

"That continued even after we went ashore. And this is something that we really haven't practiced; this full integration, of the Marine capability in the overall ability to both to project force, and to protect those naval assets that are projecting that force."

The exercise was focused on redesign of the current force structure to achieve the desired combat effect in order to lay down a template for the changes to come. As Brig. Gen Owens put it: "I think flexibility is a key word. In this exercise, we focused on today's forces for today's fight. What it really was about was getting the greatest impact, the greatest benefit out of the capabilities we have. For example, in our countermine effort, we recognize that in order to do countermine work here on the east coast of the U.S., it's going to involve coalition participation. So, we had Canadian mine hunters out working with U.S. divers in conjunction with Dutch divers, Canadian divers supported by the Coast Guard providing a cutter to help provide force protection for the mine hunters.

"And our Navy forces provided close in protection for both the mine hunters, and then subsequently, for some of our maritime sealift command shipping that was coming into the same areas. Thus, in addition to integrating the Marine and Navy pieces, we also expanded our search to what other capabilities that other countries, other services, for instance, the coast guard, and even the interagency could provide. We didn't really touch on the inter-agency aspect too much in Bold Alligator 12, but it is an aspiration for the future. We want to be able to tap into capabilities that will help us defeat some of these asymmetric threats, in particular, in order to project force ashore."

BGen Owens underscored a very key point about shaping a way ahead with the force you have to shaping the future force. "From this point of view, the goal of the exercise was to shape an effective concept of operations with current capabilities. *We've got to have the concept of operations in place as we integrate new capabilities going forward.*"

The latest capability which was included at the time was the Osprey. In fact, while journalists waited on shore for the insertion force, the Osprey team had led an assault deep into the battlespace. And even more interestingly, the Ospreys launched from a range of sea bases, including a Military Sealift Command ship. At the time, we highlighted how the coming of the Osprey impacted thinking about the amphibious assault force. "An assault raid was conducted from the seabase deep inland (180 miles) aboard the Ospreys with allied forces observing or participating. The Osprey was the key element operating in this exercise, which was not there during the last big "amphibious" exercise." [17]

And with the launch from an MSC ship, the Osprey was highlighting the next phase, rather than focusing on the ARG-MEU, one could think in terms of an amphibious task force. This is how BGen Owens highlighted the importance of the event. "The T-AKE is bringing in our dry cargo. So they bring in beyond what the amphibious ships carry, they'll bring in food, water, and they are ships that bring in our ammunition. That was what we exercised using the MV-22s to land on the T-AKE, and we had our logistics regiment Marines posted aboard the TAKE to work on the distribution piece."

---

17 Robbin Laird, "Bold Alligator: A Glimpse of Marine, Navy Future," *Breaking Defense* (March 21, 2012), https://breakingdefense.com/2012/03/bold-alligator-a-glimpse-of-marine-navy-future/

An MV-22 Osprey assigned to the Fighting Griffins of Marine Medium Tiltrotor Squadron (VMM) 266 makes a historic first landing aboard the Military Sealift Command dry cargo and ammunition ship USNS Robert E. Peary (T-AKE 5). The Osprey landed aboard Robert E. Peary while conducting an experimental resupply of Marines during exercise Bold Alligator 2012. February 9, 2012, photo by LTJG Michael Sheehan.

We followed up on the event of an Osprey landing on a T-AKE ship which has been the harbinger to the cross-decking revolution which the Osprey can unlock for today's navy as the U.S. Navy adds its own Osprey to the fleet. We went to the T-AKE ship involved in the exercise, the USNS Robert E. Peary and talked about the event with the ship's captain, Captain Little. We have written extensively about the Military Sealift Command on our websites and in our 2013 book on the redesign of our Pacific forces. This is what we wrote after our meeting onboard with Captain Little in our 2012 piece:

"Captain Little is a graduate of the Merchant Marine Academy and has operated off of virtually every asset Military Sealift Command operates, since he joined in 1989. He was the first chief mate for the T-AKE 5 when it was delivered to the Navy in 2008. He and his crew had just returned from a 9 ½ month tour, which included action off of Libya as well as participation in the Bold Alligator 2012 exercise. Notably, the helos, which operate off of his ship during deployments, are either USN helos, or Eurocopter

Pumas. And the ship is extremely flexible in providing supplies of various kinds, including ammunition and fuel. During the Libyan operation, the USNS Robert E. Peary worked with several allies as well.

"The men and women of the Military Sealift Command are true mariners. They operate at sea off and on during the year with only three months off. They are civil servants but are closely intertwined in support of the warfighter. As Susan Melow, Public Affairs Officer, for MSC's Military Sealift Fleet Support Command clarified for us: "A civil service mariner, or CIVMAR, is a federal government employee who pursues a civil service career while assigned aboard U.S. government-owned, Military Sealift Command-operated ships responsible for global fleet support. CIVMARs are credentialed, in their areas of expertise, by the U.S. Coast Guard and are rotationally assigned to MSC ships for stints of, at a minimum, four months. With no shore duty breaks during their civil service careers and with, generally, thirty days separating each ship assignment, CIVMARs are consummate mariners, journeymen in their fields."

"Question: Captain, could you talk a little bit about the Osprey landing on the T-AKE ship?

"Captain Little: The Osprey landing was a long-range supply demonstration. It took off from New River, landed on our ship, got refueled and then participated in a raid on Fort Pickett more than 180 miles inland. The Osprey was on deck for about 30 minutes, loaded four pallets, was able to refuel, and took off with her cargo to support the Marines ashore in Fort Pickett.

"Question: And you had sent some of your crew down to New River to prepare for the exercise?

"Captain Little: Yes, we wanted to prepare for the Osprey event. We wanted to go down to New River and get familiar with the Osprey. We wanted to prepare for the practical things like, how to tie it down on the deck.

"Comment: We talked with the Osprey squadron commander, and he was pleasantly surprised to find that you could re-fuel his plane.

"Captain Little: We are used as a refueler in fleet operations. We have limits when it comes to re-fueling ships but can refuel helicopters all day if we had to."[18]

Ed Timperlake with Captain Little onboard the USNS Robert E. Peary after our interview. Credit: *Second Line of Defense.*

In fact, the "return to the sea" energized by the training efforts in the Bold Alligator exercises came while the Osprey was making its broader impact on the USMC. There is no more dramatic case of a platform introducing disruptive change in a service than the Osprey to the USMC. The USMC is the only tiltrotor-enabled combat force in the world, and it has introduced significant change throughout the redesign of the USMC and is continuing to do so as the USMC works its evolving approach to integration with the U.S. Navy in blue water expeditionary operations. After an initial learning curve of how to integrate the Osprey with the Amphibious Ready Group-Marine Expeditionary Force, the speed and range of the

---

18 "TAK-ING the Supply Ship to a Whole New Level," *Second Line of Defense* (April 2, 2012), https://sldinfo.com/2012/04/tak-ing-the-supply-ship-to-a-whole-other-level/.

Osprey changed the ARG-MEU and reshaped how the amphibious ships would deploy in support of combatant commanders.

In Bold Alligator 2013, the working relationships between the U.S. Navy and the USMC were strengthened as the U.S. Navy began to focus more on how to support sea-based power projection with USMC force mix. As Col Bradley Weisz, Deputy Commander, Expeditionary Strike Group TWO, commented at the time about Bold Alligator 2013: "We are getting away from the legacy stove-pipe systems and moving to better collaboration, and more integration with our entire fleet force. This is essential in today's complex and constantly evolving operating environment; especially when you start talking about the increased anti-access and area-denial (A2/AD) threats that we will face and encounter in the littoral regions. Yes, we are developing and shaping some innovative approaches to deal with these emerging threats.

Col Bradley Weisz, Deputy Commander, Expeditionary Strike Group TWO, during our 2012 interview with him. Credit: *Second Line of Defense*. The quotes are taken from our meeting during BA 2013.

"As far as leveraging our sea basing capabilities in direct support of our amphibious forces, we will aggressively employ and utilize nine military sealift command ships, MSC ships, as part of our logistics task force.

We will have three fleet oilers (T-AOs) that can hold and carry a sizable amount of class I (subsistence) and class III (POL). We will also have two highly capable dry cargo/ammunition ships (T-AKEs) that can haul and deliver substantial amounts of class III (POL) and class V (ground/aviation ammunition) products.

A fleet oiler seen during a visit to the Military Sealift Command in Norfolk, VA in 2016. Credit: *Second Line of Defense*.

"Along with the T-AOs and T-AKEs, we will have one fast combat support ship (T-AOE) that can provide significant class I (subsistence), class III (POL) and class V (ground/aviation ammunition) capabilities in support of our CSG and ATF forces. Additionally, we will employ and utilize one Aviation Logistics Support Ship (T-AVB) that will provide crucial aviation intermediate maintenance support and repair services to all of our landing force aircraft afloat. This includes all fixed wing, rotary wing, and tilt rotor aircraft afloat."

And in an interview during the Bold Alligator 2013 exercise with Rear Admiral Ann Phillips, the 2nd ESG commander, and with BGen John Love, the 2nd MEB Commander, it was evident that shaping a way ahead for the kill web force was already under way. This is how Rear Admiral Phillips put it:

"Historically, when one thinks about the traditional role of the surface fleet, say in World War II, one focuses upon naval surface fire support and the role of naval guns. But in this day and age, we have a lot more options and alternatives with other weapons, and with our ability to respond, in time, to cyber activities and other challenges.

Rear Admiral Phillips during the Bold Alligator 2013 Exercise.
Credit: *Second Line of Defense.*

"Today's surface force has a greater capacity, and we'll have even more capacity in the future with capabilities like Navy's Integrated Fire Control – Counter Air to support forces ashore. We can influence the battle space to support the maneuver of Marine forces on the ground with a number of capabilities

"For example, when talking about a significant air and missile defense threat, you've got to remove that threat. Maritime forces, including Carrier Aviation and long-range TOMAHAWK Strike missiles strategically roll the threat back to gain entry and to gain space for operations. The Amphibious Task Force augmented with Cruiser and Destroyers for defense and power projection then provides the support and capability to the ground force to enter the battlespace and then continues that support once forcible entry is achieved.

"What we did here over the past several weeks in the Bold Alligator 2013 exercise was to work on combining the capabilities inherent in the Amphibious Task Force with the ground forces to shape a more effective force able to be inserted and withdrawn as needed. The fleet provides the ground force with support from a close in seabase that's taking care of intel, logistics, fire support, C^2 and close air support. All of this is managed from the seabase and projected forward in support of maneuver ashore. In the future, capabilities will continue to grow. For example, the Aegis radar over time has improved considerably. It has a much better capability and capacity over land now than it ever has. And radars of the future, such as the new Air and Missile Defense Radar will go even beyond that."

BGen Love added: "The exercise featured an anti-access and area denial threat which was dealt with primarily by carrier strike groups, but with the assistance of forward-deployed Marine forces. We placed two of our Marine Expeditionary Units, embarked upon amphibious ships, under the tactical control of the carrier strike groups and they played an important role in rolling back the threat.

"Once we moved into the amphibious objective area, we knew the capabilities that were provided by the fleet. We knew what the carriers provided, and we knew what the ESG provided. And as a consequence of that, we were able to craft a ground scheme of maneuver that took some calculated risks, knowing the capabilities inherent in the fleet.

"We conducted operational maneuver on the sea prior to conducting operational maneuver from the sea. In other words, we used the littorals as maneuver space, which allowed us to pick and choose the time and location of our landing, and also to use littorals as part of the deception plan.

"Simultaneous with our landing, we were actually using another amphibious ready group further south as part of our deception plan. We were able to disguise the location of our landing.

Brigadier General Love working the U.S. Navy team as seen during the exercise. Credit: *Second Line of Defense.*

"When we went ashore, because of the sea base, we did not need to establish a large logistics build-up, and I didn't need to worry about establishing a mature command and control apparatus ashore. I could rely on all those things coming from the Naval force and from my command post afloat.

"This allowed me to be light and agile ashore, and it allowed me to keep my lines of communication very narrow, thereby reducing unnecessary risks. I was able to reduce the force's exposure to risk ashore from either violent extremist organization or the conventional threat. And it allowed me to deal as well with an obvious political requirement of not coming in with a heavy force perceived as an occupation force. Politically, it will often be the case that a very light footprint will be required to send a message of non-occupation, and it will also allow the force to withdraw rapidly should situations politically or militarily dictate.

"In the Marine Corps, we've built our Marine air/ground taskforce specifically so that we can provide our own fire support. And that's why we have such a balanced aviation element in our MAGTFs. It is also dependent upon ashore based fire support, artillery and capabilities like the HIMARS system. In this case, we were able to put very little of this capability ashore because we knew we had the Marine aviation assets afloat and that we had two carrier strike groups that could provide that support for us."

Bold Alligator 2014 was a crisis response exercise and continued the work of Bold Alligator 2012 and Bold Alligator 2013. The exercise involved working with an evolving C^2 capability to manage forces operating throughout key objective areas. The presence of the Osprey allowed the U.S. and its allies to operate against longer range objective areas as well as other objective areas reachable by rotorcraft and reinforced by landing forces.

The seabases involved in the exercises were characterized by logistical integrity meaning the insertion forces can be supported by the seabase, and it is not necessary to build forward operating bases or to land significant supplies ashore in order to prosecute missions. It is a force tailored to crisis management, as opposed to having to rely on bringing significant forces ashore along with their gear in order to mount operations.

A key part of the Bold Alligator 2014 exercise was a major effort to rework command and control for force insertion from the seabase able to work with the maneuver forces ashore. Follow up interviews in 2015 with MajGen Richard L. Simcock II, Commanding General, 2d MEB, and Maj Marcus Mainz, lead 2d MEB planner for Exercise Bold Alligator 2014 highlighted the evolving approach. They underscored innovations in aviation which allowed the Marines to extend their reach and provide greater flexibility for amphibious operations. The reworking of the amphibious fleet to deliver capabilities to project power from the sea and the ability of the infantry to implement innovations in maneuver warfare and force insertion require creativity in operational design and C^2.

2d MEB exercises C^2 of scalable and modular forces by delegating it to a level where tactical operations are more effective. This construct facilitates mastery of the operational environment in a fluid combat situation by keeping focus at the appropriate levels. It gives the MEB CE (command element) the capability to focus on the operational art that bridges the strategic and tactical levels for political objectives.

Execution of the mission, empowerment of subordinate leaders at the appropriate level, and maintaining situational awareness of the overall situation is a key challenge for C². The complexity begins with incorporation of joint and coalition forces for Combined Joint Task Force (CJTF), operations. Given that joint and coalition capabilities enhance response time and effectiveness of global operations, C² takes on a whole new meaning when shaping the appropriate composite force for missions across the ROMO (Range of Military Operations), which makes it central to effective Marine Corps Operations as the nation shapes the challenge of prevailing in full-spectrum crisis management.

Crisis Management Force Structure

From Presence to Conflict Dominance Force

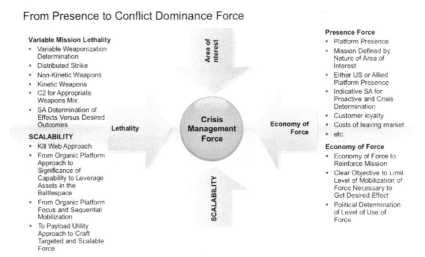

Conceptualizing the shaping of a crisis management force structure for dealing with global challenges and the engagement of peer competitors. *Credit: Second Line of Defense*

MajGen. Simcock explained in his interview that the importance of "providing the Combatant Commander with a force capable of plugging into various joint, coalition, and interagency requirements is essential. The realities of the 21st century security environment demand a smart power approach inclusive of all services of the military, our partners and interagency organizations, which play an integral role in fulfilling National Security Strategy."

Integration of allied and partner nation operational capabilities and systems with the U.S. amphibious fleet will develop, in effect, a global U.S.-Allied amphibious fleet capability. MajGen Simcock also discussed emerging demand for partnership with 2d MEB in global security "since the Marine Corps has revitalized the MEB concept capable of world-wide deployment, we have been contacted by many of our coalition partners, allies and other nations interested in training and operating with 2d MEB."

U.S. Marine Corps Maj. Gen. Richard L. Simcock II, right, outgoing 3rd Marine Division commanding general, shakes hands with Maj. Gen. Craig Q. Timberlake, left, incoming 3rd Marine Division commanding general, during a change of command ceremony on Camp Courtney, Okinawa, Japan, Jan. 20, 2017. Photo by Lance Corporal Juan Bustos.

The way Maj Mainz explained it: "Composite forces are created when you take disparate forces, which are underneath different command and control structures, and place them underneath one commander tasked with a specific mission. The 2d Marine Expeditionary Brigade is 'a receiver of forces.' We work various compositing options and shape the C^2 for those forces coming together to perform the mission."

Maj Mainz likened the 2d MEB Command Element (CE) to a Swiss army knife. "We want to be the Swiss Army knife of command and control. We want to morph or adapt into whatever environment we're in—coalition or joint. 2d MEB sees itself as a scalable CE capable of C^2 for disparate forces, coalition and/or joint, to address the unique requirements of Combatant Commanders in uncertain environment. The unique term we used during Bold Alligator is we can become a Commander of MAGTFs, not a MAGTF Commander. What that means is we see our Command Element as so flexible we don't have to go into a normal Marine construct."

We will stop with Bold Alligator 2014, but the key point is that prior to significant withdrawals from the Middle East engagement, USMC leaders focused on the return to the sea and reworking with the Navy, how to deliver an integrated force from the sea base to project force ashore and to support it afloat. And working new seabasing concepts of operations was already underway.

From the ARG-MEU to the Amphibious Task Force

The Osprey has been and continues to be a major driver of disruptive change for the USMC and with it how to operate from the sea. The speed and range of the Osprey broke the chains of the classic ARG-MEU construct and drove the USMC-USN team towards reshaping the approach to work amphibious task forces. With the coming of the F-35 and a new class of large-deck amphibious ships this dynamic of change would accelerate as well.

Shortly after the Bold Alligator 2012 exercise, we interviewed LtCol Boniface, who not only had been involved in the exercise but involved in the Libyan operations. LtCol Boniface provided a visionary projection of how the Osprey would impact USMC operations and the amphibious force. Col Boniface recently retired from the USMC with his last position being at Headquarters USMC. "The MV-22 and its capabilities are changing how we should be doing business. Traditionally, our MEU concept focuses on a radius of about 100 NM. With the speed and range of the Osprey, why can't we change this radius to 500, 1,000, or even 1500 miles? We should be able to support a concept like this and we need to think in these terms.

"It is like a game of chess. I think of a traditional or legacy ARG-MEU as being able to move a pawn one space at a time towards the enemy. If you have ever played chess, it sometimes takes a while to engage your opponent. We now have the ability to move a knight, bishop, or rook off of this same chess board and attack 180 degrees towards the rear of our enemy. We can go directly after the king. Yes, it's not really fair, but I like that fact. The speed, range, and don't forget the reliability of the MV-22, allows me to do this.

"We talk about staying ahead of the bow wave. There is a tsunami of change coming when we talk about the ability to fight an enemy and to support Marines ashore. We can increase our area of operations (AOR) exponentially because we can spread out our ships; now we have an aviation connector that can move Marines a tremendous amount of distance and in a very short amount of time. We can also use this capability to leverage our other aviation assets like our AV8-Bs, CH-53's, AH-1Ws and UH-1Ys to support the MAGTF and ultimately damage the enemy's will to fight. Let's not just move 50-100 miles ashore, but let's move 200-500 miles ashore, and do it at an increased speed, range, and lethality.

LtCol Boniface during the 2012 interview with us.
Credit: *Second Line of Defense.*

"There are still a lot of naysayers who will cast doubt on this. How are you supporting those Marines ashore? How will the fire support piece work? Harriers and the F-35 concept along with a CSG can easily answer the fire support question for limited time until organic assets like artillery catches up. I think we need to challenge the autonomy of the CSG in regard to how it fits into a modern ESG concept."

LtCol Boniface then added: "With legacy aviation assets we have had to think inside the ARG-MEU 100nm operational box. We have to get out of this mindset. And we are starting to do so by operating a more disaggregated ARG-MEU and relying on the MV-22 as an aviation connector. Now we can move from a few hundred miles away in our operational sphere to more than a 1,000-1500 in our area of influence (AOI). We need to adjust our operational mindset to align with this new capability, especially with the coming of the F-35B."

Boniface highlighted the actual impact as he had already seen it on the ARG-MEU and as he saw it with the expanded range of operation breaking apart the legacy ARG-MEU construct. He also anticipated the coming of the F-35 to the amphibious fleet which would further change how that fleet could operate and with what combat effects it could deliver.

The journey has been about the Marines moving from a significant focus on the land wars to a "return to the sea." It is one in which the force would change from a primary role of providing a greyhound bus to carry a force and deliver it to an engagement force able to operate from sea to shore and back again. It has involved shaping and understanding what an air-mobile force could do when able to operate at greater reach into littoral regions with a rapid insertion force.

Empowered by the Ospreys coupled with fifth generation capability, the ARG-MEU has become a powerful integrated seabase able to operate over a much wider area of operations, and to provide for capabilities for sea control and sea denial. Under the twin influence of these two assets, the new LHA Class the USS America was introduced and with it, significantly different capabilities for the amphibious force itself. We will next look at the twin impacts of the coming of the F-35B to the insertion force and a new large deck amphibious ship, the USS America class.

The F-35 and the Coming of the USS America

The F-35 Bravo was made for maneuver warfare. It is a short take-off and vertical landing a (STOVL), supersonic combat aircraft which has built-in integrated combat capabilities, ability to provide ISR or C^2 to the insertion force and can integrate through low latency systems with U.S. or allied F-35s operating in an area of interest.

The role of the F-35 in shaping the USMC role in the maritime kill web force was highlighted by Maj Brian Hansell, MAWTS-1 F-35 Division Head, in a 2020 interview with us: "By being an expeditionary, forward-based service, we're effectively extending the bounds of the kill web for the entire joint and coalition force."

The F-35 is not just another combat asset, but at the heart of empowering an expeditionary kill web-enabled and enabling force. On the one hand, the F-35 leads the wolfpack. This was a concept which Secretary Wynne highlighted when we worked for him in DoD. His perspective then is now reality and one which empowers an expeditionary force. As Maj Hansell put it in the 2020 interview: "During every course, we are lucky to have one of the lead software design engineers for the F-35 come out as a guest lecturer to teach our students the intricacies of data fusion. During one of these lectures, a student asked the engineer to compare the design methodology of the F-35 Lightning II to that of the F-22 Raptor. I like this anecdote because it is really insightful into how the F-35 fights. To paraphrase, this engineer explained that "the F-22 was designed to be the most lethal single-ship air dominance fighter ever designed. Period. The F-35, however, was able to leverage that experience to create a multi-role fighter designed from its very inception to hunt as a pack."

The capability of the F-35s to hunt as a pack and through its communications, navigation, and identification (CNI) system and data fusion capabilities, the pack can work as one. The integration of the F-35 into the Marine Corps and its ability to work with joint and coalition F-35s provides significant reach for F-35 empowered mobile bases afloat or ashore.[19]

Simply put, the F-35 does not tactically operate as a single aircraft. It hunts as a network-enabled, cooperative four-ship fighting a fused picture, and was designed to do so from the very beginning. As Maj Hansell noted: "We hunt as a pack. Future upgrades may look to expand the size of the pack." The hunt concept and the configuration of the wolfpack is important not just in terms of understanding how the wolfpack can empower the ground insertion force with a mobile kill web capability but also in terms of configuration of aircraft on the seabase working both sea control and support to what then becomes a land base insertion force.

An F-35B landing on the USS Wasp during 2015 sea trials which we witnessed as well, Credit Photo: *Second Line of Defense.*

The F-35 wolfpack has reach through its unique C^2 and data fusion links into the joint and coalition force F-35s with which it can link and

---

19 "The F-35, CNI Evolution, and Evolving the Combat Force," *Second Line of Defense* (December 4, 2019), https://sldinfo.com/2019/12/the-f-35-cni-evolution-and-evolving-the-combat-force/. *The F-35 and 21ˢᵗ Century Defence: Shaping a Way Ahead* (Second Line of Defense, 2016).

work. And given the global enterprise, the coalition and joint partners are working seamlessly because of common TTP or Tactics, Techniques, and Procedures. As Maj Hansell put it: "From the very beginning we write a tactics manual that is distributed to every country that buys the F-35. This means that if I need to integrate with a coalition F-35 partner, I know they understand how to employ this aircraft, because they're studying and practicing and training in the same manner that we are. And because we know how to integrate so well, we can distribute well in the extended battlespace as well. I'm completely integrated with the allied force into one seamless kill web via the F-35 as a global force enabler."

With the changing capabilities of strategic adversaries, sea control cannot be assumed but must be established. With the coming of the F-35 to the amphibious force, the role of that force in sea control is expanding and when worked with large deck carriers can expand the capabilities of the afloat force's ability to establish and exercise sea control.

With the coming of the USS America Class LHA, the large deck amphibious ship with its F-35s onboard is no longer a greyhound bus, but a significant contributor to sea control as well. As Major Hansell noted: "The LHA and LHD can plug and play into the sea control concept. It's absolutely something you would want for a sea control mission. There is tremendous flexibility to either supplement the traditional Carrier Strike Group capability with that of an Expeditionary Strike Group, or even to combine an ESG alongside a CSG to mass combat capability into something like an expeditionary strike force. This provides the Navy-Marine Corps team with enhanced flexibility and lethality on the kill web chessboard."

The USS America is the largest amphibious ship ever built by the United States. The USS America class is a key part of changing how an amphibious task force can operate. It is designed from the ground up to support the aviation assets which allow combat ships to deal with the tyranny of distance in the Pacific. It can operate as the flagship of a very diverse amphibious task force complimentary to a large deck carrier as well. The USS America is designed to support the full gamut of USMC aviation and can be configured with a significant F-35B and Osprey force and has been dubbed as a "Lighting Carrier" when it would operate in that role.

The USS America at the time of its christening ceremony which we attended in 2012. Photo Credit. *Second Line of Defense.*

The ship can hold up to 20 F-35Bs. Ospreys could be used to carry fuel and or weapons, so that the F-35B can move to the mission and operate in a distributed base. This is what the Marines refer to as shaping distributed STOVL ops for the F-35B within which a sea base is a key lily pad from which the plane could operate or move from. Alternatively, the F-35B could operate for ISR, which complements U.S. assets networked through satellites.

The other new onboard asset will be Sikorsky's CH-53K, which will be backbone for an airborne amphibious strike force. It will be able to carry three times the load external to itself than can a CH-53E and has many operational improvements, such as a fly-by-wire system. These elements constitute a true enabler for a 21st century amphibious assault force.

When one looks at the outside of the USS America and sees a flight deck roughly the size of its predecessors, one would totally miss the point of how this ship fits into USN-USMC innovation.

Looking under the decks, understanding how a radical change in the workflow, enabling, and operating with 21st century USMC strike and insertion assets, is how to understand the ship and its impact.

A major change in the ship can be seen below the flight deck, and these changes are what allow the assault force enabled by new USMC aviation capabilities to operate at greater range and ops tempo. The ship has three synergistic decks, which work together to support flight deck operations. Unlike a traditional large deck amphibious ship where maintenance has to be done topside, maintenance is done in a hangar deck below the flight deck. And below that deck is the intermediate area, where large work-spaces exist to support operations with weapons, logistics and sustainment activities.

In an interview which we did in 2014 with the ship's first Capt. Robert Hall, the CO highlighted some of the ship's capabilities: "The ship has several capabilities, which allow us to stay on station longer than a traditional LHA and to much better support the Ospreys and the F-35Bs which will be the hallmark of USMC aviation to enable long range amphibious assault. These aircraft are larger than their predecessors. They need more space for maintenance and this ship provides it. We have two high-hat areas to support the maintenance, one of them located behind the aft flight deck elevator to allow movement through the hangar. We have significantly greater capacity to store spare parts, ordnance, and fuel as well. We can carry more than twice as much JP-5 than a traditional LHA."

The ship has three synergistic decks, which allow for a significant enhancement of the logistical or sustainment punch of the amphibious strike force. According to Capt. Hall: "I like the synergistic description. The flight deck is about the size of a legacy LHA. But that is where the comparison ends. By removing the well deck, we have a hangar deck with significant capacity to both repair aircraft and to move them to the flight deck to enhance ops tempo. With the Ospreys, we will be able to get the Marines into an objective area rapidly and at significant distances. And when the F-35B comes, the support to the amphibious strike force is significantly enhanced. And we will be able to operate at much greater range from the objective area. With the concern about littoral defenses, this ship allows us the option to operate offshore to affect events in the littoral. This is a major advantage for a 21st century USN-USMC team in meeting the challenges of 21st century littoral operations. The USS America will provide a significant boost to the ability to both maintain and to provide operational tempo to support the force."

A photo shot from the bridge of the USS America shortly before its trip around South America to the West Coast of the United States. Credit: Maj David Schreiner

And in an additional interview in 2014 with Maj David Schreiner, the ship integration officer within Headquarters USMC Aviation, working the synergy among the three decks will be crucial to shaping the workflow to support operational tempo. "Your next aircraft for the flight deck can be positioned down below for a quick elevator run thereby enabling a larger volume of flights off the deck. You could then work into the deck cycle and elevator run to bring up those extra aircraft as a way not only to provide backups but to provide extra sorties for the flight deck.

"Synergy and enhanced workflow are really the two outcomes which come from a ship designed for 21st century assault assets. Instead of having to do all the maintenance topside you have the spaces down below from the heavy maintenance with the use of upright cranes and the work centers that are collocated right on the hangar bay with the supporting equipment work centers, the control work centers, and just below it on the intermediate deck below.

"You have all your supply centers and then you have your intermediate level maintenance as well for that sensitive calibration, for the more complex repairs. This creates a cycle or synergy where you have supervisors that the work centers are collocated with the maintenance that's being done on the hangar. You have maintenance actions being produced. They are brought in; they are logged into the system, they are evaluated, they can go downstairs, and they can either be fixed on the spot, calibrated, the part could be reworked or the supply system being right there, a new part in the supply could be issued back up, turned. There will be very little waste of time between different parts of the ship all supervised, brought back up, and repaired on the plane.

The USS America: A 21st Century Assault Ship
Shaping a Workflow to Support Enhanced Operational
Tempos for Multi-Spectrum Operations At Significantly
Greater Distances than Before

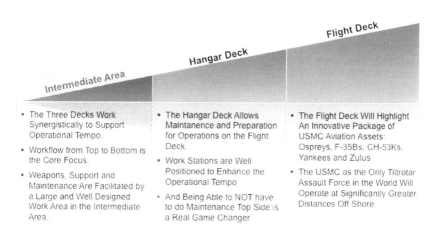

* The Three Decks Work Synergistically to Support Operational Tempo.

* Workflow from Top to Bottom is the Core Focus.

* Weapons, Support and Maintenance Are Facilitated by a Large and Well Designed Work Area in the Intermediate Area.

* The Hangar Deck Allows Maintanence and Preparation for Operations on the Flight Deck.

* Work Stations are Well Positioned to Enhance the Operational Tempo

* And Being Able to NOT have to do Maintenance Top Side is a Real Game Changer

* The Flight Deck Will Highlight An Innovative Package of USMC Aviation Assets: Ospreys, F-35Bs, CH-53Ks. Yankees and Zulus

* The USMC as the Only Tiltrotar Assault Force in the World Will Operate at Significantly Greater Distances Off Shore

Conceptualizing the workflow enabled by the design of the USS America.
Credit: *Second Line of Defense.*

115

Clearly, this workflow is a work in progress as the crew and the Marines shape ways to work the decks to optimize what can come off the flight deck. And most assuredly the F-35 has arrived and with it the capability for a seabase like the USS America to integrate with other allied F-35s in the Pacific and expand both the reach of the sea base as well as providing significant operational flexibility to a land-based force of F-35s as well.

PHILIPPINE SEA (Aug. 20, 2021) An F-35B Lightning II fighter attack aircraft from An F-35B Lightning II fighter attack aircraft from VMFA 211, embarked on the Royal Navy aircraft carrier HMS Queen Elizabeth (R08), prepares to take on ordnance and fuel on the flight deck of the forward-deployed amphibious assault ship USS America (LHA 6) during flight operations between the Queen Elizabeth and America. (U.S. Navy photo by Mass Communication Specialist 3rd Class Jomark A. Almazan)

How to Drive Change in the Amphibious Fleet: The Viper Case

As the U.S. Navy reworks how it is operating as a distributed maritime force, which is being reshaped around the capability to operate a kill web force, the question of how best to leverage and evolve the amphibious force is a key part of that transition itself.

This is a work in progress, and one in which a determination of various paths to the future are in evolution and will be subject to debate as well. Part of that evolution are changes in other elements of the amphibious task force which can over time play roles different from how various "legacy" platforms can be reworked to provide for new or expanded capabilities for the U.S. Navy overall. With changing capabilities onboard the amphibious ships, the U.S. Navy can leverage the evolving amphibious fleet capabilities for enhanced capabilities to conduct successfully maneuver warfare at sea.

A case in point is how the AH-1Z or Viper attack aircraft can evolve its roles AT SEA with the addition of key elements being generated by the digital interoperability effort, as well as adding a new weapons capability to the Viper, namely, the replacement for the Hellfire missile by the JAGM. What this means is that the Viper can be a key part of the defense of the fleet while embarked on a variety of ships operating either independently, or as part of an amphibious task force.

Four U.S. Marine Corps AH-1Z Vipers with Marine Light Attack Helicopter Squadrons (HMLA) 169 and 469, Marine Aircraft Group (MAG) 39, 3rd Marine Aircraft Wing (MAW), hover during exercise Viper Storm at El Centro, Calif., Dec. 11, 2019. The AH-1Z Viper gives MAG-39, the 1st Marine Expeditionary Force and the joint force the ability to deter potential adversaries and provide combat-ready units the capability to engage from the sea and over long distances against a near-peer threat. (U.S. Marine Corps photo by Lance Cpl. Juan Anaya)

Because the Viper can land on, and operate from, a wide range of ships, thus enabling operational and logistical flexibility, and with integration of Link 16 and full motion wave forms as part of digital interoperability improvements, it can become a key member of the kill web force at sea. In discussions in 2020 with Maj Thomas Duff and Mr. Michael Manifor, HQMC Aviation, APW-53, Attack and Utility Helicopter Coordinators, we discussed the evolving mission sets which Viper was capable of performing with the digital interoperability upgrades.

They argued that "with the upgrades coming soon via the digital interoperability initiative, the Viper through its Link 16 upgrade along with its Full-Motion video access upgrade, can have access to a much wider situational awareness capability which obviously enhances both its organic targeting capability and its ability to work with a larger swath of integrated combat space. This means that the Viper can broaden its ability to support other air platforms for an air-to-air mission set, or the ground combat commander, or in the maritime space…. Because it is fully marinized, it can land and refuel with virtually any ship operating in the fleet, which means it can contribute to sea control, which in my view, is a mission which the amphibious task force will engage in with the expanded reach of adversarial navies."

That discussion was followed by a discussion in 2020 with Maj "IKE" White the AH-1Z Division Head at MAWTS-1. In that conversation, Maj White highlighted that the Marine Corps' utility and attack helicopters have been part of integrated operations and escort tasks throughout the land wars and can bring that experience to bear in return to the sea. The Viper and the Venom have provided airborne escorts for numerous Amphibious Ready Groups over the last decade, partnering with destroyers, MH-60 Sierra, and MH-60 Romeo to protect amphibious warships as they transited contested waterways.

With the addition of the Joint Air-to-Ground Missile (JAGM) to the aircraft, the strike capability for the maritime force in providing for both sea control and sea denial is significantly enhanced. This missile provides increased lethality through a dedicated maritime mode, enhanced moving target capability, and selectable fuzzing, providing capability against both fast attack craft and small surface combatants. Millimeter wave (MMW) guidance increases survivability by providing a true fire-and-forget capability, removing the requirement for a terminal laser. Coupled with the AIM-9 sidewinder, the Viper will be able to engage most threats to naval vessels. The Viper's flexibility will provide even the most lightly defended vessels with a complete air and surface defense capability.

By working integration of the MH-60 Romeo helicopter with Viper, the fleet would gain a significant defense at sea capability. Integration of the two helicopters within the amphibious task force would allow them to provide an integrated capability to screen and defend the flanks of the afloat force. The MH-60 crews are optimized to integrate into the Navy's command and control architecture, and with onboard sensors can help detect potential targets and direct Vipers to engage threats.

The integration of Link-16 will make this effort even more seamless. This proposal from the Marines was welcomed by the Romeo community with whom discussions were held, as well both on the East and West coasts in 2020. Clearly, integrating Romeos which fly onboard the amphibious class ships with the Viper would provide a significant enhancement of the flank defense capabilities for the amphibious task force. And working a Romeo/Viper package would affect the evolution of the Romeos as well that would fly off the L class ships as well. And all of this frees up other surface elements to support other missions at sea, rather than having to focus on defending the amphibs as greyhound buses.

In a discussion in June 2020 with Cmdr. Nathaniel "Velcro" Velcio, Commanding Officer of the School Helicopter Maritime Strike (HSM) Weapons School, Atlantic based at Mayport, we focused on the potential impact operationally of integration of P-8 Triton, Seahawk and Vipers to provide a whole new role for the L class ships. Rather than being greyhound buses, the new LHA's could spearhead a whole new sea control and denial capability. With Romeos onboard then their ability to integrate with Link-16 enabled Vipers could provide for data flowing from the P-8/ Triton dyad and sensors on the MQ-25 to shape new capabilities, simply by wave form linkages, cross training, and new kill web enabled concepts of operations.

The evolution of the Viper with digital interoperability and with a new weapons package can clearly contribute to the evolution of the amphibious task force as it embraces sea control and sea denial missions, and these missions will be crucial to supporting insertion forces moving onshore to expeditionary bases as well.

After the completion of the first testing of the new connectivity package on the Viper in June 2021, the former Deputy Commandant of Aviation, LtGen (Retired) George Trautman highlighted the importance of this capability being added to the assault force in an interview with us:

"The benefit to the force of digital connectivity or digital interoperability is really exponential. It's not linear. If you're talking about F-35, V-22, and then the two 83% identical H-1 aircraft, all as a package, you're talking about a very powerful combination of capabilities whose sum is greater than its parts. And that's always been the vision going back to over a decade inside the Marine Corps. This is a major step forward in the Marine Corps' ability to not only interact with itself, but also to interact with the combined and joint force, in particular Naval Forces, in the context of operating from the seabase and the ability to use systems like the TPS-80 G/ATR radar."

Shaping a Way Ahead for the Amphibious Fleet

The enhanced efforts at digital interoperability within the USMC aviation force needs to be accompanied by upgrades of the elements of the amphibious task force regarding C^2/ISR capabilities as well. We are seeing MISR or Maritime ISR officers placed within the Carrier Strike Groups, but they could be proliferated more broadly within the fleet to enable better use of joint ISR capabilities, from undersea, to surface, to air to space for the various distributed combat assets working tailored integratability.

The importance of upgrading the C^2 capabilities in the amphibious fleet is a crucial and, compared to building new ships, very cost-effective effort. In an interview in 2015, with the Commander of Expeditionary Strike Group Two Rear Adm. Cindy Thebaud, and Capt. Michael M. McMillan then the Commander of Amphibious Squadron Eight who had just returned from command of the Iwo Jima Amphibious Ready Group off of the waters of Yemen, the importance of C^2 upgrades was highlighted.

Rear Adm. Cindy Thebaud, commander, Expeditionary Strike Group 2, speaks with Chief Warrant Officer 4 Mark Bradford, assigned to Beachmasters Unit 2, during the multi-national exercise Bold Alligator 2014 (BA14). November 5, 2014. U.S. Navy photo by Mass Communication Specialist 3rd Class Shane A. Jackson/ Released.

The importance of the U.S. making better use of its amphibious fleet was highlighted by Rear Admiral Thebaud this way: *"We already have 80% of the ships and other major equipment we'll have 20 years from now. The key is to evolve its capability and to draw upon the new systems to shape a more effective combat force."*

The evolution of amphibious capabilities will allow the rest of the surface fleet, and the aircraft carriers to evolve as well. Capt. McMillan's operational experience provided many examples of the evolving capabilities of the Amphibious Ready Group and challenges to be met in enhancing its capability to deliver joint effect. As McMillan put it, "We felt that what we did during the operation was unique, but I think that over time, our 'unique and unusual' will become the norm."

He added, "Put another way, our unique joint capabilities as a Navy-Marine Corps force can be mixed or matched to deal with a variety of tasks in the battlespace, and that flexibility is probably becoming the norm as a requirement, and we are looking to enhance that flexibility going forward."

Normally, the Navy is supporting the Marines in sustaining their air and ground combat force readiness and operations; the Amphibious Ready Group is supporting the Marine Expeditionary Unit. But with the crisis in Yemen, there was immediate need for maritime security, sea control and the ability to monitor the situation off the coast of Yemen and in surrounding waters.

McMillan noted that during his deployment, "The Marines supported the Navy by providing air assets to build the recognized maritime picture, conduct presence ops and non-traditional ISR.

"We shaped packages consisting of a mix of the Air Combat Element aircraft to conduct sea control and maritime security missions. In addition, we moved aircraft throughout shipping to enhance flexibility and effectiveness.

"For instance, the combination of 3 MV-22s with 3 new Hueys provided the LPD excellent capability for the missions of Tactical Recovery of Aircraft and Personnel (TRAP), Casualty Evacuation (CASEVAC), Quick Reaction Force (QRF) and Rotary-Wing Close Air Support (CAS). These flexible packages provided capability, which historically would have only been on the large deck carrier (LHD/LHA), albeit on a smaller scale. But we were able to provide the 5th Fleet commander with essential core capabilities."

This kind of joint capability can be missed if one simply subsumes this under a notion of historical or classic amphibious operations. And the fleet was able to contribute significant command and control for the force as well. Notably, the upgrades on the San Antonio-class LPDs provide an added option for command and control not seen historically in the amphibious fleet. But this capability needs to be enhanced throughout the amphibious fleet and Captain McMillian argued that organic ISR and better C^2 capabilities need to come to the LSD and the follow on LXR (LSD Replacement) class ships as well.

We have spent time onboard the USS Arlington talking to staff and sailors. Here is a photo from a 2013 visit with the senior staff. *Credit: Second Line of Defense.*

The evolution of the amphibious force and shaping amphibious task forces can contribute significantly to expanded capabilities for maneuver warfare at sea. By leveraging the new air capabilities, adding new defensive and offensive systems on the fleet, and expanding the C^2 and ISR capabilities of the fleet, the contribution of the amphibious task force can be reimagined, redesigned, and thereby enhance the combat power of the U.S. Navy in maneuver warfare at sea.

In a way a shift is underway from the amphibious fleet operating an Amphibious Ready Group/Marine Expeditionary Unit to an amphibious task force whereby the reach and range of the Osprey-F3F-B-CH-53K combination, certainly built around the new class of LHAs can operate as modular task forces supplementing the classic carrier strike group to an expeditionary action group which can exercise sea control and sea-denial leveraging capabilities from the sea and to the sea integrated with the joint and coalition force. And building out the expeditionary seabasing enterprise can provide an additional way ahead for mobile basing as a strategic joint and coalition force capability,

As Jim Strock has highlighted, the U.S. Navy's hull description system provides the following symbols to highlight the relevant ships in the build out of expeditionary seabasing.

Cluster 1
- SD: Dock Landing Ship
- LPD: Amphibious Transport Dock
- LHA: Amphibious Assault Ship (General Purpose)
- LHD: Amphibious Assault Ship (Multi-Purpose)
- LCC: Command Ship

Cluster 2
- ESD: Expeditionary Transfer Dock (formerly known as MLP: Mobile Landing Platform)
- ESB: Expeditionary Sea Base (one that correlates!!!)
- EPF: Expeditionary Fast Transport (formerly known as JHSV: Joint High-Speed Vessel)

Cluster 3
- T-AKE: Dry Cargo and Ammunition Ship
- T-AO: Fleet Replenishment Oiler

The classic ARG-MEU has been built around Cluster 1 ship classes sustained at sea by Cluster 3 ship classes. With the transformation of the ARG-MEU under the impact of the Osprey. the F-35B, and the CH-53K, the LHA has certainly been revolutionized and has become more aircraft carrier like, as seen in the concept of the Lightening carrier. But the purpose has been different as than a large deck aircraft carrier – the focus is upon the extended reach of the ground troops as a projection force, with the ability to move back and forth from the sea to the land and back again. And the cluster 1 package has sustainability built into it which extends the duration as well as the reach with the new aircraft capabilities, which will only be further enhanced as the CH-53K comes into the force.

But with the U.S. Navy creating a new ship grouping called "Expeditionary Support and Seabasing Support" a new operational capability is being presaged, namely, the creation of modular task forces which can support both the joint force as well as the USMC operating from the sea. To unleash the capability of this new ship class requires not simply focusing on the hull form but how that hull forms fits into the broader evolution of the force, in terms of kill web integrability, and modularity.

We attended the 2013 christening ceremony in San Diego for the USNS Montford Point, one example of the new class of hull types. The photo shows the ship being built at the yard. Credit: *Second Line of Defense.*

The new class of ships can enable this transition but are empowered by it. Kill webs rely on networks, wave forms, connectivity, distributed C^2, and platforms which can leverage all the former. Platforms are the time-space entities which enable the force; integrability allows a distributed force to deliver the desired combat effect. The kill web is about networks of sensors that can provide assessment data for shooters operating over an extended battle space. The kill web provides enhanced resilience and more capability to respond deliberately as needed, not as forced to respond in terms of loss of capability. It also allows for target assessments being coupled with evolving risk assessments in terms of deterrence risks and consequences.

As the Navy rethinks how to use its aircraft carriers, how to use its amphibious forces and how to use the whole gamut of its surface and subsurface forces to fight as a fleet, an opportunity for change is clear: Why not rework how air assets move across the sea bases to provide the fleet with a wider variety of combat capabilities tailored to specific combat scenarios? Notably, moving helicopters and tiltrotor assets across the fleet provides for a wider variety of options than simply having a set piece of equipment onboard each class of ship.

The mobility of the fleet is a baseline capability which the seabase brings to a more agile combat force. Ships provide for presence, but mobility at sea, with variable degrees of speed and stealth. But added to this are a range of other mobility capabilities which can work effectively with the fleet to expand its reach, range, and lethality. This is certainly part of the wider kill web approach.

In short, the new class of ships – expeditionary support class – provides moving islands from which capabilities can deploy, move deep into the extended battlespace, and be sustained as this class of ships can operate not as classic combat ships but as mother ships for a deployed kill web force. Put another way, simply looking at the hull form without considering the platforms or payloads which can operate from that hull form makes no sense. And furthermore, it is the evolving concepts of operations enabled by revolutions in strike, defense C^2 and ISR systems, which are crucial as well to work ways for the hull forms to be woven into new combat capabilities.

In many ways, a "re-imaging" of the amphibious fleet can open up shaping new ways to build seabases — manned and autonomous systems – which can create in effect new ways to operate expeditionary seabases.[20] Seabasing is a key capability which the joint and coalition force needs to leverage and shape ways to integrate the force, rather than simply having the Navy focus on its own discussion of the way ahead for classic naval combat conversations.

With the reshaping of C^2 and ISR capabilities and by working of distributed firing solutions with the emergence of kill web approaches,

---

20 The emergence of realistic ways to work with autonomous systems is a focus of discussion within our book, *Defence XXI: Shaping a Way Ahead for the U.S. and its Allies.* They are also discussed in our report on the Williams Foundation seminar on next generation autonomous systems, https://sldinfo.com/2021/06/next-generation-autonomous-systems-a-williams-foundation-special-report/.

the mobile basing approach leveraging the seabase elements can provide a significant capability for joint and coalition forces to both distribute and integrate force at the point of crisis management or combat effect.

This is how Jim Strock put it in our interview with him: "The other part of mobile basing we worked on 10 years ago was the afloat piece. We were focusing on Navy and Marine Corps capabilities across amphibious ships, across maritime repositioning ships, across joint high-speed vessels, across a variety of connectors at the strategic operational and tactical level to move units around.

Another example of the new ship class is the USNS Lewis B. Fuller. In this photo, a U.S. Marine Corps MV-22 Osprey assigned to Marine Medium Tiltrotor Squadron (VMM) 263, is prepared to be refueled aboard the USNS Lewis B. Puller, July 5, 2017. U.S. Marine Corps photo by Cpl Austin A. Lewis.

"And certainly, those assets today are key enablers for any sort of mobile basing concept of operations we would construct, but to expand this thinking to the joint or coalition force is really the new dimension that I don't think anyone has seriously thought through as well as finding ways to integrate fully those capabilities for the force design and operations of those forces.

"Moreover, with the greater range of seabasing capabilities that have been fielded over the past 10 years, we now need to think through how integrate those capabilities with shore-based mobile capabilities, i.e., multiple nodes within an operational network, so joint and coalition forces have a greater range of options with which to execute assigned missions. Experimentation, exercises, and proof of concept events will collectively get us where we need to be."[21]

In short, the USMC provides a critical piece of the kill web puzzle, as the United States and its allies rework their warfighting and deterrence strategies to deal with peer competitors worldwide. It is clearly a work in progress, but new platforms are coming to the Marines, such as the CH-53K which clearly can support more effectively than the legacy asset, mobile basing, as well as the digital interoperability approach which make the Marines more effectively woven into the kill web approach as well.

---

21 Robbin Laird, "Mobile Basing as a Strategic Capability," Defense.info (January 18, 2022), https://defense.info/re-thinking-strategy/2022/01/mobile-basing-as-a-strategic-capability-continuing-the-conversation/.

CHAPTER FIVE:
THE LARGE-DECK CARRIER AND KILL WEB TASK FORCES

The U.S. Navy is unique in the world's navies in terms of the role of large deck aircraft carriers in its global operations. The famous phrase which President's ask in times of crisis: "Where are my carriers?" highlights the demonstrated flexibility of the carrier battle group in providing responses to crises affecting the United States and its allies.

As Jeffrey G. Barlow noted in a 1997 article: "The U.S. government has employed military force in responding to foreign crises more than 200 times since 1945, and in two-thirds of these instances the U.S. Navy task forces sent into harm's way have had aircraft carriers as their major offensive component....An examination of how U.S. aircraft carriers have been used in a number of international crises during the past 50 years reveals just how the versatile carriers can influence the outcome in the United States favor. On-scene carrier task forces can serve to deter aggressors from taking actions detrimental to U.S. or allied interests or to compel them to accept otherwise unpalatable consequences. If, however, the crises escalate into open warfare, forward-deployed carriers can transition almost immediately from peacetime operating tempos to active combat status."[22]

Throughout the Cold War, the carriers were indeed a key part of dealing with Soviet actions globally, with significant presence and combat flexibility. Their role has remained significant throughout the past twenty years as the carrier battle groups have engaged and provided support for the land wars in the Middle East and continue to do so as required.

---

22 Jeffrey G. Barlow, "Answering the Call: Carriers in Crisis Response Since World War II," *Naval Aviation News* (February 1997).

In these operations, the large deck carriers and their task forces have been used in relatively close-in operations with their land attack capabilities coordinated by the joint force commanders in relatively uncontested air space. With the return of Great Power competition, the carriers as centerpieces of U.S. Navy operations are leveraging past Great Power confrontations and reworking how to work in contested air-sea environments. Notably, the growing impact of long-range strike by the Chinese and Russians pose new threats which clearly affect the concepts of operations associated with the large deck carriers and how they will play their role with a distributed maritime force and with air and ground force capabilities woven into new ways to defend and attack via kill web combat approaches.

In so doing, the role of the large-deck carrier is being re-imagined and adapted to the overall innovations in the fleet, and in the joint and coalition forces. Put bluntly, the large deck carriers provide significant flexible capabilities whose overall impact is linked to how the integrated distributed force overall evolves and develops its offensive and defensive capabilities. It is not just about what is on a large deck carrier or what is resident in the organic carrier task force; it is about its ability to empower the wider kill web force and to leverage that force to enhance its own lethality and defensive capabilities as well.

Back to a Focus on Blue Water Combat Operations

In some ways, the return of Great Power competition presents back to the future considerations. What did we learn in World War II, when the last greater carrier battles unfolded, and island hopping was a core requirement? Which of these lessons are relevant as we return to a priority focus on blue water combat? And how does a kill web approach provide a different role for the large-deck carrier and for distributed task force management and enablement? And why is a kill web approach a key part of shaping the fleet's capability to deal with emerging high-end threats like hypersonic cruise missiles?

Some of these answers have been provided by Rear Adm, John Meir, who is currently the Commander Naval Air Force Atlantic, and prior to that the Navy Warfare Development Commander. He also was the first captain of the USS Gerald R Ford, a position which certainly posed in a concrete way the question of the future of the large deck carrier in the integrated distributed combat force. The question of the back to the future aspect of the return of the large deck carriers to blue water combat operations was addressed in the discussion between Rear Admiral Meier had with Matthew Danehy, Director of Concepts, Naval Warfare Development Command which we quoted earlier. Rear Admiral Meier noted in that discussion: "Many of the principles that we're kind of going back to our roots and somewhat foundational, not just to our history and heritage as a Navy, but really pulling that and advancing that into distributed maritime operations and the technologies of the future."

Clearly, what is being focused upon is blue water operations. In many ways, this is drawing upon experiences in World War II but in a new technological age. This rebirth, as Rear Adm. Meier was a key focus of another podcast which he did, this one with Rear Adm. (Retired) Samuel J. Cox, director of the Navy History and Heritage Command. The discussion highlighted a look back in terms of the culture which delivered an innovative fighting Navy which would fight and win the Pacific maritime battle. As Rear Adm. Meir concluded the podcast: "I think our Navy is founded on the ideals of the American fighting spirit and skill that carried the day in the Pacific, certainly through the battles that we discussed today, Coral Sea, the early raids, Midway. The aspect of learning from history is enormously important. And for our next podcast, I want us to shift our discussion to the subject of the evolution of the Air Wing…Our evolution of the Air Wing today and the Air Wing of the future, we are focused on leveraging technology to enhance our range of operations where we are increasingly able to operate at extreme ranges, at distance, bringing in low observables and unmanned aircraft to do so....[23]

Rear Adm. Meier in an interview we did with him in November 2020, laid out very clearly how he saw the way ahead for the large deck carrier and its role within a broader spider or kill web. He argued that "in some ways, it is back to the future, and remembering what we did in World War II in the Pacific but significantly updating it with our new technologies, connectivity, distributed maritime operations and understanding the nature of the adversaries we are dealing with. It is more of a focus on maneuver and raid concepts where we pick the time and choose the place and location to be. Fundamental to that is the capability to do that in a manner that our adversary doesn't track, detect, target us. And that does get a little bit harder as technology advances in terms of overhead sensors, space, long range, ISR, those sorts of things as well as emissions control. We are working to minimize the likelihood of our detection or operating in ways unanticipated by the adversary."

Rear Admiral Meier onboard the USS Ford at Sea November 2020.
Credit: Second Line of Defense.

---

23 "Rear Admiral John Meier, Commander, Naval Air Force Atlantic, interviews the Director of the Navy's History and Heritage Command," *Defense.info* (September 4, 2020).

In that interview Rear Adm. Meier highlighted how he saw the large-deck carrier and its concept of operations within a distributed maritime force being worked. "Our force is not designed nor intended to be an offensive force, yet if deterrence fails, we certainly have that capability. That capability is enhanced with range and speed. Range and speed can refer to the platform, the shooter, or the weapon itself. I will tell you after really a generation of naval service where we have focused on land wars in Asia, we've really woken up to the need for longer range strike. It will not be long before we have maritime strike tomahawk, and hypersonics will be here before we know it. We're making great advances in those areas.

"We're talking about a very fluid battlespace, where both blue and red are maneuvering within that battlespace. The next war we expect to be a maritime fight at extreme ranges. From a 'fighting navy' perspective, I think it's imperative that we maintain our tactical and operational edge that includes forward presence, lethality, and increasing lethality at range and at speed, which are things that quite frankly we have not focused upon during the land wars. But when you talk about the maneuver capability of a Ford-class aircraft carrier, with the air wing range beyond that and the weapons that the aircraft carry, we are delivering significant reach into the battlespace. We're engaging in training drills exercises and operating at some ranges that we have not ever done off of the decks of aircraft carriers; it's really impressive."[24]

We now turn to the question of how the next generation large deck carrier and its projected concepts of operations within a distributed maritime force are being crafted and shaped.

Envisaging the Role of the Greatest Warship Ever Built

There is little doubt, having visited the USS Gerald R Ford several times and having spent time briefly with the warship at sea, that this is the

---

24 Robbin Laird, "The Way Ahead for the Large Deck Carrier: The Perspective of Rear Admiral Meier, Commander, Naval Air Force Atlantic," *Second Line of Defense* (November 3, 2020).

greatest large deck carrier ever built and clearly a candidate to be considerd the greatest surface combatant ever built. But this is not a question of the warship itself, it is also the question of how it is designed, along with operating the integratable air wing onboard, and working within the evolving 21st century context of a distributed maritime fleet able to operate interactive maritime kill webs with the joint and coalition force.

In other words, it is not just about the ship itself; it is the context into which it is being birthed and the evolving capabilities to fight and win in the extended battlespace which are crucial to understand how the new large deck carrier can play its role driving further innovation.

It is important to understand that a platform can only do so much; it is the combat culture, and overall capabilities of the force with which it is integrated which delivers the full meaning of what a new combat platform can deliver. A good case in point was the greatest battleship built in World War II, the Bismarck and its fate. In their magisterial work on the Bismarck, the authors of *Battleship Bismarck* provide their assessment of the operational context which Bismarck actually engaged in compared to what was planned. The original concept of operations was a joint maritime task force of submarines and sister surface ships, became translated into one where it would be paired with a sister ship only to meet the convoys and the Royal Navy.

Bismarck was designed to provide the firepower to attack protected convoys. The formidable striking power of the Bismarck would provide long range strike with the U-boats and the cruiser fleet providing closer in strike against the convoys and the adversary's fleet. The authors noted: "A worried Admiral Lütjens…pointed out that the deployment of only two ships would be an individual and isolated undertaking the Royal Navy could easily contain, Lütjens was also concerned about the dangers of air attack from British carriers, having barely escaped during his rush to make Brest at the end of Operation Berlin."[25] It was also obvious that to

---

25 William H. Garzke, Jr., Robert O. Dulin, Jr, and William Jurens with James Cameron, *Battleship Bismarck: A Design and Operational History* (Naval Institute Press, Annapolis, Maryland, 2019), pp. 153-54.

succeed the Kriegsmarine task force would need to find a way to leverage the air superiority which the German Air Force had established in continental Europe and to work as effectively as possible with land-based air as emergency cover or supplementary strike where possible.

The Bismarck experience highlights the importance not only of a building and deploying a significant warfighting asset but the importance of the warfighting ecosystem to which it contributes and can draw from. In this part of the chapter, we address the new class of large-deck carriers, then the ecosystem synergistic with it.

We have visited the USS Gerald R. Ford three times over the past few years, and discussed with then Rear Adm. Moran, when he was head of N-98, the naval air warfare command, the initial thinking about how the USS Gerald R. Ford would intersect with the new "spider or kill web" approach of the carrier with the evolving combat eco system.[26] Although the USS Ford draws on the generations of experience operating large deck carriers, the USS Ford is no more a Nimitz class replacement than the F-35 is a replacement for legacy aircraft.

The ship has a number of capabilities which allow it to have substantial increases in sortie generation rates and which allows the ship to deliver mix and match force packages into the expanded battlespace. And these capabilities will work differently with the fleet, understood more broadly, as inclusive not only of the Navy but with the U.S. Air Force and Marine Corps as well.

The kill web warfighting context within which the USS Gerald R. Ford will operate will be shaped by several key elements: the integratable air wing, new approaches to working fleet wide combat integrability, enhanced capabilities to work with the various elements of the joint and coalition forces more effectively, reworking blue water expeditionary operations, and shaping dynamic targeting options.

---

26 Robbin Laird and Ed Timperlake, "The Ford-Class Carrier, the F-35C and Spider Web War at Sea," *Breaking Defense* (May 15, 2013), https://breakingdefense.com/2013/05/navy-the-f-35c-the-ford-class-carrier-spider-web-war-at-sea/.

In other words, it is not just a new ship; it is a new blue water capability empowering maritime and air power to operate in ways symmetrical with the challenges of full spectrum crisis management and escalation control. As such, the ship will benefit from the various operational changes which the United States and its allies are generating but it will also drive further changes in concepts of operations and capabilities as well.

In many ways, it is an untold story. For most discussions of the USS Gerald R. Ford have revolved around the new systems onboard the ship; not what those capabilities enable both for the fleet and the joint and coalition force, and, in turn, how those capabilities enable the new ship to leverage innovations being shaped for operations in the extended battlespace by the joint and coalition forces.

During visits to the USS Gerald R Ford in October and then November 2020, the changing nature of the workflow enabled by the new systems onboard the ship as well as the very significant shift in capabilities of the new generation large deck carrier to operate in an information warfare kill web approach were highlighted. Several changes in the workflow onboard the ship allows not just greater sortie generation rates but a much more rapid speed to deployment and to do so with an ability to arm the aircraft for a wide range of missions. The workflow changes can be readily seen in two areas: the process of weapons load out and the flexibility to manage new weapons coming into the inventory; and how the flight deck operates with a new landing and launch system to enable an ability to work with mix and match carrier combat packages to be able to handle tailoring the launch packages much more effectively than a legacy carrier.

There are several elements of the workflow shift for weapons. On a Nimitz class carrier, there is a "weapons farm" on the ship's flight deck from which weapons are worked for assembly and worked with components brought from various levels of the ship and then transported by a hydraulic system which pulls the elevator up with wires and ropes. The weapons need to be moved through one of the two mess decks before being transported on deck. And prior to loading the weapons onto the aircraft, there is the challenge of finishing the weapons preparation prior to weapons loading.

This process changes onboard the USS Gerald R. Ford. Below the flight deck are two very large weapons assembly and loading areas, where the weapons are prepared to be transported to the flight deck for loading onto the aircraft. These two large areas allow the ordinance team to prepare weapons of various complexity out of the weather, which makes the process much more rapid and safer. And it is clear when one stands in these "weapons handling transfer areas" that the ship will be able to accommodate the various new weapons which during its lifecycle which will be developed, built, and delivered to the U.S. Navy.

One of the two below deck weapons and loading areas
on the USS Ford. Credit Photo: *U.S. Navy*

In other words, it is better now for today's arsenal and has significant capability to support the weapons revolution underway. As Rear Adm. Clapperton, Commander, Carrier Strike Group Twelve, summed up during the October 2020 visit: "We can move more weapons in a safer way, a faster way to a flight deck that is larger and more flexible. And that all contributes to the kind of agility, lethality, and flexibility the Ford brings to the fight."

The Next Generation Large-Deck Carrier

This workflow and the other modifications for flight deck operations are changing how the metrics for USS Gerald R. Ford versus Nimitz class carrier performance should be measured. As Rear Adm. Clapperton highlighted: "We are working with Carrier Strike Group Four, the group which certifies when a strike group is ready for deployment. We are working with them to determine realistic and reasonable measures applicable to Ford versus Nimitz class. What are the metrics for launch and recovery, for ordnance delivery, for sortie generation, and weapons employment that we are going to use for a Ford class carrier versus a Nimitz class carrier?"

It is also clear that the new carrier will be able to operate with significant capabilities to support multi-mission operations. There is enhanced capability for the crew to build diverse weapons packages below deck and then to transport them rapidly to the flight deck for loading. This will give the ship the ability to mix and match flight strike packages or even ISR packages much more rapidly. As Rear Adm. Clapperton underscored: "Clearly, we can more rapidly support multiple options, from ASW to fleet defense, to surface warfare, to information warfare or air to ground."

Discussion onboard the USS Ford with Rear Admiral
Clapperton, October 2020. Credit: *U.S. Navy.*

The other key aspect of workflow changes that allow for more support for multi-mission operations and enhanced speed to deployment is the flight deck and all the changes which allow that deck to support the integratable air wing differently from the legacy carrier. A major difference can be seen right away when one steps onto the flight deck. The island on the USS Gerald R. Ford has been moved 140 feet aft and is 30% smaller. What this allows is significant additional space for aircraft refueling and weapons loading operations, with the area forward of the island able to accommodate more combat aircraft. During flight operations, Ford's design increases the amount of usable space forward of the island and reduces the amount unusable space aft. As the ship's captain, Capt. J.J. Cummings put it during the October 2020 visit: "If you think of the ship as a gun, and the strike force as bullets, then we have increased the size of the clip because we can load it with more bullets because of the island being further aft on Ford versus Nimitz."

Captain J.J. Cummings onboard the USS Ford November 2020.
Credit: Second Line of Defense.

There is more operational space on the USS Gerald R. Ford's flight deck and the new launch and landing systems as well as a significant redesign of how refueling is done on the flight deck provide key tools for a significant reshaping of the operational tempo for the large deck carrier. The new launch system allows for a wider range of aircraft to operate from the carrier; the new arresting gear system can recover them. The ability to mix and match the current air fleet and the future one is significantly enhanced with the new Electromagnetic Aircraft Launch Systems (EMALS). The launch system has a larger aircraft weight envelope that exceeds what is available with steam catapults so EMALS can launch very light aircraft or heavy aircraft which means this system can accommodate future manned or unmanned aircraft. The same flexibility exists in the Advanced Arresting Gear (AAG) with larger current operating wind and weight envelopes and the capability to recover future aircraft designs with minimal modifications required. The refueling system is designed to keep a clear path to the catapult by reducing flight deck obstructions caused by refueling hoses, weapons' skids, and weapons elevator access points. This highly efficient flight deck flow allows for the Ford to sustain higher launch and recovery rates.[27]

Preparing for a launch at sea with the EMALS system onboard the USS Ford, November 2020. Credit: *Second Line of Defense.*

---

27 It should be noted that the French will incorporate such systems onboard their next generation carrier through the close cooperation between the two navies as well. See Pierre Tran, "The United States clears EMALS sale to France for their next generation carrier," *Second Line of Defense* (December 27, 2021), https://sldinfo.com/2021/12/the-united-states-clears-emals-sale-to-france-for-their-next-generation-carrier/.

During the October 2020 visit to the USS Gerald R. Ford there was a chance to discuss the new flight deck systems with Lt. Cmdr. Andy Kirchert, Ford's Top Catapult Officer (TOPCAT). There are several advantages of the system over the legacy steam catapult system which he highlighted. First is the flexibility and adaptability of the system. The EMALS system has more room for growth for future aircraft systems. Steam catapults are not able to shoot super light aircraft. They can shoot heavy aircraft but that causes serious wear and tear on the catapult when it shoots heavy shots. Heavy/light shots are not an issue at all with EMALS. Second, the new system has reduced manning requirements for the launch function. There is reduced manning by 50%. Third, longer fly days are enabled due to reduction in the pre-flight and post flight procedures. For example, steam catapults require a heat up to be ready for launch. Fourth, the system is easier on aircraft which should lead to reduced stress on the aircraft due to launch. The system delivers very precise endspeeds for the launch process. Fifth, the system delivers enhanced safety margins. The system will not allow an aircraft to launch if it sees something wrong in the process.

Discussion with Lt. Cmdr. Kirchert onboard the USS Ford, October 2020. Credit: U.S. Navy

The counterpart to the EMALS is the AAG which offers capabilities to recover the current fleet of aircraft in environmental conditions that exceed what is possible with the Nimitz class system. And like EMALS, AAG is designed to have the ability to operate with aircraft of varying weights, including future aircraft systems. When one visits the AAG system below deck, it is amazing to see the extent of automation and how little manpower is required to operate it.

The refueling system is a major aspect of the redesign of workflow on the flight deck. Aviation Boatswain's Mate (Fuels) Second Class Thomas Drew Watson highlighted the changes and their impact. Post flight, aircraft are parked along two isles for refueling—one on the deck edge and the other just outside the landing area. This parking arrangement allows unobstructed access to the catapults. The in-deck refueling stations which are unique to the *Ford* keep refueling hoses out of the taxi paths to the catapult and these refueling stations can refuel two aircraft at those stations. This has a major impact because on the *Nimitz,* the refueling crew must carry several, lengthy, connected fuel hoses which are heavy from the starboard side of the Nimitz class to do mid-deck refueling. On the Ford, the hoses are right there beside the in-deck refueling stations and rather than needing a crew of five people to bring the hoses 150 feet to mid-deck for refueling, you only need two crew to man the in-deck refueling stations.

One of the in-deck refueling systems onboard the USS Ford, November 2020. Credit: *Second Line of Defense.*

As impressive as the workflow changes are in terms of ramping up sortie generation rates and speed to deployment, this discussion can look like the USS Gerald R. Ford is an upgrade on the legacy carrier. Such an impression rapidly dissipates when visiting below deck and talking with the information warfare officers or the weapons officers serving on the ship. This shift was already anticipated by then Capt. John Meier, now Rear Adm. Meier, when we visited the ship in 2015. In our 2015 interview Capt. Meier stated: "Clearly, the ship is designed to enhance the sortie generation rate of the airwing. But less noticeable is that the Ford is a vastly improved command and control platform as well. The new phased array radars are going to be the most capable ones on the water. They will open up a window on new levels of C^2 and new ways of fighting and communicating and controlling communication flows."

Capt. Meier then added: "The super computers onboard the ship, with the power to support them as well as having significant power available for system cooling along with the deployment of future laser weapons is a crucial baseline for building out of C^2 capabilities. The next generation in active sensor technology in the dual band radars provides a solid foundation, not simply for the organic defense and strikes capability of the carrier, but for the battle fleet as a whole. Significant increase in bandwidth is a fundamental requirement for an expanded C^2 capability at sea which can support land, sea, and air operations. And the unique rapidly reconfigurable command suites on board allow for C^2 to be provided for joint or coalition partners in a manner appropriate to the mission set."

Captain Meier during our 2015 visit to the USS Ford.
Credit: *Second Line of Defense.*

The command deck and capabilities onboard the ship are significant. During the October 2020 visit to the USS Gerald R. Ford, there was a chance to tour the command deck and to discuss the changes with Rear Adm. Clapperton and CSG-12's Information Warfare Commander, Capt. Steve "Shep" Shepard. There is a much more significant working area for mission planning, which can incorporate a numbered fleet as desirable or joint force command elements as well. For example, with the coming of the U.S. Air Force's B-21, a B-21 command element could sit right in the Ford's mission planning area to work integrated combat effects in real time. The B-21 could operate as the Ford class carrier's wingman, or the Ford could operate as the B-21's wingman.

What is clear is that with the power generation systems and the cooling systems onboard Ford, the ship can accommodate the evolution of technology onboard the ship, and above all, the evolution of computational power and digital technology. Ford has only about half of its power capacity being taken up and as such the ship can incorporate new weapons systems, whether it is directed energy, a new C^2 system, or new wave forms to operate in a denied environment. Ford is harvesting lessons learned over decades of experience for the Nimitz class with regard to command at sea. Notably, those lessons relate to sharing information across the fleet and how to use the IW commander as the integrator of all those other warfare commanders.

Capt. Steven Shepard is a key member of the team standing up Ford for its first deployment. This means, as Rear Adm. Clapperton put it: "As a Strike Group, we are building IW into the ship from the ground up, and Shep and his team are working our mission planning and C² systems with an eye to enhanced IW capabilities which can be delivered by the ship and are interactive with the fleet and the joint force." Notably, the two officers served together towards the end of the Cold War, and that memory is also an anchor point to building out the Ford for the peer competitor world.

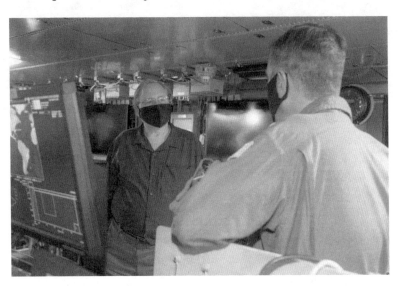

Visiting the command deck for the USS Ford, October 2020.
Credit: U.S. Navy

Viewing the mission planning spaces onboard the ship, one can see how the spaces are optimized and positioned in a better way to enable those warfare commanders to work together. They also allow for additional services, partners, and allies to work onboard the Ford and then to share that level of understanding and that level of awareness with those partners and across the strike group. Rear Adm. Clapperton noted: "The Ford is well positioned as we move into this future where an aircraft carrier and the strike group can be considered enablers of other weapon systems. We can function as an integrator of all of those capabilities, or as enabler of the fleet and joint assets, but equally benefit from the joint capabilities operating in the extended battlespace."

The ship also has several reconfigurable mission planning bays. When visiting the new British carriers, we noticed as well that they have also incorporated this important aspect of shaping a carrier for the kill web-enabled fleet. These bays can accommodate systems across the spectrum of classification. This means that the challenge of operating across the spectrum of crisis management can be managed by partners, allies or U.S. joint force elements onboard the ship as well. Taken as a whole, this means that "we have more flexibility for the missions we do and more flexibility for evolving technologies to meet the changing security environment," according to Rear Admiral Clapperton.

He then described how he viewed the capabilities of the ship to deliver more effective integrated operations. "When you get into mission command scenario and when you get into a coms denied environment scenarios where the commander forward needs to make real-time risk decisions, there is no time to go back to a 'mother may I' kind of C^2 process. We need platforms like this which enable coordination in such an environment. If we want to do naval integration, with the command space we have on Ford, we can, for example, bring onboard the command element for an expeditionary task force or expeditionary strike group. We can liaison with them and put them right there in the command suites next to the guys who do surface and underwater warfare for us. They could be working hand in glove to ensure complete integration of the maritime domain awareness picture. We could have those people sitting side by side working those issues making sure integration is happening."

View of the flight deck from the bridge of the USS Ford,
November 2020. Credit: Second Line of Defense

It is no accident that the next flag assignment for Rear Adm. Clapperton leveraged his experience as the Commander, Carrier Strike Group Twelve. He is now serving as commander, Combined Joint Task Force, Cyber, U.S. Tenth Fleet, Ford Meade Maryland. No better statement with regard to synergy between the reworking of the carrier and the information age could be made.

The discussion with Capt. Shepard—a third-generation military officer with more than 30 years of experience in the U.S. Navy—highlighted the expanded role for IW as part of the carrier maneuver warfare approach. And in that approach, we discussed the coming of the new Maritime Intelligence, Surveillance, and Reconnaissance or MISR officers as well. He argued that the role of carrier maneuver was to provide flexibility to respond to threats. It is to create uncertainties for adversaries, and clearly IW and combat in the electro-magnetic spectrum is a key part of that effort. All of which means that ability of the C^2/ISR deck is a key part of the warfighting capability of the ship.

While it is much cooler watching aircraft take off from the deck, many of the decisive effects delivered by a Ford-led task force will be delivered in the spaces below deck. Capt. Shepard sees the creation of the Information Warfare Commander (IWC), a warfare commander equal to the Air Wing and Destroyer Squadron commander, as critical to the Navy in operating and managing the Information Warfare domain in Great Power

Competition. Additionally, the coming of the MISR officers as part of the expansion of the kind of situational awareness which allows for more effective maneuver warfare at sea.

As Rear Adm. Clapperton put it: "Much like the F-35 makes the other fighters more survivable and more lethal, the Ford will make the entire fleet more survivable and more lethal. The direction we need to take the ship is leveraging advances in situational awareness to empower the fleet."

Operating on the Kill Web Chessboard

Clearly, the USS Gerald R. Ford is coming to the fleet, as the fighting Navy refocuses and prioritizes blue water operations and blue water expeditionary operations commence. At the heart of such a return is maneuver warfare at sea. The U.S. Navy has clearly done this before but is now doing so in the context of new technologies, and new joint and coalition capabilities and the new threat environment posed by the 21st century authoritarian powers.

A good sense of how the large-deck carrier and its operations are being reworked and reimagined was discussed with a senior U.S. Navy officer we talked to in 2020 about the way ahead for the large-deck carrier. "The carrier strike group battlespace has gone from being where the engagements occur to a situation in which the carrier strike group itself becomes a piece on the larger chessboard, which will, from a Navy perspective, be managed at the numbered fleet level. Because of the sensor and communications technologies and the weapons evolution, the chessboard is bigger, and the large deck carrier is feeding into the interactive kill webs through which we operate on that chessboard. The numbered fleet becomes the command-and-control node, which is why we are seeing the numbered fleets standing up in maritime operations centers that we did not have before. The size of the chessboard is enlarging significantly, with kill webs, that can stretch for thousands of miles, when you add in things like Triton or satellites."

The Navy's focus on distributed maritime operations is part of a broader joint coalition warfare approach built around a distributed but integrated force. It entails working with very flexible modular task forces, which can reachback to other combat capabilities to deliver strike and defense capabilities over much wider distances than where they are operating geographically. We see the large deck carrier and its partnered assets as moving beyond a focus simply on its proximate operating area to supporting a larger region, to be understood in terms of the size of the numbered fleet. It is very clear that the USS Gerald R Ford and its sister ships will provide very effective infrastructure for such an approach.

Visiting the USS Ford in October 2020. Credit: U.S. Navy

Such a reworking of large deck carrier concepts of operations facilitated by the coming of the USS Gerald R Ford is not a surprise to senior Naval leadership, which has been focused for some time with regard how to deliver a maritime distributed force integrable to deliver the desired combat effect. When we interviewed then Rear Adm. Moran, then head of Air Warfare on the naval staff in 2013, he described how he saw the way ahead:

"The Ford will be very flexible and can support force concentration or distribution. And it can operate as a flagship for a distributed force as well and be tailored to the mission set. When combined with the potential of the F-35, Ford will be able to handle information and communications at a level much greater than the Nimitz-class carriers. People will be able to share information across nations, and this is crucial. We call it maritime domain awareness, but now you've included the air space that's part of that maritime domain."[28]

There are multiple ways to discuss how the reworking of the roles of the large deck carrier provides insight into its intersection with an evolving ecosystem. At the heart of the change is reworking modular task forces and the evolving combat clusters with which the task force integrates with for offensive and defensive operations. For the large deck carrier, it is a question of thinking beyond its organic warfighting capabilities to how it can be the supporting or supported element of the wider kill web force. It is about the flexibility of combat packages which can come off a carrier flight deck and how those combat packages can work with distributed forces in the areas of interest.

The airwing of the future understood as the integratable air wing entails shaping new approaches fleet wide combat integrability, enhanced capabilities to work with the various elements of the joint and coalition forces more effectively, reworking blue water expeditionary operations, and shaping kill web dynamic targeting options, all provide the strategic context within which the USS Gerald R Ford will operate.

What is underway is a shift from integrating the air wing around relatively modest and sequential modernization efforts for the core platforms to a robust transformation process in which new assets enter the force and create a swirl of transformation opportunities, challenges, and pressures. How might we take this new asset and expand the reach and effectiveness of the carrier strike group? How might it empower maritime,

---

28   Robbin Laird and Ed Timperlake, "The Ford-Class Carrier," (May 15, 2013).

air, and ground forces as we shape a more effective (i.e., a more integrat-able) force?

We suggested in an earlier chapter how one aspect of rethinking is how the large deck carrier intersects with the various aspects of basing on the relevant combat chessboard. Fixed bases are prime targets for the kind of strike capabilities which the Russians and Chinese and other author-itarian states are deploying and developing. The large deck carrier is the most mobile and protected air base which can flexibly move throughout the extended battlespace. How can this capability intersect with other U.S. and allied forces working on mobile or expeditionary basing?

The large-deck carrier can provide significant capability to work a distributed basing approach into an enhanced integrated combat capa-bility. It can do so in multiple ways, such as deploying targeted combat capability to marry up with what a force partner has deployed to a mobile or expeditionary base, which can be an island, a ship, or clusters of auton-omous systems operating in the area of the interest. Clearly, the kind of C^2 capabilities on the Ford can provide a key contribution to being able to weave distributed capabilities into an extended kill web.

Landing on the USS Ford, November 2020. Credit: *Second Line of Defense.*

There is probably no area in which the reworking or reimaging of the large deck carrier is more significant for the U.S. Navy than reworking how the surface fleet can be built, designed, and operated as a distributed force. In the classic configuration of the carrier task force, the primary focus is upon a task force understood with regard to the underwater and surface assets which are integrated with the carrier to provide for both the defense of the carrier and augmentation of its strike capacity. Although the question of defense of the carrier and augmentation of its strike capability remain key considerations, what has happened is that the surface fleet itself is becoming a primary strike and defense asset which the large deck operates to support and enhance its defense and strike capabilities.

In many ways this began with the growing role of the Aegis fleet in the missile defense mission. And with the coming of the F-35, working sensor integration between Aegis and the F-35 extends the reach of the Aegis combat bubble.[29] And those F-35s can come from land, mobile bases, or sea bases.

The arrival of a global fleet of F-35s with which the fleet can tap into, as well as operate of its carriers, its amphibious ships and tap into in terms of allied maritime sea bases is a significant change in understanding what a large deck carrier task force looks like going forward. The reach which the F-35 provides throughout a deployed fleet of U.S. and allied F-35s is part of the kill web capabilities which the carrier can tap into and contribute to.

The reach which an integrated F-35 force can provide to the seabases is an often-neglected part of what the F-35 enabled amphibious and large deck carrier force can provide to the maritime fight. The F-35 has been designed from the ground up to be networked within the battlespace. To do this, it needs low latency communications capabilities that are also low observable. The F-35 is designed to operate as a wolfpack that can then be leveraged throughout the kill web.[30]

F-35 wolfpack operations moving forward highlights and provides a case study of the importance of shaping a more integrated combat force one which can operate in distributed battlespace but be aggregated at the

29 Robbin Laird, "The Long Reach of Aegis," *Proceedings* (January 2012).
30 For a further look at the nature of F-35 information systems and how they intersect with the combat force, see the following: *C2/ISR and the Integrated Distributed Force* (Defense.info, August 12, 2020), https://defense.info/highlight-of-the-week/c2-isr-and-the-integrated-distributed-force/.

point of attack as the opportunity and need arrives. It is about reshaping the combat force to become more integratable and when considering new platforms ensuring that integratability is built into these platforms. It is also a leverage point into shaping a broader approach of C^2/ISR capabilities necessary to enable the kind of combat force which can operate across the spectrum of conflict. The F-35 is a unique platform, but its build-out and operational experience sets a dynamic background against which a broader shift in understanding a way ahead to enhance the integratability of a multi-domain force.

As Rear Adm. Meir put it in an interview prior to the October 2020 visit to the Ford: "The F-35 is a key element of making the air wing integratable in the sense you have described. The MADL data links in the Pacific fleet of F-35s can provide the kind of significant reach we need in the Pacific. Obviously, we will need to work the handoffs among aircraft and the security dynamics as well. But the technical foundation is clearly there." Multifunction Advanced Data Link or MADL is the unique low latency wave form onboard the F-35 which is used to support machine to machine interactions between platforms as well. The MADL wave form along with how F-35s process and manage data enable F-35s to operate as an integrated combat package able to collectively fuse data, and to do so within a specific force package which by being interactively fused provides higher levels of accuracy than any one combat aircraft operating by itself could provide.

An F-35C operating with the USS Carl Vinson in 2018. Photo
by Seaman Apprentice Ethan Soto. Credit: U.S. Navy

The coming of the F-35 to the multi-domain combat force is a part of
the evolving ecosystem for the large deck carrier but it also intersects with
two other key elements of that evolution as well: the weapons revolution
and the evolutions within the surface fleet. Regarding the weapons revolution, for the large deck carrier, the coming of directed energy weapons
in the defense of the carrier will be a major step forward in reshaping
how weapons can be deployed throughout the extended battlespace. As
the power systems on the Ford enable significant self-defense capabilities
through a network of directed energy weapons on the carrier itself, weapons it might have needed onboard flying combat assets can be directed
to other tasks.

The question of the future of joint force missile development and operations is opening a new chapter. Part of it is associated with the emergence
of the kill web, an era in which evolving ISR capabilities are reshaping
strike and the role of third-party strikes which can be called in from a wide
variety of platforms to prosecute diverse target sets. Part of it is the end
of a particular TLAM era, because of their vulnerabilities in the denied
combat environment domain, or the question of vulnerabilities from the
space links or the challenges posed by adversary electronic or tron warfare.
And the Chinese dynamic of missile development and proliferation will
reshape how to deal with strike, requiring both offensive and defensive

capabilities and creative mixes of the two into new strike denial capabilities. As blue water maneuver returns along with blue water expeditionary operations, a new chapter is opening on weaponization.

Another aspect of that dynamic is the question of weapons mixes, stockpiles, and target utility. "Why use a million-dollar missile to kill a low value target," was how one U.S. Navy officer put it to us. Stockpiles are too low for 21st century warfare; and the weapons mix is out of skew with the nature of the threat environment.

And we are already seeing how things can change even before the USS Gerald R. Ford goes to sea as a fully operational carrier. During a visit to the ship in November 2020, two-thirds of the air wing was operating from the ship doing cyclic air operations. Also onboard the ship were the full complement of warfare officers, bringing the various warfare competencies to the command deck. One notable member was the commander of an Aegis destroyer, as Aegis will have a combat officer onboard the Ford working the various ways Aegis and the carrier will work together in the blue water maneuver space.

One marvelous moment in the visit, after having traversed the cavernous ship for several hours, was sitting down in the briefing room to be briefed by one of the squadron commanders. This commander gave a rapid-fire brief bristling with information and enthusiasm, and one might have missed an interesting development he referred along the way. On November 9, 2020, the Ford air wings operated with ACC in a counter-air defense exercise with F-22s, and F-15s to shape a joint warfighting package. This obviously would carry with it the C^2 collaboration from land to sea in a warfighting training exercise. And again, this is not the kind of exercise one would be expecting for the work up of a new carrier.

A U.S. Air Force F-22 Raptor assigned to the 525th Fighter Squadron takes from Joint Base Elmendorf-Richardson, Alaska, during a training sortie with several F/A-18E Super Hornets from Strike Fighter Squadron 192, June 5, 2019. VFA-192 set up a detachment of F/A-18Es in Alaska to provide integration and support training with JBER's F-22 Raptors. U.S. Air Force photo by Staff Sgt. James Richardson.

And in the first quarter of 2021, there was another illustration of how the USS Gerald R. Ford is entering into a period of history different from how its predecessor did. When the small Italian carrier, ITS Cavour, came to the East Coast of the United States for the certification of its F-35Bs, it had a chance to operate with the new, large deck carrier. One could describe this as a large deck carrier at sea with a smaller carrier but that would really miss the point.

From the standpoint of what we are seeing with the launch of 2nd Fleet and JFC Norfolk (which we discuss fully in chapter eight), the U.S. Navy and the relevant NATO nations are reworking how to shape a distributed integrated force. And having a significantly redesigned large deck carrier on the U.S. side configured to operate with the fleet differently, and with a small deck carrier operating F-35s off its deck, these two platforms together deliver new capabilities to the 360-degree combat force.

With the ITS Cavour switching from Harriers to F-35s, its contribution to the coalition force ramps up exponentially. The F-35s operating off the Cavour can integrate with U.S. and allied forces also flying the F-35. And with the F-35 global enterprise, the global reach of information surveillance and reconnaissance is significant along with the ability to shape a common operating picture for the kind of time urgent decision-making needed for full spectrum crisis management.

The Ford-class aircraft carrier USS Gerald R. Ford (CVN 78) and the Italian aircraft carrier ITS Cavour (CVH 550) transit the Atlantic Ocean March 20, 2021, marking the first time a Ford-class and Italian carrier have operated together underway. U.S. Navy photo by Mass Communication Specialist Seaman Trenton Edly.

But that is really the point. This is not just a replacement for the Nimitz class carrier this is a whole re-imaging of the large deck carrier being introduced into the new strategic situation and shaping new combat capabilities with the fleet, the joint services, notably the USAF and with coalition partners. With three times the onboard power systems compared to the Nimitz class, new C^2 capabilities, an ability to host directed energy weapons, and to configure C^2 cells differently, the USS Gerald R. Ford conducting blue water operations could operate as a key epicenter for supporting multiple kill webs or reintegrating into a tightly integrated defensive force dependent on the evolving combat situation.

CHAPTER SIX:

AN ISR-EMPOWERED FORCE

he U.S. Navy is crafting a significant paradigm shift, one which we call the kill web. In some ways, this shift is akin to the famous comment in a play by the 17th-century French playwright Molière that Monsieur Jourdain has been speaking prose for all his life but not knowing that he had. The kill web shift with the current force lays down a foundation from which to incorporate new platforms and technologies over the next phase of maritime force operations and development.

No better case in point is the maritime patrol reconnaissance force. This is a force which was defined by the P-3 anti-submarine warfare (ASW) aircraft flying "alone and unafraid" to its displacement by a "family of systems" which work together to deliver distributed but integratable kill webs capabilities to the force, both naval and joint. And as this "family of systems" shapes a new ecosystem working with the fleet, that ecosystem shapes key challenges which need to be resolved as part of the expansion of maritime autonomous systems or passive sensors added to platforms throughout the fleet.

Resolute Hunter and Navy-led ISR Innovation

At Naval Air Station, Fallon, in November 2020, the U.S. Navy hosted the third iteration of a relatively new exercise called Resolute Hunter. This exercise is about how to shape a new paradigm for 21st century so that Intelligence, Surveillance, and Reconnaissance (ISR) capabilities can be worked to provide enhanced mission execution. Much like how NAWDC has added two new warfighting competencies to its program, namely, dynamic targeting and Maritime ISR, Resolute Hunter is complementing

Air Wing Fallon (AWF) for the U.S. Navy and the Red Flag exercise series for the U.S. Air Force, but in some important ways launching a new paradigm for the ISR forces to provide a more significant and leading role for the combat forces.

With the significant upsurge in the capabilities of sensor networks, and the importance of shaping better capabilities to leverage those networks, the role of the ISR platforms and integratable forces are of greater significance going forward in force development and evolving concepts of operations. Rather than being just collectors of data and providing that data to the C^2 decision makers, or to specific shooters, the ISR force is becoming the fusers of information to provide for decisions distributed in the battlespace to deliver the right combat effect in a timely manner. According to Rear Adm. Meier, Naval Air Force Atlantic, in our 2020 interview, Resolute Hunter is different from Red Flag and AWF. "The origins of Red Flag and of TOP GUN were largely tactically focused. Resolute Hunter is focused on shaping an evolving operational approach leveraging the sensor networks in order to best shape and determine the operational employment of our forces and the delivery of the desired combat effect." In other words, such an exercise is about shaping and training for a kill web concept of operations approach for the maritime force.

The exercise in November 2020 was shaped around a crisis management scenario. In a fluid political and combat contested area, where friendly and hostile forces were operating, ISR assets were deployed to provide proactive capabilities to assess that fluid situation. A number of U.S. Navy and USAF assets were deployed along with USMC intelligence capabilities to operate in the situation. The assets were working together to assess the fluid situation, but the focus was on fusion of information in the battlespace by assets operating as decision nodes, not simply as collectors for decision makers elsewhere in the battlespace.

What the exercise was working toward was the importance of assets being used in a broader ISR-led role which evolving sensor networks can provide, as well as training the operators to both work the networks as well as to consolidate what these asset operators judged to be happening in a fluid battlespace. It was about how ISR is shifting from a collect intelligence to go somewhere else role to parsing information to facilitate rapid decision-making.

Not surprisingly, this is MISR-led exercise. Cmdr. Pete "Two Times" Salvaggio, the head of the MISR Weapons School (MISRWS), was in charge of the Resolute Hunter exercise. In a discussion with "Two Times" in his office during the November 2020 visit, he underscored the shift underway. The goal of the training embodied in the exercise is for operators in airborne ISR to operate as "puzzle solvers." Rather than looking at these airborne teams as the human managers of airborne sensors, "we are training future Jedi Knights." And to be clear, all the assets used in the exercise are not normally thought of as ISR platforms but are platforms that have significant sensor capabilities. It really was about focusing on sensor networks and sorting through how these platform/networks could best shape an understanding of the evolving mission and paths to mission effectiveness.

The ISR sensor networks with men in the loop can deliver decisions with regard to the nature of the evolving tactical situation, and the kinds of decisions which need to be made in the fluid combat environment. It may be to kill or to adjust judgements about what that battlespace actually signifies in terms of what needs to be done. And given the speed with which kill decisions need to be made with regards to certain classes of weapons, the ISR/C^2 network will operate as the key element of a strike auction. Which shooter needs to do what at which point in time to degrade the target? How best to determine which element of the shoot sequence— not the kill chain—needs to do what in a timely manner, when fighting at the speed of light?

What ISR capabilities can deliver are "moments of clarity" with regard to decisive actions. At a minimum, the ISR teams are shifting from providing information for someone else to make a decision to being able to deconstruct the battlefield decision to craft real time understanding of the situation and the targeting options and priorities.

But what is an effective metric of performance? At AWF and Red Flag the measure is to make kills and avoid getting killed; with Resolute Hunter, what are the metrics? Clearly one is the speed to deconstruct the combat situation and determine actionable decisions. It is the speed to provide for kill enablement by the right information delivered to the right shooter at the right time. The speed function is complex in that it is not about simply determining for a particular platform a simple targeting solution; it is about situational determination, not simply awareness.

Perhaps one might put it this way. The evolving role of the C^2/sensor networks are redefining the role of ISR. And that role is shaping domain knowledge of the extended battlespace and determining and detecting priority targets and then auctioning off in the battlespace to the platforms best positioned with the right payloads for rapid and timely kills or, in other words, shaping a kill web concept of operations.

Resolute Hunter is about shaping new capabilities, skill sets, and training for the evolving kill web fighting navy, one embedded in and capable of leading the joint force. It is a question of evolving the relevant skill sets by the ISR teams of operators and decision-makers. And a key part of the challenge facing the ISR teams is to understand adversary intent and not misreading the red side's ISR actions or chess moves with weapons into the engagement area. With USAF, USMC, U.S. Army, U.S. Navy and allied participation, the challenge will be to be able to work together as collaborative teams operating in the battlespace to shape appropriate "moments of clarity" for combat decisions and mission effectiveness.

The Transformation of the MPRF

Rear Adm. Peter Garvin, then head of the MPRF and now Commander, Naval Education and Training Command, provided a very good overview of the transformation of the MPRF in a series of interviews he gave us in 2020. A 1989 US Naval Academy graduate, he witnessed the last 30 plus years of change in the political/military environment as a P-3 pilot. This meant as well that he was entering the force coincident with the perceived sunsetting of the Soviet naval threat and transition to a new era of maritime patrol operations. He began his deployed operational experience at Keflavik, Iceland, as part of the U.S. and NATO ASW force prosecuting former Soviet, now Russian submarines. Contrast this with his last operational deployment which focused almost entirely on over land ISR contribution to CENTCOM forces. Despite the decades-long increase in overland ISR and combat focused missions, the Navy did not abandon its key ASW/USW mission set.

Petty Officer 3rd Class Sean Robertson, aviation electronics technician, from Portland, Ore., washes the underside of a wing on a P-3 Orion on the flightline at Ali Air Base, Iraq. Robertson is assigned to CTG 57.18 supporting Operation Iraqi Freedom. September 3, 2009.

Rear Adm. Garvin described the shift from the P-3 to the P-8/Triton dyad and the Romeo helicopter as follows: "We are following a similar mission construct working with our allies, but the thinking and modality has advanced significantly. We are taking full advantage of the leap forward in many sensors and communications technology to interoperate in ways that were previously impossible. Faced with a resurgent and challenging ASW threat, we have not given up on the old tool sets, but we are adding to them and weaving them into a new approach.

"We are clearly shifting from linear or sequential operational thinking into a broader understanding and implementation of a web of capabilities. In the past, when operating a P-3, you operated alone, you had to be the sensor and the shooter. To be clear, it remains necessary that every P-8 aircraft and crew be ready and able to complete the kill chain organically, but the fact of the matter is that is not the way it always has to be, nor is it the way that we're planning for it to have to be going forward.

"On any given mission, the P-8 could be the sensor and perhaps the allied submarine is the shooter. Or vice versa. Or maybe the destroyer is the one that happens to get the targeting solution and the helicopter is the one that actually drops the weapon. Sensor, shooter, communications node, or perhaps several at once, but each platform is all part of a kill web."

The teaming arrangement between P-8 and Triton is a very innovative way of training operators to work both a manned and a remotely piloted aircraft to deliver the desired outcome to the fleet. As Rear Adm. Garvin described the approach: "There are several ways to look at this. The first is to understand that both platforms are obviously software-driven and are modernized through spiral development. We focus on spiral development of the dyad in common, not just in terms of them as separate platforms. It is about interactive spiral development to deliver the desired combat effect.

"Another key element of teaming is that during the course of their career, the operators of P-8 and Triton have the opportunity to rotate between the platforms. This gives them an innate understanding of the mission set and each platform's capabilities. They, better than anyone, will know what the dyad can deliver, up to an including a high level of platform-to-platform interaction. The goal is to be able to steer the sensors or use the sensor data from a Triton inside the P-8 itself.

Aviation Machinist Mate First Class (AW/SW) Daniele Dominic Foci, assigned to Carrier Airborne Early Warning Squadron 120 re-enlisted this morning in-front of turret #3 aboard the decommissioned Iowa-Class Battleship USS Wisconsin (BB-64). Rear Admiral Peter A. Garvin, CO of Commander, Patrol and Reconnaissance Group served as the re-enlisting officer. August 9, 2019, Photo by Max Lonzanida.

"The idea of P-8 and Triton operators working closely together has proved to be quite prescient. Our first Triton squadron, VUP-19 is down in Jacksonville, Florida under Commander, Patrol and Reconnaissance Wing 11. And when we build out the full complement of Tritons, we'll have VUP-11 flying out of Wing 10 in Whidbey Island, Washington. Triton aircrew literally work down the hall and across the street from their P-8 brothers and sisters.

"The Maritime Patrol and Reconnaissance aviator of the future will be well-versed in the synergy inherent in both manned and unmanned platforms. The unblinking stare of a Triton enhances the Fleet Commander's MDA and understanding of an adversary's pattern-of-life by observing their movements in the optical and electromagnetic spectrum.

"Moreover, Triton serves as a force multiplier and enabler for the P-8. Early in Triton program development, we embraced manned and unmanned teaming and saw it as a way to expand our reach and effectiveness in the maritime domain. One key software capability which empowers integration is Minotaur. The Minotaur Track Management and Mission Management system was developed in conjunction with the Johns Hopkins University Applied Physics Laboratory. Minotaur was designed to integrate sensors and data into a comprehensive picture which allows multiple aircraft and vessels to share networked information. It is basically a data fusion engine and like many software capabilities these days, doesn't physically have to present on a platform to be of use. These capabilities ride on a Minotaur web where, if you are on the right network, you can access data from whatever terminal you happen to be on."

He argued that the U.S. Navy was not taking a simple evolutionary approach but a leap ahead with how they were working the manned with the remotely piloted aircraft to deliver the desired combat effect to the fleet. "I think of it this way, rather than taking an evolutionary or iterative approach, what this allows for is a step change approach. We're thinking beyond just the iterative."

Clearly, the U.S. Navy has worked the relationships between Triton and P-8 to provide a comprehensive ISR/Strike solution set. Triton can provide the long-haul wide-angle view of the battlespace with P-8 and its organic and third-party targeting capabilities playing the focused targeting role. To work coordinated operations, the Triton and P-8 crews need to understand from the ground up how each platform works independently and together, to shape an integratable sensor-strike system.

The Triton can have the dwell time to identify a much wider range of targets than P-8 which then enables P-8 to focus their operation on high priority targets. In the kind of extended battlespace which has and will emerge, knowing where critical choke points are with regard to an adversary's system or force becomes a priority. An integratable Triton and P-8 working together can provide significantly greater capability to deliver this outcome, rather than simply operating separately.

By having crews which have operated on the P-8 as well as the Triton, they share an ability to do the kind of ISR appropriate for dynamic targeting. By working on one platform, then on the other, it is not so much cross-learning as shaping an integrated knowledge base and skill sets to operate in the ASW kill web. Triton can inform the P-8 before it takes off about the threats in the extended battlespace which then the P-8 can prioritize.

With the amount of surface targets on the ocean today in certain regions of the world, the Triton software can work with Automatic Identification System (AIS) data and other systems to help the operators identify threats to be further studied, evaluated, and potentially targeted. According to one analyst, "Automatic Identification System (AIS) is an automated tracking system that displays other vessels in the vicinity. It is a broadcast transponder system which operates in the VHF mobile maritime band. Your own ship also shows on the screens of other vessels in the vicinity, provided your vessel is fitted with AIS. If AIS is not fitted or not switched on, there is no exchange of information on ships via AIS. The AIS onboard must be switched on at all times unless the Master deems that it must be turned off for security reasons or anything else. The working mode of AIS is continuous and autonomous."[31]

From the outset, the U.S. Navy's work with industry has focused on building, operating, and supporting a dyad to deliver the common operational picture driving the next round of anti-submarine warfare and maritime domain awareness. This P-8 dyad with Triton delivers a new capability for the fleet. This is manned-unmanned teaming being put into practice today, not in some distant combat future.

---

31 Shilavadra Bhattacharjee, "Automatic Identification System: Integrating and Identifying Marine Communication Channels," *Marine Insight* (December 25, 2020), https://www. marineinsight.com/marine-navigation/automatic-identification-system-ais-integrating-and-identifying-marine-communication-channels/.

Training for the Kill Web

During a visit to Jax Navy in June 2020, discussions with P-8 operators provided insights into how training to operate the aircraft and to work with Triton or Seahawk are not enough for Naval aviators in support of the fleet in the kill web age. Lt. Jonathan Gosselin, a P-8 Weapons and Tactics Instructor at the Maritime Patrol Reconnaissance Weapons School, provided insight into the change. For Lt. Gosselin, at the heart of the effort is really understanding, training for, and executing third party targeting. He argued that moving from a stove-piped mentality where the operators of the platform focus on their role as being both the sensor and the shooter, to a kill web perspective where the P-8 could provide the sensors for a firing solution, or whether the P-8 would deliver a weapon provided by another asset to perform the firing solution is at the heart of the change.

According to Lt. Gosselin: "What I am working on right now is shaping a curriculum to bring that capability to the MPRA community." He added: "We are working to develop con ops and integrate with other platforms such as the B-1, the B-52 and eventually with the B-21. This is where we're trying to go with the force. We've realized that we've put ourselves in a stovepipe, and we have to break ourselves out of that stovepipe and understand that we are not going to win this fight alone. It does not matter who the adversary is. This is a joint fight."

In effect, the focus is upon dynamic targeting across a distributed integrated force. As Lt. Gosselin put it: "We're talking about taking targeting data from one domain and quickly shifting to another, just like that. I have killed the target under sea. I am now going to go ahead and work the surface target and being able to understand the weapon sensor pairing network and being able to call in fires from different entities using commander's intent to engage the target. That's what we're trying to do: to get our operators to understand that it is not just a one-piece answer. There may be a time when you have to kick to another shooter."

To do so, he is engaging significantly with the Triton squadron as well to shape a way ahead for kill web dynamic targeting. Lt. Gosselin noted:

"With the P-8 and Triton we are able to expand our envelope of situational awareness. We can take that and now take the baseline concepts from what the P-3 did and apply them to a more advanced tactics, techniques, and procedures in the form of integrating with the B-21, the B-1, the F-18s, the F-35 joint strike fighter in a dynamic targeting kill web."

And with regard to the cultural shift, this is what he added: "It's important to talk not about how can I defeat this target, but really it should be, how can we defeat this target? Let's break ourselves out of this stovepipe and understand that I may not always be the best shooter. I may be the best sensor, but I might not be the best shooter." He argued that the Maritime Patrol Reconnaissance Weapons School is playing a key role within the U.S. Navy to shape this cultural shift.

Triton, Orbital Operations, and Network Challenges

The P-8/Triton dyad has already introduced significant changes in terms of working the challenge of operations of manned aircraft with remotely piloted ones in shaping a common operational picture and targeting effort. The challenges are compounded by working a manned aircraft doing sortie generated ISR operations, supported by working with another manned asset, the Romeo helicopter, with a remotely piloted aircraft doing orbital concepts of operations are significant. But learning how to deal with those challenges, along with the network management challenges are crucial parts of shaping the way ahead as new sensors operating from a variety of sensor-rich manned and autonomous platforms enter the kill web combat force.

The Triton, as an orbital concept of operations node in a network, is challenging the data management systems which the U.S. Navy currently operates. There clearly needs to be progress on the data infrastructure side to better handle real time data and to deliver it the combat edge to support operations which increasingly face the challenge of fighting at the speed of light.

The Triton/P-8 dyad poses a significant challenge to reworking the C^2/ISR enabled force. On the one hand, decisions can be pushed to the tactical edge. On the other hand, at the fleet command level, decisions need to be made rapidly at the strategic level.

But there is another challenge facing both industry and the Navy: how to maximize the advantages generated by an orbital concept of operations set of platforms versus a sortie generated set of platforms? Triton does the first; P-8 does the second; and the U.S. Navy's legacy is only the second.

The Triton community is starting to build some experiential depth, the kind of depth crucial for the knowledge revolution which the Triton can bring to the fleet. And given that the Triton is engaged in tasking, collecting, processing, exploitation, and dissemination of information in real time, learning how to do this for the fleet is a crucial challenge facing the future of a kill web enabled force. And looking forward, as the Triton adds high-band multi-intelligence (multi-INT) capabilities, it will become a more effective platform to contribute to the collaborative effort where multiple sensors can be cross-referenced to provide greater fidelity on targeting, and notably when it comes to smaller vessels of interest as well.[32]

It is early days for sorting out how to get the number of aircraft up to do the kind of orbital concepts of operations for which Triton was designed. But without enhancing the data management network side of the challenge, the ability to leverage the data generated by Triton will not be maximized. Unlike Global Hawk, which has its own dedicated pipe to deliver data, the Triton is working through the Navy's mission data collection systems. This creates challenges in terms of how to best handle the data and how best to ensure it gets delivered to the right place at the right time.

---

32 Jeff Newman, "Unmanned Triton Gets Signals-Intelligence Upgrade," *Naval Aviation News* (March 14, 2017), https://navalaviationnews.navylive.dodlive.mil/2017/03/14/triton-upgraded-with-signals-intelligence-sensor/.

Chief of Naval Operations (CNO) Adm. Mike Gilday is briefed on the MQ-4C Triton Unmanned Air System during a tour of Naval Air Station Patuxent River. U.S. Navy photo by Mass Communication Specialist 1st Class Raymond D. Diaz III/Released. November 4, 2020.

There is also clearly a cultural learning process as well. The MPRF community has operated throughout its history based on a concept of operations driven by air sortie operations. The Triton is based on a multi-airplane orbit concept of operations which yields a very different data stream than one gets from an air sortied aircraft. And it is one which is layered between what the space systems deliver and what the sortied air collection platforms can deliver.

Triton, like the F-35, is not being used in terms of storage of data coming off the aircraft, which makes little sense if the ISR/C^2 side of the force will indeed drive the way ahead for the combat force. The data backbone which was assumed to arrive with Triton is not yet there. And the challenges which data-rich aircraft already operating with the fleet—such as F-35 and Triton—face pose a significant roadblock to adding more ISR contributors: how to shape networks which facilitate rapid decision-making rather than impede it at both the tactical and strategic levels?

While the P-8 can operate with autonomy and networkability, the Triton is a network-generating, network-enabling asset. The vast amounts of data provided by Triton is requiring the Navy and the joint force to rework how to handle data flows from the unmanned asset to gain combat advantages. Put another way, traditional methods of handling data are not adequate to manage properly such massive amounts of information. In fact, learning how to manage data from Triton has been a key driver for change in how to redesign the ISR to C² empowerment systems, which the U.S. Navy seeks to execute for distributed maritime operations.

The unmanned asset operates differently from the P-8 or the Romeo in a way that is also leading to adjustments. For instance, both the P-8 and Romeo sortie into an operational area, operate for a period of time and land (either on land in the case of the P-8 or on a ship in the case of the Romeo helicopter). The concept of operations for the Triton, however, is very different. Triton provides the U.S. Navy with a whole new level of situational awareness that the Navy would attain no other way. With 24/7 coverage of the area, and in continuous orbit at 3000km, the Triton can provide domain awareness knowledge crucial to informing the threat and opportunity calculus for the area of operations.

The Triton/P-8 dyad then, poses a significant challenge to reworking the C²/ISR enabled force. Without enhancing the data management network side of the challenge, the ability to leverage the data generated by Triton will not be maximized. The data backbone for Triton is not yet completely there. But by deploying Triton, the Navy and the Air Force are moving forward with new ways for data management and to flow ISR more effectively into decision-making systems. But again, this is being driven by the operational experience of the Triton and other new air systems, and adaptation is based on real-world experience, not an abstract science project.

There is clearly a cultural learning process as well. The MPRF community has operated throughout its history based on a concept of operations driven by air platform sortie operations. The Triton is based on a multi-aircraft orbit concept of operations which yields a very different data stream than one gets from an air sortied aircraft—somewhere between what space systems deliver and what the sortied air collection platforms can deliver. And given that the Triton is engaged in the tasking, collecting, processing, exploiting, and disseminating of information in real time, learning how to do this for the fleet is a crucial challenge facing the future of a kill web enabled force.

As Triton gains multi-INT or multi-intelligence capabilities, it will become a more effective platform to contribute to the collaborative effort where multiple sensors can be cross-referenced to provide greater fidelity on targeting, and notably when it comes to smaller vessels of interest as well. What the Triton experience has demonstrated, without a doubt, are the challenges that unmanned or autonomous systems pose to the C^2 and ISR networks.

Leveraging MPRF Transformation

Three key elements of the MPRF transformation are crucial for shaping a way ahead with adding sensor networks, which can be provided by passive sensing additions to platforms, by new active sensors deployed onboard maritime or airborne, or space-based autonomous systems. The first element is the impact of software-enabled platforms, and how to manage operational adaptations and changes. The second is the question of designing networks to handle data either in terms of a local combat cluster or with regard to enabling a larger integrated force. The third is enabling enhanced cyber warfare, and machine management capabilities within the fleet.

The simple point is this: the MPRF is currently working all these challenges, and how they manage these challenges will provide an important input guiding the fighting navy as it works in new ISR capabilities, rather than simply reducing its combat capability by just adding new platforms without understanding how to use them in today's fight. One can always remember how useful it was for the Navy to have radar in Hawaii prior to December 7, 1941.

The software dynamic piece is often ignored when discussing the way ahead in the near to mid-term and how being able to leverage such software can lead to rapid operational changes. The MRPF is already experiencing significant change in this area and shaping a way ahead regarding the advantages of software upgradeability for the fighting navy, as already discussed in chapter one when we highlighted the interview with Lt. Sean Lavelle.

Put simply, part of the innovation being done in the MPRF community is about reaching towards a much more rapid process of software upgradeability and integrability for the distributed force. There is little doubt that success in this domain will proliferate throughout the operational naval forces in the years ahead and shape new ways to manage platforms and payloads to enable both a more survivable and lethal combat force.

A second challenge is working network management for an integrated distributed force. There is a wide range of opportunities to deliver more ISR enablement for the force through the introduction of new sensor networks, passive sensing capabilities on new platforms like the CMV-22B replacement for the C-2 transport aircraft and the growing opportunities to deploy a range of maritime remotes.

But this will not happen until the kind of network overload challenges already experienced within the MPRF are solved and managed. The current Chief of Naval Operations has highlighted how to look at the challenge. Referring to maritime autonomous systems, he had this to say: "Those vessels are useless unless we can command and control them with a very high degree of precision and reliability. And so that's where we start talking about the Navy's Project Overmatch, that falls underneath, or nests underneath JADC-2. And so, there are four big pieces to that. It's the networks. It's the infrastructure. It's the data standards. And then finally, it's the capabilities, whether they're battle management aids or whether they're artificial intelligence and machine learning capabilities that we apply to that data that allow us to decide and act faster than the bad guy, and then deliver ordnance faster out of these unmanned platforms."[33]

---

33 "Statement of Admiral Michael M. Gilday, Chief of Naval Operations," (Senate Armed Services Committee Subcommittee on Readiness, December 2, 2020).

What the quote from the CNO highlights is the importance of addressing C²/ISR networking in two related but different ways. The first is the integration of the presence force, which forms a lego block within a DMO concept of operations. And the second, is the reachback capabilities enabled by wider range, and scope to incorporate non-organic presence force platforms and capabilities thereby shaping a much more lethal and survivable modular task force.

The third challenge which the current operational experience of the MPRF community can assist the fighting navy resolve is how to manage manned-unmanned assets and to do so with regard to the cyber fight as well. There is no point in having more unmanned or autonomous assets if all they are is the weak link in the kill web networked combat force. With both the more rapid rewriting of software code, which Lt. Lavell highlighted in our quotes from him in chapter one, and the working of local and wider area networks to deliver the kind of situational awareness that will give strategic and tactical advantage with which the integration of the transformed MPRF can provide the fleet, the fighting navy is already gaining the kind of operational experience with how to work an effective way ahead.

From P-3 to Kill Web MPRF

From "Flying Alone and Unafraid" to the Kill Web

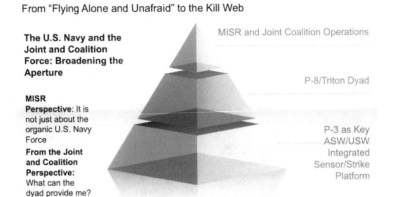

The U.S. Navy and the Joint and Coalition Force: Broadening the Aperture

MISR and Joint Coalition Operations

MISR Perspective: It is not just about the organic U.S. Navy Force

P-8/Triton Dyad

From the Joint and Coalition Perspective: What can the dyad provide me?

P-3 as Key ASW/USW Integrated Sensor/Strike Platform

Conceptualizing the kill web shift for the ISR-empowered
maritime forces. Credit: *Second Line of Defense.*

But the shaping of a kill web concept of operations for the "family of systems" for the MPRF is simply a foundational element for a broader ISR-enabled effort. From a MISR perspective, it is the ability to leverage all of the available and relevant joint and coalition force ISR-generators that are significant to deliver decision information to the operating fleet, not just the ones with the correct U.S. Navy markings on the outside of the air frame.

As the first deployed MISR officer. LCDR Maddox, put it in an interview with her in 2020: "The MISR perspective is a very different mindset shift for the U.S. Navy." [34] And that mindset change was very well expressed by CDR Salvaggio, the MISR head at NAWDC who underscored that the role of a MISR officer was to be familiar with joint and coalition capabilities which could deliver the right information to the maritime operating forces. This meant that the challenge would be to become

---

34 Robbin Laird, "The Coming of MISR to the Fleet: The Perspective of the First Deployed MISR Officer," Second Line of Defense (August 5, 2020), https://sldinfo.com/2020/08/the-coming-of-misr-to-the-fleet-the-perspective-of-the-first-deployed-misr-officer/.

familiar with joint and coalition platforms rather han simply knowing about what the U.S. Navy owned and operated. This is about opening the aperture with regard to what could be available at the point of operational interest, not simply being the world's leading expert on P-8, Triton, and Romeo helicopters.

In addition, there is the reverse point of the ISR information flow. How do Triton, Romeos, or P-8s inform the joint and coalition force? Are they integratable with what the joint and coalition forces needed to know for operational lethality and survivability? Are the MPRF platforms able to integrate with the data streams which joint or coalition partners can use?

Lance Cpl. Luke Seiler from Marine Wing Support Squadron 271 Aviation Mobility Company, FARP Platoon, along with Sailors from Navy Cargo Handling Battalion ONE receive and refuel a Navy P-8 Poseidon, from Patrol and Reconnaissance Squadron (VP) 8 at a forward arming and refueling point (FARP), demonstrating the integration of force capabilities at Kinston, N.C. as part of Large-Scale Exercise (LSE 2021), Aug. 13, 2021. Photo by Senior Chief Petty Officer RJ Stratchko.

This is a major challenge, but one which is certainly highlighted if one is focused on kill web concepts of operations. The effort to enhance the utility of data which a P-8 could provide to the USMC, for example, is certainly important to get full value out of what the P-8 senses and what a USMC asset like the G/ATOR radar senses as well. But the blunt fact is that the two core and impressive combat assets were NEVER built to work together. A Fall 2021 exercise by the U.S. Navy involving the USMC did in fact start the process of working this kind of integration. In an interview with MAG-29 at 2nd Marine Air Wing in August 2021, we discussed the upcoming naval exercise and an element of the integration with the U.S. Navy being worked. In that exercise, the assault force was to bring the G/ATOR radar to an expeditionary base and to operate that radar in support of an Aegis ship and its targeting and tracking functions. But instead of using the P-8 as a relay element in the effort, they had to use a USAF asset as the P-8 could not work with the data stream coming from the G/ATOR radar.[35]

In short, the MPRF is a key part of the operating navy building out the future force from working more effective integration of current capabilities with the fleet, the joint, and the coalition force. And it is how key allies working with the U.S. Navy and the joint force to shape an expanded cluster of combat capabilities which can contribute to the integrated fight across the spectrum of warfare to which we now turn.

---

35 Robbin Laird, "Shaping a way ahead for the assault support community: Visiting the War Eagles of MAG-29," *Second Line of Defense* (August 10, 2021), https://sldinfo. com/2021/08/shaping-a-way-ahead-for-the-assault-support-community-visiting-the-war-eagles-of-mag-29/.

CHAPTER SEVEN:
KILL WEB MATESMANSHIP

The United States Navy simply cannot build enough ships to compete with the numbers the Chinese are putting out. But our book highlights how the U.S. Navy is building a more survivable and lethal force to deal precisely with the Chinese naval build-up and Russian force modernization. We are focused on how to shape a maritime force able to work with the joint forces and allies to deliver distributed combat capability for escalation and crisis management effectiveness.

A key part of being able to do so is to continue to work how the presence force provided by allies and partners can be integrated into a wider political-military force to deliver the kind of crisis management and combat effect necessary for the global competition with 21st century authoritarian powers. Then CNO Admiral Mike Mullen proposed in 2005 to build out a global maritime partnership with his "thousand ship navy" concept.

With a focus on kill web concepts of operations, where seabases provide for presence, and those presence forces are integrated with evolving C^2/ISR capabilities to get enhanced capability out of the deployed presence forces, and with expanded reachback capabilities allowing the presence force to flow into a more lethal and survivable modular task force, the focus on distributed integratability with allies receives an enhanced prospect of success. And it also about the most neglected aspect in discussing maritime capabilities, namely sustainability. As core allies focus on ways to enhance their own sustainability, the engagement of the U.S. sea services with those allies, also can provide sustainable depth as well.

This is why using the metric of a 30-year shipbuilding program is not one which indicates maritime combat capability, effectiveness or crisis management dominance. The U.S. Navy's thirty-year shipbuilding program has been overtaken by the need to look at the concepts of operations which the maritime force can deliver in combination with the joint force and to find ways to capitalize the workforce already created for existing ship types. And to then make judgements with regard to the kinds of ships that need to be built, and to avoid, at all cost, building orphan ship classes like the littoral combat ship.

In this chapter we focus on two allies—Australia and Britain—who are building out their forces to provide for national capabilities but in a manner that is integratable with the U.S. maritime services to deliver full spectrum operational forces. By shaping interactive kill web capabilities with the American forces, the Australians and the Brits extend the reach and combat effectiveness of their forces. In turn, with an ability to leverage the presence and scalability of allied forces, the U.S. Navy can provide for a combat force with greater reach than simply relying on what the deployed numbers of U.S. warships could deliver.

Our colleague, Marcus Hellyer of the Australian Strategic Policy Institute, and a leading expert on military systems in Australia, highlighted in a January 28, 2021, article how the U.S. Navy can deal with the challenge of the Chinese maritime build out. This is how he puts it: "Whether under the name of mosaic warfare, distributed lethality, or some other term, they involve disaggregating capabilities such as weapons, sensors, processing power and communications systems into smaller vessels and vehicles, some manned, some unmanned. The individual components would be cheaper, but when linked into a resilient network or mesh enabled by artificial intelligence, together they would provide greater, more responsive lethality while being able to suffer attrition. Such concepts have made some progress towards reality, but overall have struggled to gain traction."[36]

---

36 Marcus Hellyer, "The U.S. Navy Needs to Admit that it can't Outbuild China," *ASPI Strategist* (January 28, 2021).

Hellyer and Laird both have both focused on the new build Offshore Patrol Vessels in Australia as a platform which could be leveraged significantly, notably in light of shaping a kill web enabled navy.[37] When you shift from set piece design ship combat task forces to modular task forces which can incorporate land and air systems not formally part of a classic maritime task force, one can rethink how to innovate with regard to ship builds. Ships can operate as presence forces with scalability through kill webs to tap into joint and coalition strike and defense capabilities.

Laird visiting the Australian West Australia shipyard building the new Australian OPVs. This picture was shot in March 2020 as the COVID-19 lockdown was starting in Australia.

In his November 2021 report on the Australian Navy, Hellyer drew upon his earlier paper on the OPV to highlight what in effect is a recognition of the kill web enabled maritime force. Hellyer identified two approaches which could leverage what is already in place but re-imagined, re-worked and integrated.

---

37 Marcus Hellyer (June 3, 2020), https://www.aspi.org.au/report/concentrated-vulnerability-distributed-lethality-offshore-patrol-vessels and Robbin Laird, *Joint by Design: The Evolution of Australian Defence Strategy* (2020), chapter eight.

The first is "building vessels based on the OPV hull but fitted with missile systems and smart autonomous systems—air, surface and undersea. Not every maritime platform needs to be able to do every task and defeat every threat by itself. Breaking this mindset opens new possibilities.

"An armed version of the OPV that doesn't pretend to be a multi-role platform but has useful offensive or sensor capabilities looks attractive as a near-term addition to the Navy's lethality that complicates any adversary's decisions. They won't be multi-role vessels, which avoids the spiralling complexity and cost we see with the Hunter (the new Australian frigate class) but would operate in tailored taskforces with other vessels.

"This approach would be part of a broader strategy of making greater investments in the 'small, smart and cheap'—disaggregated uncrewed or minimally crewed systems that employ autonomous technologies to generate distributed mass and effect."

This of course is a pure statement of a kill web approach. What the kill web approach to integratability highlights is focusing on how to connect relevant platforms to shape an integrated force package based on shared situational awareness and C^2 decision making capability. It is not about how much capability one can pile onto to one exquisite platform.

But having platforms, and enough of them to operate in the extended battlespace, is crucial. This means that building out of what you can build now is not a bad idea, rather than putting your eggs in the future X class frigate, destroyer, or carrier. And in the Hellyer report he focuses on the Australian variant of this point, namely rather than waiting for the future frigate class, it would behoove the Navy to build out what they have already succeeded in doing, namely building a first-class Aegis ship.

"The second approach is the option of building more Hobart-class air warfare destroyers. We've already been through the pains and challenges of getting the design right and learning how to build them. While they mightn't have quite the same antisubmarine warfare capability as the Hunter is intended to have, they're still very capable antisubmarine platforms. Moreover, their 48 missile cells offer advantages over the Hunter in air defence and strike—and for deploying missiles made in Australia through the emerging guided weapons enterprise.

"With the design mature and the build process well understood, there's the realistic prospect of getting a second batch of three Hobarts into service before the Hunter program delivers, the first of them well before the end of the decade.

"As with any complex undertaking, there will be challenges, such as managing facilities and workforce between the major shipbuilding programs at Osborne in South Australia and restarting supply chains, but the shipyard was designed to have more capacity than simply producing one frigate every two years.

"The reason the government retained ownership of the shipyard (and the taxpayers funded its development) was to retain the flexibility to produce different vessels from different designers as required. Moreover, a new air warfare destroyer program will help generate the ecosystem of skilled tradespeople, designers, engineers, combat systems integrators, project managers and local suppliers that will be needed for the build and sustainment of the future SSNs. It would avoid a cold start to the SSN program and so help mitigate its schedule risks."

Hellyer makes the core point, which is too often lost in discussions of shipbuilding: "If the National Naval Shipbuilding Enterprise can't deliver meaningful capability well before 2030, then its entire purpose needs to be reconsidered. Ultimately, delivering actual capability in strategically relevant time frames will address risk as well as rebuild public confidence in the shipbuilding enterprise."[38]

Working more effectively with allies in shaping an integrated distributed force is crucial way ahead for the U.S. Navy and to achieve kill web integratability, sharing of information and of effective decision-making at the tactical edge are crucial. Hellyer emphasized: "If the key threat is the growing Chinese navy, then effective, timely responses will require

---

38 Marcus Hellyer, "Delivering a Stronger Navy, Faster," ASPI (November 2021), https://www.aspi.org.au/report/delivering-stronger-navy-faster.

moving beyond focusing on ships to be built in future decades to planning for joint responses drawing on all U.S. assets. The U.S. Marine Corps' reconceptualization of itself as a ship-killing force is one hint towards a different way of thinking. Resuscitating the U.S. Air Force's bomber fleet's role as ship-killers is another. Even the U.S. Army can play a role here with its own long-range strike platforms. And that's before we think about the role the U.S.'s coalition of allies can play."[39]

The U.S. Side of the Equation

In a December 2020, in a U.S. Department of Defense publication, the heads of the USMC, the U.S. Coast Guard and the U.S. Navy signed off on a way ahead on how to respond to the growing assertiveness and capabilities of the 21st century authoritarian powers. "America's Naval Service defends our Nation by preserving freedom of the seas, deterring aggression, and winning wars. For generations, we have underwritten security and prosperity and preserved the values our Nation holds dear. However, China's behavior and accelerated military growth place it on a trajectory that will challenge our ability to continue to do so. We are at an inflection point. Our integrated Navy, Marine Corps, and Coast Guard must maintain clear-eyed resolve to compete with, deter, and, if necessary, defeat our adversaries while we accelerate development of a modernized, integrated all-domain naval force for the future."[40]

What the document lays out is at the heart of the focus of our book, namely, how to build and operate an integrated distributed force that can combine presence with scalability to deliver what we call full spectrum crisis management capabilities. We discussed earlier in the book how the USMC is refocusing on naval integration and how the U.S. Navy is training differently and leveraging ISR and C^2 assets to reshape its combat capability. But the full spectrum piece often gets hung up in discussing the question of gray zone capabilities, and frankly this is an area where the

---

39 Hellyer, "The U.S. Navy."
40 *Advantage at Sea: Prevailing with Integrated All-Domain Naval Power* (U.S. Department of Defense, 2020), foreword.

U.S. Coast Guard plays a key role, and its underfunding in recent years affects not only the capability of the maritime services to deliver greater capability in the gray zone but to also work with allies and partners in this crucial area where our authoritarian adversaries are focusing significant attention.

In our 2013 book entitled *Rebuilding American Military Power in the Pacific: A 21st Century Strategy*, we began by speaking on the presence mission with a detailed look at the U.S. Coast Guard and its role.[41] The central role of the USCG in a maritime security and defense role is far too often overlooked. For example, from Seattle to San Diego, many key U.S. cities lie in the Pacific Basin. And the economic impact of the Asian relationship is evident everywhere in the region. The impact of maritime trade is central. And these cities and their ports are part of the conveyer belt of goods transferred from Asia to the United States and beyond. Also underscored are the trade routes for the conveyer belt, which follow the Great Circle Route from the Asian ports south of Alaska and then down the West Coast of the United States.

The defense of these littorals is a major task and challenge. Maritime trade and commerce are a big part of the picture, but one must recognize that such trade and commerce largely comes via the Great Circle Route from Asia, then south of Alaska and then to America's West Coast ports. Defense of the littorals requires working safety and security of maritime trade and commerce, managing environmental threats and the management of the fisheries and building a sound and safe security system end-to-end from Asia to the United States. This means that the ports must be safe from the intrusion of terrorist threats or asymmetric actions by potential adversaries in the Asian region. Safety, security, and defense of the littorals lie at the center of a sound Pacific strategy.

A way to conceptualize the fusion of the commercial with security and defense concerns is to combine the role of the maritime transit system as

---

41 Robbin F. Laird, Edward Timperlake and Richard Weitz, *Rebuilding American Military Power in the Pacific" A 21st Century Strategy* (Santa Barbara, California: Praeger, 2013).

a conveyer belt with the role of SLOCs for military operations. The two are fused at the middle but are two parts of a continuum of operations on the sea and from the sea. At the heart of the 21st-century reality is the need to manage escalation and de-escalation as well as the pivot point between multiple-sum and zero-sum security and defense dynamics. Confrontations such as those between China and the United States and its allies currently in the South China Sea can escalate and get out of control. But to demonstrate dominance, the Chinese are positioning themselves for escalation. It is necessary to counter such efforts and to put on reverse pressure, but it is also necessary to master when to manage de-escalation as well as escalation.

The Maritime Vortex

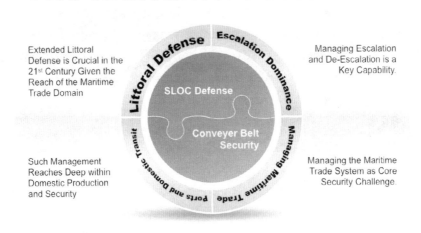

Extended Littoral Defense is Crucial in the 21st Century Given the Reach of the Maritime Trade Domain

Managing Escalation and De-Escalation is a Key Capability.

Such Management Reaches Deep within Domestic Production and Security

Managing the Maritime Trade System as Core Security Challenge.

The graphic highlights the intersection of maritime trade or the maritime conveyer belt security with littoral defense operations. This is why the intersection between commercial maritime trade and non-kinetic and kinetic defense of the littoral are so significantly connected. Credit graphic: *Second Line of Defense*.

The Coast Guard plays a special joint agency role in providing for U.S. littoral defense. In that role, it is a Title X or defense agency in the United States, not simply a homeland security agency. If you cannot protect the entry points into the United States, the nation will clearly not have an effective foundation for a defense and security strategy in the Pacific. Threats are embedded in the normal operations of the maritime trade system; managing these threats is a foundation element for the defense of the United States in the Pacific.

The USCG's national security cutters operate throughout the Pacific and indeed the Pacific USCG is much neglected piece of the puzzle. In several years of working with the USCG, there was a clear opportunity to see the launch of the new National Security Cutters and their impact. The ship has the flight deck, C^2 and ISR systems which make it a mature partner in a kill web force.

In a 2011 interview with Adm. Currier, then the Deputy Commandant (Mission Support) for the USCG, the impact of this new ship on the USCG was highlighted as follows: "It is a multi-mission system. What I've just described to you is the detection, monitoring and interdiction of a surface or subsurface suspect vessel, a narco-terrorist threat. But the NSC has additional utility in that this ship is a protected asset as well. It can operate in a contaminated environment, whether it is chemical, bio, or nuke. It can go into an incident area as a completely protected, self-contained command and control platform to support at sea or land operations as well.

"And due to the USCG's unique capability to operate with DOD in a joint task force environment, or unified commands on the civil side, the NSC can bring them together, house them, provide them communications, and translate between the two from a planning and execution standpoint. In other words, the National Security Cutter is a unique asset for national security. It can go to the scene of a major disaster, whether it is an earthquake in San Francisco, or a WMD attack in the New York City area and be able to provide the responders with sustained and protected communication facilities capable of co-joining unified commands with DoD JTF's."[42]

---

42 "The National Security Cutter Opportunity," *Second Line of Defense* (August 2, 2011), https://sldinfo.com/2011/08/the-national-security-cutter-opportunity/.

If one thinks that gray zones are important, then the significance and commitment to the USCG and its foreign operational role needs to be significantly enhanced. There is no clearer case of this than dealing with the USCG Pacific. In a 2011 interview with Vice Adm. Manson Brown, Pacific Area Commander, he highlighted the key role the USGG plays in the Pacific. "Many people believe that we need to be a coastal coast guard, focused on the ports, waterways, and coastal environment. But the reality is that because our national interests extend well beyond our shore, whether it's our vessels, or our mariners, or our possessions and our territories, we need to have presence well beyond our shores to influence good outcomes.

"As the Pacific Area Commander, I'm also the USCG Pacific Fleet Commander. That's a powerful synergy. I'm responsible for the close-in game, and I'm responsible for the away game. Now the away game has some tangible authorities and capabilities, such as fisheries enforcement and search and rescue presence. But it's also got some softer type of capability. We do a lot of nation building. We perform a lot of theater security cooperation for PACOM. We'll send ships over to Japan. We've got ships going over to China just to exchange ideas, and discuss common objectives and capabilities, and demonstrate American engagement in the region. As I travel around, I realize that the USCG is respected internationally because of our law enforcement and regulatory capabilities and our history. When people see our response to Katrina, or to Deep Water Horizon, they want a piece of us."[43]

For the USCG to play its role in the December 2020 strategy, there is little doubt that they need more national security cutters and to ensure that those cutters can lead task forces or plug into task forces as we have described within the context of interactive kill webs. A huge opportunity was missed by the maritime services by building the littoral combat ships which draw much and contribute little to a kill web force. The opportunity was to build out the National Security Cutters and to buy with them a new

---

43 "The USCG in the Pacific," *Second Line of Defense* (August 13, 2011), https://sldinfo.com/2011/08/the-uscg-in-the-pacific/.

frigate class which could enable a more capable presence force which could leverage the kind of scalability which a fifth generation-enabled air and naval force can surge to the national security cutter.

In the book edited by Andrew S. Erickson and Ryan D. Martinson on Chinese maritime operations, they provide a detailed look at gray zone operations, namely, operations short of the use of lethal force but empowered by a well worked out chain of maritime power elements up to and including the presence of combat forces.[44] The goal is to reshape the external environment in favorable ways without the need to engage in kinetic operations. In the hybrid war concept, lethal operations are the supporting element, not the tip of the spear, to achieve what the state actor is hoping to accomplish tactically or strategically. Their book argues that this is a phase short of what the Russians have done, which has been labelled hybrid warfare.

Both gray zone ops and hybrid war ops are part of a broader strategic reality, namely, the nature of crisis management and ongoing limited conflicts or wars facing the liberal democracies competing with the authoritarian states in a peer-to-peer competition. The challenge can be put bluntly—deterrence has been designed on the Western side with large-scale engagement of enemy forces in mind. What if deterrence in this sense is the necessary, but not sufficient capability to constrain the actions of the authoritarians? What if you can deter a full-scale war, but by so doing are not able to control what your adversary is doing in terms of expanding his global reach and reshaping the strategic environment to his benefit? What if you have organized yourself for deterrence but not effective crisis management? The gray zone concept should be subsumed in this broader strategic shift and challenge, rather than being a separate field of study.

The December 2020 strategic document highlights how these capabilities need to be shaped: "Generating Integrated All-Domain Naval Power. By synchronizing the capabilities, capacities, roles, investments,

---

44 Andrew S. Erickson and Ryan D. Martinson (eds), *China's Maritime Gray Zone Operations* (Naval Institute Press, 2019).

and authorities of the Naval Service, we will expand our influence across the competition continuum and in all domains—from the sea floor to space; across the world's oceans, littorals, and coastal areas ashore; and in the cyber domain, information environment, and electromagnetic spectrum."

"Strengthening alliances and partnerships. The Naval Service will foster a global unity of effort to secure unfettered access to the maritime domain. A strong, worldwide network of maritime partnerships, united in common purpose, serves as an enduring advantage over our rivals."

"Prevailing in day-to-day competition. The Naval Service will uphold maritime governance and counter malign behaviors below the threshold of war through assertive and persistent operations. We will enable our success by building unity of effort within joint, whole-of-government, allied, and partner activities."

"Controlling the seas. In conflict, the Naval Service will establish, maintain, and exploit sea control in contested environments from the littorals to open ocean, including critical chokepoints. Investments in increased lethality, capacity, targeted capabilities, and transformed naval expeditionary forces capable of sea control and sea denial will support this effort."[45]

To do so requires the cross-cutting multi-domain interactive kill web force we are highlighting in our book but to do so in ways that allies, and partners are not just part of the solution but generating ways for the United States to find new and innovative paths forward as well. There are no more significant allies in this context than Australia or the United Kingdom.

The Australians Shape a Fifth-generation Combat Force

When the Australians decided to buy the F-35, they did so with a serious commitment not just to replace an aircraft—the Super Hornet—with a next

---

45 *Advantage at Sea: Prevailing with Integrated All-Domain Naval Power* (U.S. Department of Defense, 2020), p. 21.

generation one, but to leverage its capabilities to drive change throughout the force. The RAAF Chief of Staff at the time of the F-35 acquisition decision was Air Marshal Geoff Brown and from the outset he focused on how bringing the new "flying combat system" into the force could be leveraged not just to make the RAAF more capable, but to spearhead change throughout the force to become more capable in conducting integrated multi-domain operations.[46]

Today, the RAAF has the most modern air force among the liberal democracies, and as they have added platforms, the focus has been upon shaping integrated air operations in support of a multi-domain force. The migration began with the acquisition of the C-17 as a strategic lift aircraft which complimented the RAAF C-130s and then the later acquisition of C-27s. Given the size of Australia, just to operate in Australia requires the RAAF to do so as a power projection force.

The flight deck of the KC-30a with an Australian C-17 in the background during a visit to 33rd Squadron at Amberly Airbase in 2014. Credit: *Second Line of Defense.*

---

46 For a detailed look at the evolution of the Australian defense strategy and transformation of the Australian Defence Force, see Robbin Laird, *Joint by Design: The Evolution of Australian Defence Strategy* (2020).

They then added the KC-30A or the Airbus A330MRTT, transport and tanker aircraft. This innovative tanker offloads its fuel from storage in the wings, leaving the ability to leverage the inside of the aircraft for a wide variety of uses, including MEDIVAC, transport, or future innovations in combat systems which can be located onboard the aircraft. They then added the E-7 Wedgetail, air battle management aircraft, whose unique software and hardware systems allow the aircraft to migrate from a core responsibility to deliver air battle management to providing various electronic or information warfare capabilities to the force.

When the Australians came to the Middle East to support what they called Operation Okra, they brought an integrated self-supported air task force to the Middle East. This was the first time that they did not need USAF support to fly their core combat capabilities to an area far from Australia. This kind of integration has allowed the RAAF to drive significant change in the ADF and given its role in supporting maritime operations, the reset of the Australian Navy is being driven in part by the RAAF transformation.

During a 2016 to Williamtown Airbase, Laird met with 42 Wing which operates the Wedgetail within the RAAF. Credit: *Second Line of Defense*.

In a 2016 discussion at Williamtown Air Base in Australia with then Commander of the Air Combat Group Air Commodore Steve Roberton, he explained how the fifth-generation transition affected Air Force-Naval integration. He argued that the new fifth generation approach was shaping a way ahead with regard to force integration. And for the RAAF, this approach is crucial because unlike the USAF or the USN, the RAAF does not have a large force of specialized aircraft to operate in an evolving approach to integration; the RAAF with the Navy and the Army need to lead a process of force structure integration shaped by a key driver like the F-35.

This is how he put it: "The Australian Defense Force is in a different position than the U.S. Navy or Air Force, in that we are largely being air asset led. Our aviation assets are out ahead of where we are with development of our surface combatants. For Australia, the F-35 is not just about making everything else in the battle space better and more effective. It's more about providing options for commanders to accord them the right time to choose how to deploy force so that the right asset can be where it needs to be to get the desired effect. Increasingly, for us, that's going to be both kinetic and non-kinetic. The F-35 is going to provide us a level of temporal control that we haven't really had but this will only happen if we get the information sharing right. But we're still in a position where we are waiting for some of the other force structures to become more effectively integrated in the way ahead."

The RAAF operates the P-8 and Triton which only reinforces Roberton's point about how the Australians do air to surface integration between their Air Force and their Navy. This photo was shot during a 2017 visit to RAAF Edinbourgh to talk with the RAAF about both P-8 and the coming of Triton. Credit: *Second Line of Defense.*

As Air Commodore Roberton sees it, there is a three-phase process underway and "we are only at the first step. "We need to be in the position where our maritime surface combatants are able to receive the information that we've got airborne in the RAAF assets. Once they've got that, they're going to actually be trying to be able to do something with it. That is the second level, namely where they can integrate with the C^2 and ISR flowing from our air fleet. But we need to get to the third level, where they too can provide information and weapons for us in the air domain. That is how you will turn a kill chain into a kill web. That's something that we want in our fifth-generation integrated force."

He went on to emphasize: "In a fifth-generation world, it's less about who is the trigger shooter but actually making sure that everybody's contributing effectively to the right decisions made as soon as possible at the lowest possible level. And that is why I see the F-35 as an information age aircraft. I'm less concerned about the load outs on the F-35. You can give it another ten weapon stations and you would miss the core point.

What's actually important is how the F-35 makes other weapon providers or effect providers out there fare better and shape faster reaction times. A lot of people seem stuck in the old mindset of how many weapons we are going to stack on each aircraft. That's almost two generations ago. In some ways, we are going back to the concept of military aviation early in World War I where we are the eyes and ears for the combat force forward operating."[47]

With the RAAF in the process of transformation, the Australians began the largest naval recapitalization since World War II. And the recapitalization was not just about adding hulls, it was about reshaping how those hulls would be configured in terms of integration within the national fleet and in terms of how to work more effectively with the U.S. Navy and the U.S. joint force and other coalition allies like Japan in the decades ahead. Aegis combat systems have been selected for the new surface fleet going forward to ensure national integratability, and to reinforce the connectivity with the U.S. and Japanese navies going forward.

A key architect in shaping the new way ahead was the Chief of Navy, Vice Adm. Tim Barrett. In a presentation made to the Williams Foundation in 2016, the Chief of Navy focused on the opportunities and challenges of the largest recapitalization of the Australian Navy since World War II. New submarines, destroyers and amphibious ships and associated fleet assets are being built in Australia to shape a new maritime capability for Australia. But this force is being built in the time of significant innovation in the Pacific whereby new force concepts are being shaped, such as kill webs, distributed lethality, and fifth generation airpower. Barrett made it very clear that what was crucial for the Navy was to design, from the ground up, any new ships to be core participants in the force transformation process underway, in other words con-ops driven.

---

47 The quotes are taken from the interview, Robbin Laird, "Shaping the Airpower Transition: The Perspective of 'Zed' Roberton, Commander Air Combat Group (RAAF), *Second Line of Defense* (April 6, 2016), https://sldinfo.com/2016/04/shaping-the-airpower-transition-the-perspective-of-zed-roberton-commander-air-combat-group-raaf/.

Vice Admiral Barrett addressing the Williams Foundation Seminar
in Canberra, Australia. Credit: *Second Line of Defense.*

In his presentation at the conference, he underscored that "we are not building an interoperable navy; we are building an integrated force for the Australian Defence Force." He drove home the point that ADF integration was crucial for the ADF to support government objectives in the region and beyond and to provide for a force capable of decisive lethality. By so doing, Australia would have a force equally useful in coalition operations in which distributed lethality was the operational objective. He noted that it is not about amassing force in a classic sense; it is about shaping a force which can maximize the adversary's vulnerabilities while reducing our own.

And he reinforced several times in his presentation that this is not about an add-in, after the fact capability, but rather it was necessary to design and train from the ground up to have a force trained and equipped to be capable of decisive lethality. He quoted Patton to the effect that you fight war with technology; you win with people. It is about equipping the right way with right equipment but training effectively to gain a decisive advantage.

The recapitalization effort was a "watershed opportunity for the Australian Navy." But he saw it as a watershed opportunity, not so much in terms of simply building new platforms, but the right ones.[48] And with regard to the right ones, he had in mind ships built from the ground up which could be interoperable with the F-35, P-8, Growler, Wedgetail and other joint assets. "We need to achieve the force supremacy inherent in each of these platforms, but we can do that only by shaping integrated ways to operate."

Group Captain Braz during Laird's April 2017 visit to Amberley Airbase in Australia to discuss the arrival of the Growler into the RAAF and joint force. Credit: *Second Line of Defense*.

Vice Admiral Barrett highlighted that the Australian Navy was in the process of shaping a 21st century task force concept appropriate to a strategy of distributed lethality and operations. A key element of the new approach is how platforms will interact with one another in distributed

---

48 This clearly has affected how the Australians have approached their shipbuilding program and how to design new ships as part of a modular task force. Due to space limits of the book, we cannot discuss this at length here. But during a March 2020 visit to Australia, Laird visited the new shipyard for the Offshore Patrol Vessel and wrote a report on that program. The case study can be found in his book *Joint by Design: The Evolution of Australian Defence Strategy* (2021), chapter eight.

strike and defensive operations, such as the ability to cue weapons across a task force.[49]

Shaping a new fleet which is both integratable with the Australian Defence Force and with their key coalition partners, the United States and Japan, requires reworking how to network the force. One of the clearest expressions of the way ahead along these lines was in our 2016 interview with Rear Adm. Mayer, the commander of the Australian Fleet. This is how he characterized the C^2 side of the weapons enterprise for an integrated but distributed force. "The potential of each of the individual platforms in a network is such that we've actually got to preset the limits of the fight before we get to it. The decisions on what we'll do, how much we'll share, and what sovereign rights we will retain have to be preset into each one of the combat systems before you switch it on and join a network. There is no point designing a combat system capable of defeating supersonic threats and throttling it with a slow network or cumbersome C^2 decision architecture. Achieving an effective network topology is so much more complex in a coalition context in which the potential for divergence is higher."

---

49 The quotes from Vice Admiral (Retired) Barrett are taken from Robbin Laird, "Vice-Admiral Barrett on the Way Ahead of the Australian Navy: Design the Force for Decisive and Distributed Lethality," *Second Line of Defense* (September 6, 2016), https://sldinfo.com/2016/09/vice-admiral-barrett-on-the-way-ahead-of-the-australian-navy-design-the-force-for-decisive-and-distributed-lethality/.

Rear Admiral Manazir with Rear Admiral Mayer at the second Williams Foundation Seminar in 2016. Credit: *Second Line of Defense*.

He further elaborated the network enablement of strike as follows: "The paradox is that a coalition network is much more likely a requirement than a national network, and yet what investment we do make is based on national systems first. If we don't achieve the open architecture design that enables the synergy of a networked coalition force, then the effectiveness of the coalition itself will be put at risk. The moment we insert excess command and hierarchical decision authority into the loop, we will slow down the lethality of the platforms in the network."

Rear Adm. Mayer then added: "Before we even get in the battlespace, we have to agree the decision rights and preset these decisions into the combat system and network design; the fight for a lethal effect starts at the policy level before we even engage in combat operations. The network and C^2 rather than the platforms can become the critical vulnerability. This is why the decision-making process needs to be designed as much as the network or the platforms. If the C^2 matrix slows the network, it will dumb down the platform and the capability of the system to deliver a full effect."

Rear Adm. Mayer compared the new kill web approach to understanding ecosystem dynamics. "The nature of the force we are shaping is analogous to a biological system in which the elements flourish based on their natural relationship within the environment. We have an opportunity to shape both the platforms and the network, but we will only achieve the flourishing ecosystem we seek if each harmonize with the other, and the overall effectiveness is considered on the health of the ecosystem overall. For example, an ASW network will leverage the potential of the individual constituent platforms and that in turn will determine the lethality of the system. A discordant network connection will, at the least, limit the overall force level effect of the network and at worst break the network down to discordant elements."

Clearly, a key part of the evolution is about shaping a weapons revolution whereby weapons can operate throughout the battlespace hosted by platforms that are empowered by networks tailored to the battlespace. And that revolution will have its proper impact only if the network and C^2 dynamics discussed by Rear Adm. Mayer unfold in the national and coalition forces.

As Rear Adm. Mayer put it: "The limiting factor now is not our platforms; it's the networks and C^2 that hold the potential of those platforms down. When the individual platforms actually go into a fight, they're part of an interdependent system. The thing that will dumb down the system will be a network that is not tailored to leverage the potential of the elements, or a network that holds decision authority at a level that is a constraint on timely decision-making. The network will determine the lethality of our combined system."[50]

The Australian approach was highlighted as well by the surprise announcement in the Fall of 2021 that they had reached an agreement with the United States to procure nuclear submarines. The United Kingdom was

---

50 Robbin Laird, "The Network as a Weapon System: The Perspective of Rear Admiral Mayer, Commander Australian Fleet," *Second Line of Defense* (September 10, 2016), https://sldinfo.com/2016/09/the-network-as-a-weapon-system-the-perspective-of-rear-admiral-mayer-commander-australian-fleet/

also part of that agreement largely because the Astute class submarine was built with significant U.S. technical assistance and those agreements are very likely to be applicable to the Australian case.[51]

Laird visited HMAS Rankin at the Royal Australian base HMAS Stirling which is part of Fleet Base West in March 2020. The submarine has an advanced combat system and several capabilities interoperable with the U.S. Navy but providing additional capabilities for ASW as well.

While most press assessments focused on the future Australian nuclear submarine variant, the heart of the arrangement really revolves around providing strategic depth and sustainability for both the United States and Australia in dealing with the Pacific-based threats. Western Australia and the Northern Territories are becoming increasingly significant geopolitically in dealing with the China challenge.

---

51 We have focused on the Australian submarine decision and its ripple effects in Robbin Laird, editor, *Defense XXI: Shaping a Way Ahead for the United States and its Allies.* (2022)

Already Australia has the key elements of addressing the ASW and USW challenges which this area of operations extended out beyond their first island chain provides, including their own effective diesel submarines sensors, P-8s, Tritons, F-35s, etc. They are clearly working a kill web approach to ASW and USW which we discuss in the next chapter.

The Australians will build out the infrastructure and ecosystem for operating their future nuclear submarines and almost certainly build that in advance of getting their own submarines and will work with the U.S. Navy's operational fleet as well. This means that the sustainability of the U.S. fleet is enhanced as well by the Australian decision.

As the Australians face the challenges which China poses in the Indo-Pacific region, they are focused on enhanced resilience and self-reliance. But they are doing so in part by shaping an integrated distributed force designed to work more effectively with the United States, Japan, and other key allies in the region. And in so doing they are driving further change in American forces as well. As Air Vice-Marshal (Retired) John Blackburn put it in our 2017 interview: "We want to learn from the U.S., follow it closely, but actually take a step which is hard for the U.S. to do because of its size, and that's go truly integrated by design across the whole of the joint force."[52]

This means that from the United States point of view, the Australians will drive innovations differently from the United States, with the clear opportunity for the United States to enhance its own fleet innovativeness by adopting relevant Australian practices and changes in concepts of operations.

---

52 Robbin Laird, "The Challenge of Designing an Integrated 21ˢᵗ Century Combat Force," *Second Line of Defense* (April 21, 2017), https://sldinfo.com/2017/04/the-challenge-of-designing-an-integrated-21st-century-combat-force-air-vice-marshal-john-blackburn-retired-looks-at-the-way-ahead/.

The UK Shapes an Integrated Operating Concept

The United Kingdom faces major challenges associated with its withdrawal from the European Union as it reorients its regional and global roles. With the dynamics of change in the direct defense of Europe, there is a priority upon refocusing United Kingdom support to the Northern region at the expense of its Cold War focus, as well as upon what was referred to as the Central Front.[53]

During a 2019 visit to London, a senior defense official flat-out stated to us: "With the return of geography, the focus needs to be clearly on our Northern and Southern Flanks, and this means the emphasis needs to be placed upon air–naval integration. The Royal Navy and the RAF need to find ways to work much more effective integration. And our new carrier provides a means whereby we can do so."

With Brexit Britain, there is a natural withdrawal of military attention from what used to be called the Central Front during the Cold War days, and a renewed focus on the flanks. France and Germany are to provide the maneuver forces and space for the defense of Europe's new frontline in Poland and the Baltics, and the UK's contribution will be reduced to reinforcing efforts, not leading them in this continental European sector.

The new Queen Elizabeth class carriers are a key piece of sovereign real estate around which flank defense will be generated. It is also a focal point for the RAF and Royal Navy integration of the sort which a transformed force will need to deliver to the nation. The new UK carrier provides a mobile basing capability by being a flexible sea base, which can complement UK land-based air assets and provide a flexible asset that can play a role in the Northern Flank or the Mediterranean on a regular deployment basis and over time be used for deployments further away from Europe as well.

---

53 For a more detailed discussion of the refocus of UK defense policy and its challenges, see Robbin Laird and Murielle Delaporte, *The Return of Direct Defense in Europe: Meeting the Challenge of XXIst Century Authoritarian Powers* (2020), chapter seven.

Laird (center of the photograph) and senior Royal Navy and Royal Air Force personnel visiting HMS Queen Elizabeth during the build stage in Scotland in 2015. Photo Credit: Royal Navy.

The Commander of the UK Carrier Strike Group at the time, Cmdr. Andrew Betton, and Col. Phil Kelly, Royal Marines, COMUKCSG Strike Commander, discussed the coming of the new UK aircraft carrier during a visit to Portsmouth in 2018. It should be noted that Betton has since become Rear Admiral Betton and the deputy to U.S. Vice Adm. Andrew Lewis in the new NATO Atlantic Command, and there is little doubt that the coming of the UK carrier is part of the reworking of the UK role within NATO defense.

Cmdr. Betton and Col. Kelly both underscored the flexible nature of the HMS Queen Elizabeth. The UK is building out a 21st century version of a carrier strike group, one which can leverage the F-35 as a multidomain combat system and to do both kinetic and non-kinetic strikes based on these aircraft, as well combines them with helicopter assault assets to do an F-35-enabled assault, or if desired, shift to a more traditional heavy helicopter assault strike. As Cmdr. Betton put it: "Our new carrier offers a flexible, integrative capability. The carrier can play host and is intended absolutely to play host to a carrier air wing. At the same time, it can provide something very different in terms of littoral combat operations, primarily using helicopters."

He emphasized that the Royal Navy was building new escort ships as well as new submarines and the approach to building a maritime strike group meant that working through the operational launch of the carrier was also about its ability to be integrated with and to lead a 21st century maritime strike group. And the new maritime strike group was being built to work with allies but just as importantly to operate in the sovereign interest of the UK. The F-35B onboard was a key enabler to the entire strike group functions.

Cmdr. Betton noted that "the airwing enables us to maneuver to deliver effects in the particular part of the battlespace which we are operating in. You cannot have sea control without the air wing. Our air wing can enable us to do that and have sufficient capability to influence the battlespace. You clearly do not simply want to be a self-sustaining force that doesn't do anything to affect the battlespace decisively. The F-35 onboard will allow us to do that."

Squadron Leader Hugh Nichols standing in front of a UK F-35B at USMC Air Station Beaufort where he was training with the USMC. The photo was taken during our visit to Beaufort in 2015 after attending the F-35B ship trials onboard the USS Wasp.

Col. Kelly added that with the threat to land air bases, it was important to have a sea base to operate from as well, either as an alternative or complement to land bases. "The carriers will be the most protected air base which we will have. And we can move that base globally to affect the area of interest important to us. For example, with regard to Northern Europe, we could range up and down the coastlines in the area and hold at risk adversary forces. I think we can send a powerful message to any adversary."

The new carrier is being built with "growthability" in mind, in terms of what it can do organically, what it can leverage and contribute to the maritime task force, and how it can reach out into the battlespace to work effectively with other national or allied assets operating in the area of interest. And the carrier is not simply a new asset for the RAF and the Royal Navy—it is coming into its operational life as the post-Brexit alliance structure is being shaped as well.

The UK political leadership has emphasized that they would like to enhance their military force's ability to operate globally, and clearly an integrated air and sea force is a key building block for doing so. This is illustrated by the decision to take the carrier to the Pacific to join the United States and France in a joint exercise with the Japanese in 2021.

And prior to its voyage to the Pacific, HMS Queen Elizabeth was engaged in exercises in the North Atlantic. Already, the new carrier is being given a key role in UK defense in terms of participating in the reworking of North Atlantic defense being spearheaded by Second Fleet and Allied Joint Forces Command Norfolk, which we discuss in the next chapter. And the fact that the first commander of the HMS Queen Elizabeth is the deputy commander of Allied Joint Force Command Norfolk is not by chance.

At first blush, exercises in the Pacific for the UK carrier may seem at odds with its primary mission in European defense. But given the nature of the threats posed by the 21st century authoritarian powers as well as the way ahead for the reshaping of the blue-side defense forces associated with an integrated distributed force enabled by kill webs, it is not. As the then head of the RAF, Air Chief Marshal Stephen John Hillier, put it in a seminar in Australia in 2018: "You asked me to speak about high-intensity warfare in Europe. Perhaps I've not really provided that much of that specific geographical context. But then as I said right at the start, I don't believe that what I've described can be bracketed within a particular geography. The challenges I've described are truly global and truly common to us all. I believe that airpower's inherent characteristics and capabilities make it especially able to respond effectively to those challenges."[54]

What Hillier discussed throughout his 2018 presentation in Australia was the presaging of what would be introduced in 2020 at the new integrated operating concept for the UK forces. That operating concept which is rooted in the kill web approach was officially launched in the Fall of 2020. Chief of Defence Staff, General Sir Nick Carter, at the 2020 version of the annual Royal United Services Institute address by Chief of Defence Staff, highlighted the launch of the new strategy. "What should be our response to this ever more complex and dynamic strategic context? My view is that more of the same will not be enough. We must fundamentally change our thinking if we are not to be overwhelmed. Hence, we are launching this Integrated Operating Concept.

---

54 "Shaping a Way Ahead: The Perspective of Air Chief Marshal Stephen John Hillier, the Royal Air Force," *Second Line of Defense* (April 18, 2018), https://sldinfo.com/2018/04/shaping-a-way-ahead-the-perspective-of-air-chief-marshal-stephen-john-hillier-the-royal-air-force/.

Air Chief Marshal Stephen John Hillier speaking at the Williams Foundation Seminar in 2018 in Canberra, Australia. Credit: *Second Line of Defense.*

"It has several big ideas: First of all, it makes a distinction between 'operating' and 'war-fighting'. In an era of persistent competition our deterrent posture needs to be more dynamically managed and modulated. This concept therefore introduces a fifth 'c'—that of competition—to the traditional deterrence model of comprehension, credibility, capability and communication. This recognizes the need to compete below the threshold of war in order to deter war, and to prevent one's adversaries from achieving their objectives in fait accompli strategies. As we have seen in the Crimea, Ukraine, Libya and further afield.

"Competing involves a campaign posture that includes continuous operating on our terms and in places of our choosing. This requires a mindset that thinks in several dimensions to escalate and deescalate up and down multiple ladders— as if it were a spider's web. One might actively constrain in the cyber domain to protect critical national infrastructure in the maritime domain.

"This campaign posture must be dynamically managed and there must be a preparedness to allocate consistent means over longer term horizons, while adjusting the ways to anticipate a rival's response. The ways will include actions being communicated in a manner that may well test the traditional limits of statecraft.

"This posture will be engaged and forward deployed—armed forces much more in use rather than dedicated solely for contingency—with training and exercising being delivered as operations. It will involve capacity building and engagement in support of countries that need our support. This could include partnered operations against common threats, particularly violent extremism. And this may involve combat operations.

"It will also place a premium on building alliances and improving interoperability to make us more 'allied by design' and thus able to burden share more productively. It is important to emphasize that the willingness to commit decisively hard capability with the credibility to war fight is an essential part of the ability to operate and therefore of deterrence.

USMC and UK officers working integratability onboard the USS Wasp during F-35B sea trials in 2015. Credit: *Second Line of Defense.*

"The second important idea is that we cannot afford any longer to operate in silos—we have to be integrated: with allies as I have described, across Government, as a national enterprise, but particularly across the military instrument. Effective integration of maritime, land, air, space and cyber achieves a multi-domain effect that adds up to far more than simply the sum of the parts, recognizing—to paraphrase Omar Bradley—that the overall effect is only as powerful as the strength of the weakest domain.

"And third, we have to modernize. We must chart a direction of travel from an industrial age of platforms to an information age of systems. Warfare is increasingly about a competition between hiding and finding. It will be enabled at every level by a digital backbone into which all sensors, effectors and deciders will be plugged. This means that some industrial age capabilities will increasingly have to meet their sunset to create the space for capabilities needed for sunrise. The trick is how you find a path through the night. We know this will require us to embrace combinations of information-centric technologies. But predicting these combinations will be challenging."[55]

The introduction of the new carriers is part of how the UK is generating the kind of change which General Sir Nick Carter underscored in his comments. Such an approach was highlighted in a meeting we had at the UK Ministry of Defence in 2014 with RAF and Royal Navy officers involved in working the standup of the carrier operational approach, As then Commander and later Captain Nick Walker who was serving at the time as Chief of Staff Carrier Strike in the Carrier Strike and Aviation Division within the Navy Command Headquarters in Portsmouth argued: "This evolving capability will give the decision maker a lot of flexible tools to respond or prepare for crises. The Maritime Task Force can be well integrated with land-based air but does not need a lot of forward ground presence to generate combat effects. This can give decision makers significant flexibility with regard to a crisis or to have the ability to move to crises rather than having to generate force build up in a particular place in order to intervene."

---

55 "Chief of the Defence Staff, General Sir Nick Carter Launches the Integrated Operating Concept," *UK Ministry of Defence* (September 30, 2020).

In his presentation to the Williams Foundation Seminar on air-sea integration on August 10, 2016, Captain Walker added to his earlier comments and highlighted that the carrier was coming into service as part of the overall transformation of UK power projection capabilities. Indeed, the CEPP or Carrier Enabled Power Projection statement of intent highlighted the way ahead: "An integrated and sustainable joint capability, interoperable with NATO, that enables the projection of UK Carrier Strike and Littoral Manoeuvre power as well as delivering humanitarian assistance and defence diplomacy, enabling joint effect across the maritime, land and air environments at a time and place of political choosing."

The deck of the Queen Elizabeth carrier is 85% of the size (i.e., area) of a Nimitz class carrier; which can carry up to 36 F-35Bs along with a Merlin Crowsnests and a Merlin Mk2 ASW helicopter. Alternatively, the ship can be used in the projection of land forces from the sea in terms of Marines and helo insertion capabilities as well. But it is the carrier strike focus which is definitional for the new carrier. The ship has been designed from the ground up to support F-35B, in terms of weapons, C^2, and ISR integration. According to Walker: "We have also built from the ground up interoperability and have worked closely with the USN and USMC with regard to this capability. And we are working on a broader approach to NATO interoperability as well."

Much like the leadership of the Royal Australian Navy focused on in their presentations at the seminar, Walker emphasized new approaches to task forces as key part of their transformation approach. Clearly, the UK is looking at the evolving impact of introducing carrier strike upon the overall change in the RAF and Royal Navy as well. And a key aspect of this transformation is working the evolving integration of fifth gen upon legacy capabilities.

Captain Walker highlighted in his presentation the shift from a legacy mindset, which focused on thinking of maritime versus air environments to an integrated information dominance environment. "A key cultural change is that we are looking at air and maritime as an integrated domain;

and we are looking at the interaction among the environmental seams of our forces driven by a kill web approach and capability." A clear challenge is reworking C². "We need to shape a more mission order vice a directive Air Tasking Order approach to the use of an integrated air-maritime force."[56]

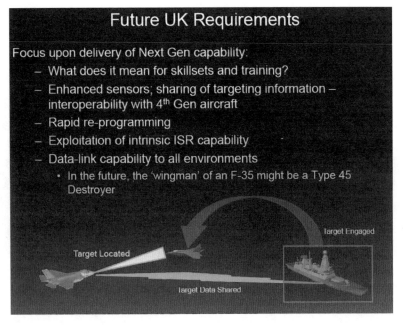

A slide from the presentation by Captain Walker to the Australian seminar highlights the way ahead as envisaged by the UK forces.

The coming of the carrier and the RAF working Typhoon-F35 integration provides strategic depth for U.S. forces when operating in the North Atlantic. Air-sea integration along with the expanded defense capabilities being shaped from the Nordics through to Poland is crucial for the operation of U.S. air and maritime forces, a subject which we address in the next chapter.

---

56   Robbin Laird, "Captain Nick Walker Provides an Update on the Queen Elizabeth Class Carrier at the Williams Foundation Air-Sea Seminar," *Second Line of Defense* (September 9, 2016), https://sldinfo.com/2016/09/captain-nick-walker-provides-an-update-on-the-queen-elizabeth-class-carrier-at-the-williams-foundation-air-sea-seminar/.

A measure of the change anticipated was highlighted during our 2106 visit to RAF Lakenheath and the discussion with the 48th Wing Commander Captain later Brigadier General Robert Novotny. He underscored that unlike setting up an F-35 base in the United States, standing one up at RAF Lakenheath was about putting the F-35 into play with the UK, the Norwegians, the Danes and the Dutch. "We are not flying alone; but joined at the hip. We will be flying exactly in the area of interest for which the plane was designed and can fly together, maintain together, and operate together leveraging the air and sea base for which the F-35 B will fly from as well. It is a unique and strategic opportunity for the USAF and for the nations.

"As we get this right, we can bring in the Danes, the Norwegians and Dutch who are close in geography and the Israelis and Italians as well to shape the evolving joint operational culture and approach. Before you know it, you've got eight countries flying this airplane seamlessly integrated because of the work that Lakenheath and Marham are doing in the 20 nautical miles radius of the two bases."

A new defense capability is staring NATO in the face as well as for UK and U.S. defense leaders. The challenge will be to do what Novotny noted in discussing the potential for synergy: "Let's not talk about what we can or we can't do. What's right to do? Everything can be changed. And if it makes sense for us to operate in a different manner, we change the written guidance to support that as long as the leadership is in full agreement. We will have to break glass. Applying yesterday's procedures and policies to this joint effort makes little sense."

An element of change as well is the importance of shaping cross-decking capabilities and operations among the seabases. The Osprey and the CH-53Ks can certainly do so from the United States side of the equation. Indeed, the first cross decking the Osprey did was to land on HMS Illustrious in 2007. Many allied nations have since seen the Osprey land on their decks and shaping a cross decking sustainment capability would make clear sense to build strategic depth while operating across bases in the areas of interest, leveraging basing as discussed earlier in the book.

With the operational introduction of the British carriers and the commitment both the USMC and the UK have given to cross training, in 2021 we saw the first cross-deck operations of the F-35 shaping a 21st century combat capaiblity. As 1st Lt. Zachary Bodner, 3rd Marine Air Wing wrote in an August 24, 2021, story: "Marine Fighter Attack Squadron 211 conducted a first-of-its-kind operation which saw F-35B aircraft launched from HMS Queen Elizabeth land on the amphibious assault ship USS America to load ordnance, refuel, and strike follow-on objectives on August 20th, 2021. The operation highlighted the interoperability of the F-35B and the strategic importance of the joint integration between the United Kingdom Carrier Strike Group and the U.S. Navy Amphibious Ready Group / Marine Expeditionary Unit.

"This mission was the first time in modern history the United States has cross-decked aircraft for a mission utilizing a foreign aircraft carrier, demonstrating naval partnerships in action. Doing so as part of the United Kingdom Carrier Strike Group 21 strengthens our alliances and partnerships through the development of interoperable capabilities, combined operations, theater security cooperation, and capacity-building efforts," said Col. Simon Doran, U.S. Senior National Representative to the UK CSG.

"DMO calls for U.S. Naval forces to operate in a less concentrated and more distributed manner to complicate an adversary's ability to find, track, and target them while still delivering decisive combat power where needed. The multi-national maritime aviation operation extends the reach of the F-35, enabling the 5th-generation aircraft to effect objectives farther away, for extended amounts of time, and with increased ordnance capacity."[57]

---

57 1st Lt. Zachary Bodner, "VMFA-211 Conducts First Cross-Deck Aviation Mission in Modern Naval History," August 24, 2021. https://www.marines.mil/News/News-Display/Article/2743788/ vmfa-211-conducts-first-cross-deck-aviation-mission-in-modern-naval-history/

U.S. Marine Corps Maj Brian Kimmins prepares to launch an F-35B from HMS Queen Elizabeth for a historic cross-deck operation with USS America in the Pacific Ocean on August 20, 2021. Photo by 1st Lt. Zachary Bodner.

The reshaping of the maritime force which has been described throughout this book in terms of an interactive kill web-enabled distributed but integratable force has clearly had a major impact on the UK's thinking. So has the Australian launch of the rebuild of their force in similar terms.

Some of this has been delivered by the impact of new equipment bought in common between the U.S. services and the Australians and the British, such as Aegis in the case of Australia, P-8 in terms of the UK and Australia, and the United States, Triton in the case of Australia and the United States, and F-35s in terms of all three. But more than this, it has been the realization that getting greater combat capability across full-spectrum operations absolutely requires better integration across the extended operational space, and not stove-piped management with top-down detailed decision making. In the case of the Australians, the coming of the F-35 drove a significant rethink; with regards to the British, it was the coming of the carrier which has done so.

Shaping Forces for Kill Web Concepts of Operations

As the United States and its core allies rework their forces for more effective collaboration, clearly leveraging common operating platforms is one way to be able to do so. But even more importantly will be the capability to integrate the force while respecting national interests and deployment priorities.

There are a number of collaborative programs which have generated significant opportunities for the U.S. Navy to work with allies and by so doing provide opportunities to build the kind of collaboration which can expand the kind of data and strike collaboration crucial to a kill web-enabled integrated distributed force. If we return to Hellyer's earlier point: "And that's before we think about the role the U.S.'s coalition of allies can play." A key way to think about this is to highlight the core allied enterprises the U.S. Navy and USMC are involved in and how managing these more effectively than simply looking them as arms sales but rather as kill web building blocks can dramatically expand both the U.S.'s and coalition combat and crisis management power.

F-35 and P-8/Triton Belts

F-35 and P-8/Triton Force

Integration of RAF Lakenheath and RAF Marham Provides Unique Impacts and Advantages.

" see there is great potential for two countries to develop in concert, side-by-side, and to set, set the model for joint operations

"As we get this right, we can bring in the Danes, the Norwegians and Dutch who are close in geography and the Israelis and Italians as well to shape the evolving joint operational culture and approach

"Before you know it, you've got eight countries flying this airplane seamlessly integrated because of the work that Lakenheath and Marham are doing in the 20 nautical mile radius of the two bases "

• P-8: Lossie, Iceland, Norway

A graphic highlighting the kind of synergy which is
driven by shaping kill web concepts of operations.

The Aegis global enterprise was clearly a pioneer in this effort, as a number of key allies have built ships to operate the Aegis combat system. The shared sensor data provides a much wider capability for the fleet than if one simply was relying on U.S. platforms alone. We have written a great deal about the coming of and building of an Aegis global enterprise, and indeed when Laird was working with Rear Admiral George Huchting the effort to include Spain in the program really was the launch point of what would become the global enterprise. As we noted in a 2009 article: "The U.S. Navy's Aegis program is an important contributor to shaping the foundation for such a global system. Through initially foreign military sales programs in Japan and eventually cooperative commercial defense programs, Aegis has become part of the allied fleet."[58]

Another key enterprise with which the Aegis global enterprise can leverage is the very formidable F-35 global enterprise. As virtually all key allies of the United States and the three air services in the United States fly the same plane, the potential for leveraging this "flying combat system" is significant.

---

58 "The Aegis Global Enterprise: Crafting a Global Defensive Capability," *Second Line of Defense* (September 18, 2009).

During their visit to the Center for Surface Combat Systems (CSCS) and CSCS' learning site, AEGIS Training and Readiness Center (ATRC), co-located onboard Naval Support Facility Dahlgren, Capt. Dave Stoner, commanding officer for CSCS, discusses U.S. Navy training with CDRE Stephen Hughes, commander, Surface Force, Royal Australian Navy (RAN), and CDRE Darron Kavanagh, director general, Combat Management and Payloads in Capability Acquisition and Sustainment Group, RAN. U.S. Navy photo by Michael Bova, October 1, 2019.

The surface for this effort has barely been scratched but is crucial in shaping a capable kill web enabled force. For the U.S. Navy this means that a wide variety of air-enabled ships, ranging from the Italians to the Japanese to the British to the amphibious ships can provide capabilities. Rather than the large deck carrier admirals arguing that these smaller ships are not aircraft carriers, they should make the case for what large deck carriers can be reimagined to do as we did in an earlier chapter.

But the coming of an at sea global fleet of F-35s fully capable of interacting with and sharing data and decision making in a contested environment with land-based F-35s ushers in a significant war winning capability for the United States and its allies. But only if integratability is leveraged and worked.

Another key enterprise which has largely been created through the U.S. Foreign Military Sales or FMAs approach is the global proliferation of the ASW and anti-surface warfare Romeo helicopters. The potential here has not even been scratched. During a 2020 visit to the HSM Weapons School, Atlantic, based at Mayport, a discussion with Cmdr. Nathaniel "Velcro" Velcio, the Commanding Officer of the School, highlighted the opportunity to do so. "We could make much better use of the global partnerships enabled by a program like the Seahawk. Regarding the Australians, their Romeos and the U.S. Navy's are virtually the same and both forces are working common TTPs. Regarding NATO, there is some commonality in operations," according to CDR Velcio, "if the ally in question is operating a dipping sonar system, such as the Canadians do with Cyclone and the Brits do with Merlin."[59]

An MH-60R helicopter from the HMAS Arunta (FFH 151) of the Royal Australian Navy prepares to be grounded on the flight deck aboard the Arleigh Burke-class guided-missile destroyer USS John S. McCain (DDG 56) during flight operations while conducting integrated maritime security operations. Photo by Petty Officer 2nd Class Markus Castaneda. October 20, 2020.

---

59 Robbin Laird, "The Seahawk in the Extended Battlespace," *Second Line of Defense* (July 12, 2020).

A final case in point is the acquisition of P-8s and Tritons by allies. The P-8 has been acquired by India, Australia, Norway, South Korea, and the United Kingdom. The Triton has been acquired by Australia. In effect, what we see coming in the Pacific and in the Atlantic are interactive sensor webs that extend the reach of core platforms and their onboard sensors. The fusing of multiple sensors via kill webs enhances the ability of the entire force, including key partners and allies, cooperatively, to engage enemy targets in a time of conflict. Interactive webs can be used for a wide range of purposes throughout the spectrum of conflict and are a key foundation for full spectrum crisis management. To play their critical role when it comes to strike, whether kinetic or non-kinetic, this final layer of the web needs to have the highest standards of protection possible.

Indian and Pacific Ocean Security

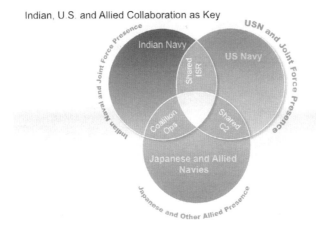

Enhanced collaboration among the US, Indian and allied navies is essential to secure 21st century maritime defense and security. Credit: Second Line of Defense

If the U.S. Navy's P-8 / Triton dyad is integratable with allied maritime patrol capabilities, the reach of both the U.S. and allied interactive web capabilities is substantially enhanced. It is also obvious that if key allies are not engaged then there are holes in the web structure which will either simply be gaps or need to be filled by other means. In simple terms, it is clear that the United States and its allies must operate within a convergent set of interactive webs to shape a shared and actionable common operating picture. The results will significantly empower a combined strike force and, even more importantly, inform decision-makers about how to prioritize targets in a fluid combat situation.

In one of our 2020 interviews with him, Rear Adm. Peter Garvin, head of the Maritime Patrol Reconnaissance Force, provided a very clear perspective on how this was happening in his domain. With regard to the P-8 / Triton partners, Rear Adm. Garvin highlighted the opportunities for co-learning, which are generated from common training that occurs at VP-30 and the Maritime Patrol and Reconnaissance Weapons School at NAS Jacksonville, Fl. He highlighted the famous quote, "You cannot surge trust."

The working relationships built during high-end tactical training carry over into operations whereby a global community of operators can share operational experience and enrich the development of the enterprise. According to Garvin: "My first international visit upon taking command was to Australia; leadership there referred to our working relationship as 'mateship.' This term accurately describes the collaborative nature of our partnership and demonstrates its importance to ourselves and the rest of the world."

"We have built similar relationships on varying scales, all around the world. These relationships serve as force multipliers, which opens the door to cooperatively leverage technology to deliver networked sensors and a shared understanding of the decisions and options we share across the extended battlespace. Our allies understand the fundamental nature of their region better than we do. If you have properly maintained these important working relationships, both interpersonal and technological, then you will have access to the cultural knowledge and human geography that might otherwise would not be available to you. We become stronger interactively with our allies by sharing domain knowledge to operate across a wider geographical area. In effect, we are shaping kill web "matesmanship."

"We clearly have closer relationships with some allies than with others, which shapes policy and data sharing. However, the technology is now out there which can allow us, within the right policy framework, to provide data at appropriate security levels much more rapidly than in the past. Our policy frameworks simply need to catch up with our technologies. History has shown us that it is infinitely more difficult to sort out our working relationships in times of intense conflict. Those partnerships need to be nurtured and exercised now to help shape our interactive webs into a truly effective strike force over the extended battlespace."

For Rear Adm. Garvin, working with partner and allied maritime patrol partners is crucial, even when those close partners are operating different platforms. For example, Japan indigenously developed their own replacement aircraft for its legacy P-3s. He highlighted the healthy sharing arrangements the U.S. Navy has with the Japanese Maritime Self-Defense Force in the MDA area. Similarly, he highlighted the very close relationship with Canada, who operates a significantly modernized P-3, the CP-140 Aurora.

Rear Adm. Garvin underscored that the aperture for increased cooperation with India was opening up as well, a process which he clearly welcomed. "Put simply, the idea of partners and allies sharing in the web you describe must have, at its core, that underlying, underpinning relationship built upon trust. Sometimes buying the same kit does make it easier. But without that relationship it doesn't matter if you bought the exact same kit."[60]

---

60 The quotations are taken from Robbin Laird, "Extending the Reach of the Kill Web: The U.S. Navy works with Allies on the Maritime Patrol Enterprise," *Second Line of Defense* (May 13, 2020).

CHAPTER EIGHT:

"IT'S NOT MY FATHER'S SECOND FLEET"

The U.S. Navy is shaping an integrated distributed force. Working connectivity throughout the force and working new ways to shape modular task forces provides the capability for the U.S. Navy to be more lethal, survivable, and effective and lays down the foundation for working new technologies into the fleet along the lines of the payload/utility kill web approach which we discuss in the next chapter.

The standup of new fleets in Norfolk to deal with the Russian threat starting in 2018 provides a case study of such change. We spent time with the command as well as with the North Carolina-based Marines to understand how the relaunch of Second Fleet and the standup of a new NATO command in the United States drive and reflect the changes in fleet operations shaping a way ahead for a distributed force within integratable kill webs.[61]

Second Fleet and Allied Joint Force Command Norfolk were placed under the command of Vice Adm. Lewis to launch the new approach and to shape the initial way ahead. According to his original deputy, Vice Adm. Mustin, who is now head of the Naval Reserves, "What made us successful over the last 20 years, post 9/11, is not what's going to make us successful into the next few decades. Working with Vice Adm. Lewis has been important as well. As Second Fleet Commander, he clearly understands that we need to shape a new approach. When I was in High School in the 80's, my father was Second Fleet Commander, so I can legitimately say that "The new Second Fleet is not your father's Second Fleet." He went on to add that "What Vice Adm. Lewis wants and what we are offering

---

61 The USMC side of this effort has been covered in detail in Robbin Laird, *The USMC Transformation Path: Preparing for the High-End Fight* (2022), chapters four and five.

started with a clean sheet of paper as it relates to the design of the reserve force for C2F."[62]

Great Lakes, ILL (March 13, 2021) Vice Admiral John Mustin, Chief of Navy Reserve, speaks with Naval Region Midwest Reserve Component Command Sailors at 2021 CO-SEL conference. U.S. Navy photo by Cdr. Todd Spitler.

The clean sheet of paper point underscores why the relaunch of Second Fleet is a case study of the kind of change underway within the U.S. Navy more generally as it shapes a way ahead to fight as an integrated distributed fleet.

---

62 The quotations in this chapter from the U.S. or Allied navies are taken from our interviews done visiting Norfolk from November 2019 through the Summer of 2020. Those interviews can be found in the following background report we did in support of the book: Robbin Laird and Ed Timperlake, "The Standup and Evolution of 2nd Fleet and Joint Force Command Norfolk: Shaping A Core Capability for North Atlantic Defense," *Second Line of Defense* (May 2021). https://sldinfo.com/2021/05/2nd-fleet-and-joint-force-command-norfolk-a-may-2021-update/.

C2F and Allied Joint Force Commands as Startup Fleets

The opportunity which the U.S. Navy has had to standup a new fleet in Norfolk to deal with North Atlantic defense as well as to work interactively with the standup of the only NATO operational command on U.S. territory has clearly allowed for shaping an innovative way ahead for fleet operations, and joint and allied integration to deal with the Russian, not the Soviet threat.

We have discussed the standup of the commands and their interaction in crafting a fully operational fleet with the leadership of both commands as well as with the Marines who are working with them. It is clear that from the outset, the approach has been to work from the ground up to have a distributed integrated force.

As Vice. Adm. Lewis put it to us: "We had a charter to re-establish the fleet. Using the newly published national defense strategy and national security strategy as the prevailing guidance, we spent a good amount of time defining the problem. My team put together an offsite with the Naval Post-Graduate school to think about the way ahead, to take time to define the problem we were established to solve and determine how best to organize ourselves to solve those challenges. We used the Einstein approach: we spent 55 minutes of the hour defining the problem and five minutes in solving it. Similarly, we spent the first two and a half months of our three-month pre-launch period working to develop our mission statement along with the functions and tasks associated with those missions. From the beginning our focus was in developing an all-domain and all-function command. To date, we clearly have focused on the high-end warfighting, but in a way that we can encompass all aspects of warfare from seabed to space as well."

In a speech in early 2021 to DSI's Fifth Annual Joint Networks Conference, Vice. Adm. Lewis underscored how he viewed the central role of allied and joint integration in shaping a way ahead for the commands. "At C2F, we have integrated officers from multiple allied nations directly into the fleet staff. The U.S. Marines, reserve component officers, and foreign exchange officers are fully functioning staff members—not just liaison officers—and they include a two-star Royal Canadian Navy officer as the vice commander of C2F. At JFCNF, an initial team of fewer than ten individuals stood up the command with the help of reserve, joint, and international officers—a testament to integration from its inception. We are also integrating the staff by functional codes (C2F N-codes in the same building with their JFCNF J-codes), and we aspire to use NATO standards for everything from classification to mission orders and associated command-and-control systems to realize our full potential."

Left-to-right Commander, U.S. Fleet Forces Adm. Grady, Chief of Naval Operations Adm. John Richardson, Commander, U.S. 2nd Fleet Vice Adm. Andrew Lewis and Fleet Master Chief U.S. 2nd Fleet Smalts salute the Ensign during the 2nd Fleet Establishment Ceremony. August 24, 2018. Photo by Petty Officer 1st Class Gary Prill.

In that speech, Vice. Adm. Lewis highlighted the importance of interoperability and interchangeability in working fleet capabilities. "Interoperability is defined as 'the ability to act together coherently and efficiently to achieve tactical, operational, and strategic objects,' often involving the ability to exchange information or services by means of electronic communications. We must then be integrated—the ability of forces to not only work toward a similar mission, but to do so as one unit. An example of this is the Mendez Nunez, who deployed as part of the Abraham Lincoln Carrier Strike Group in 2019. The final step in the spectrum of relationships is interchangeability. That is the ability to accomplish the mission, regardless of which nation is executing a particular role."

Here the Spanish Alvaro de Bazan-class frigate Mendez Nunez (F 104) is seen in the Steadfast defender 2021 exercise. U.S. Navy photo by Mass Communication Specialist 2nd Class Scott Barnes. The Álvaro de Bazán class, also known as the F100 class, is a class of Aegis combat system-equipped air defence frigates in service with the Spanish Navy.

The launch of the C2F saw the addition of Lewis's Vice Commander to be a Canadian Rear Admiral. One clearly important fact cannot be missed when visiting VADM Lewis, is that one finds his office flanked on one side by a Canadian Rear Adm. and on the other by a British Rear Adm. The first is his C2F deputy, and the second is his NATO deputy. It is hard to miss the point: this is a command focused on integration of maritime capability across the North Atlantic.

The importance of having a Canadian Rear Adm. within the American command cannot be overstated. Rear Adm. Waddell brings experience from commanding Canadian forces in the Pacific and the Atlantic. According to Waddell: "We will not be as large a command as other numbered fleets. We are designed to max out at about 250 people and currently are around 200 now. We must be different and innovative in how we get after the missions. We need to make sure we're using tools and alternative resources, because we don't have that depth and capacity of people, so you have to find a different way."

As a startup command that is FOC, they are not emulating other numbered commands in many ways. "We are not primarily focused on the business of force generation, but we focus on how to use assigned forces to shape a desired outcome. We don't want to get in the space of those responsible for force generation: we just want to be able to advocate for timely, effective outputs that optimize the use of the fleet."

He noted that the assumption that the Second Fleet was going to be the Second Fleet of old was misplaced. "The old Second Fleet was interested in sea lines of communication. But the new Second Fleet is focused on strategic lines of communication. This is an all-domain perspective, and not just the convoy missions of past battles of the Atlantic." He referred to C2F as the maneuver arm in providing for defense, deterrence, and warfighting but as part of a whole of government approach to defending the United States, Canada, and NATO allies against threats.

He underscored that "we are flexible and unconcerned with regard to whom we will work for. Operationally, we work for NAVNORTH (Fleet Forces Command) for the Homeland Defense Mission, but we can seamlessly transfer and work for NAVEUR/ EUCOM to defend forward, or to work in the GIUK Gap for an Allied Joint Force Command."

How did we end up with a Vice Commander who is Canadian? As Rear Adm. Waddell tells it, "Vice. Adm. Lewis was asked to stand up Second Fleet and given much latitude to do so. He went to a senior Canadian official to ask for a Royal Canadian Navy officer to serve as his deputy. Waddell felt that bringing a Canadian officer into the force made a lot of sense for a number of reasons. First, because of the partnership nature of operations in the area of interest. Second, because the Canadians have experience in operating in the high north, which could be brought to the renewed efforts on the part of the United States side to do so. Third, as Waddell himself works the C2F experience he can weave what he learns into Canadian approach to operations.

"It's not lost on me that we as a Canadian service honed our teeth in the battle of the Atlantic in the Second World War in the North Atlantic and then in the ASW fight through the Cold War. Those competencies, although we were collectively distracted a little bit from iterations to CENTCOM and in the Persian Gulf for some time, are crucial going forward. I think we've reinforced those capabilities and are investing in new capabilities at home in Canada, such as with the Type 26 surface combatant program, a very robust platform."

A Canadian advanced P-3 called the CP-140 is seen taxing to a halt at 14 Wing Greenwood, Canada during a visit of the Second Line of Defense team to Nova Scotia in 2017. Credit: Royal Canadian Air Force.

He discussed various tools and approaches being used to understand how to scope the challenges and priorities, including hosting a Battle of the Atlantic tabletop exercise. The goal of efforts like these are to scope out the various interactions across an extended battlespace to understand how fights influence one another.

All of this leads to a very significant conclusion about the U.S. Navy and allies integrating across an extended battlespace and operating distributed forces. "For the web of capabilities, you need to be ready to fight tonight, you need to be able to seamlessly integrate together across the fleet, inclusive of U.S. and allied forces. You fight as a fleet."

Vice Adm. Andrew Lewis, commander, U.S. 2nd Fleet, left, stands alongside U.S. 2nd Fleet Vice Commander, Rear Adm. Steve Waddell. (U.S. Navy photo by Mass Communication Specialist 2nd Class Joshua M. Tolbert, August 12, 2019.)

That means fundamental change from a cultural assumption that the U.S. Navy has run with for many years. "You need to understand and accept that a fighting force needs to be reconfigurable such that others can seamlessly bolt on, participate in, or integrate into that force. That might mean changes from the assumptions of how the Navy has operated in the past to successfully operate with allies." Reconfigurable across a coalition is clearly enabled by kill web capabilities to operate as flexible modular task forces.

The standup of Allied Joint Forces Command occurred shortly after that of the new C2F. And the concept from the outset was that both commands would work together under the leadership of a single U.S. Admiral to find ways to shape more effective leveraging of U.S. and Allied capabilities and to be able to operate as a much more effective integrated force than in the past.

JFC Norfolk was created at the 2018 Brussels Summit as a new joint operational-level command for the Atlantic. It reached an important milestone in September 2020 when it declared Initial Operational Capability. JFC Norfolk is the only operational NATO command in North America and is closely integrated with the newly reactivated U.S. Second Fleet. JFC reached its initial operating capability in September 2020.

Royal Navy Rear Adm. Betton, who was the first commander of HMS Queen Elizabeth, is the Deputy Commander of Allied JFC. According to a discussion we had with Betton in March 2021, "Coming here 18 months ago has been a really exciting professional opportunity, and genuinely a pleasure to have another run at setting up a team pretty much from scratch. The Second Fleet team was well on the way by the time I got here, but the NATO team was just about at conception, but not much beyond that."[63]

The geography and three-dimensional operational space of the NATO zone of responsibility is very wide indeed. As Betton put it: "SACEUR's area of responsibility, goes all the way from the Yucatan peninsula in the Gulf of Mexico to the North Pole. I've always loved the phrase from Finnmark to Florida, or Florida to Finnmark. But it is also important to realize all domain challenges and threats that we face. It's everything from seabed infrastructure, through the sub-sea water column, the surface, the airspace above it, and up into the satellite constellation above that."

The allies are bringing new capabilities to the fight, such as P-8s, and F-35s, and new combat ships as well. Finding ways to integrate evolving allied capabilities by the "relevant nations" is crucial to shaping a more effective allied deterrent and warfighting strategy in the North Atlantic. As Betton put it: "The U.S. is by far the dominant figure of NATO, but it's not the only piece. And it's not always just the heavy metal that is relevant. It's the connectivity, it's the infrastructure and the architecture that enables the 30 nations of NATO to get so much more than the sum

---

63 When Rear Admiral Betton referred to having another run at setting up a team from scratch, he is referring to his earlier role as a key player in standing up the new UK carrier capability. We discussed this with him during a visit to Portsmouth in 2018.

of the parts out of their combined effort. But it's particularly the relevant nations in the operational area and their ability to work together which is an important consideration."

The Rear Adm. underscored the importance of the only operational NATO command on U.S. soil. "The idea of integrating it with the second fleet headquarters under a dual-hatted command was a fantastic move because it emphasizes bluntly to Europe that the U.S. is fully committed to NATO. It's not NATO and the U.S. The U.S. is part of NATO. And having an operational headquarters here in CONUS really emphasizes that point in both directions."

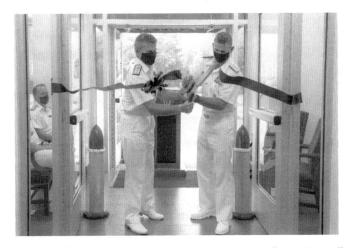

Royal Navy Rear Adm. A. Betton, Deputy Commander, JFCNF, (left) and U.S. Vice Adm. A. Lewis, Commander, JFCNF at JFCNF's Initial Operational Capability ceremony at Naval Support Activity (NSA) Hampton Roads, Virginia. September 2020. Photo Petty Off. 1st Cl. Th. Green.

He noted that there are 16 nations at the command currently with three more arriving in the next few months, namely, Portugal, the Netherlands, and Bulgaria. And reworking how to create the most effective defense is also a work in progress. As Rear Adm. Betton put it: "One of the key efforts we are pursuing in this integrated command is not just stitching together NATO and U.S. assets, but it's also stitching together teams within teams. It could be the U.S. cooperating with Norway, Sweden, and Finland, with Admiral Lewis commanding a multinational command.

"And a crisis might grow and evolve into something that the North Atlantic Council agree to respond to and therefore activate the JFC to command in a NATO sense. But because the Commander has that flexibility to go from a unilateral U.S. only under second fleet, through a growing coalition, there's the opportunity to coordinate activity with a whole diverse range of entities before it becomes a formal NATO response."

It is clear that agility and scalability are a key part of the way ahead for 21st century full-spectrum crisis management. And the JFC working in an integrated manner with C2F certainly is working such capabilities. This is a case of startup fleets working core capabilities which are clearly needed across the combat force.

And there is a third command as well that is part of the startup, and maturation process as well. The Combined Joint Operations from the Sea Center of Excellence (CJOS COE) is the only NATO Centre of Excellence on U.S. soil. According to the Center's website: "The Combined Joint Operations from the Sea Centre of Excellence (CJOS COE) was established in May 2006. Representing 13 nations, CJOS is the only Centre of Excellence in the United States, and one of 27 NATO accredited Centers worldwide, representing a collective wealth of international experience, expertise, and best practices.

"Independent of the NATO Command structure, CJOS COE draws on the knowledge and capabilities of sponsoring nations, United States Fleet Forces, United States SECOND Fleet, and neighboring U.S. commands to promote "best practices" within the Alliance. CJOS COE also plays a key role in aiding NATO's transformational goals, specifically those focused on maritime-based joint operations. We enjoy close cooperation with Allied Command Transformation (ACT), Allied Maritime Command (MARCOM), other NATO commands, maritime COEs, and national commands.

"Comprised of 30 permanent staff and 20 U.S. Navy reservists, CJOS COE is highly flexible and responsive to its customers' needs. The Centre cooperates, whenever possible, with industry and academia to ensure a comprehensive approach to the development of concept and doctrine."[64]

But the story is even more interesting than this description provides. For the Centre continued to exist while Second Fleet did not. And in that period between Second Fleet's stand down in 2011 and its standup again in 2018, the Centre worked hard to shape the reworking of how maritime operations NATO wide contribute to Atlantic defense and, in the wake of the events of 2014, focused on the coming reset of North Atlantic maritime operations. When Vice Adm. Lewis came, he understood how important what the Centre was doing was to the core operations of Second Fleet itself, not just in terms of managing a NATO effort, but the kind of distributed integrated force which needs to be shaped to deal with the new strategic environment.

The Deputy Director of the Centre, Cmdr. Tom Guy from the Royal Navy underscored that 2nd Fleet was focused on its role as a coalition and joint command and control force. Vice Adm. Lewis has, from the outset, focused on distributed command and control and shaping the command as a warfighting instrument. This was simply not going to happen unless the U.S. Navy becomes much more part of the European NATO navies, and to work more effectively as an integrated force.

Cmdr. Guy emphasized to us in discussions in the spring of 2021, that the Centre was focused on supporting the Second Fleet's mission of being able to fight tonight more effectively. The Centre of Excellence effort is near to mid-term. In other words, it is very much "the art of the possible," and leveraging the practical near-term can greatly inform discussions for insightful longer-range planning for future maritime operations.

Cmdr. Guy underscored that getting that paradigm right allows for future iterations of combat technology to be worked in a more integrated manner going forward. Here the Centre plays a key supporting role to Allied Command Transformation, which is also located in the Norfolk

---

64 http://www.cjoscoe.org/?page_id=147

area.[65] Because the foreign military community in Norfolk is very close and in a practical sense a place where folks know one another and thus allows for a significant cross fertilization between the Centre's role in support of Second Fleet with ACT's longer term thinking as well. As Cmdr. Guy put it: "We need the second fleet staff to innately to have the understanding about what it takes to integrate with a UK or French or Italian carrier strike group."

Distributed Command and Control as a Core Capability

In our discussions with Vice. Adm. Lewis it has been clear that a core focus of the activity for his commands has been upon command and control or C^2. If the fleet is going to fight as a distributed force and one integratable with relevant joint or coalition capabilities, mission command is crucial. And with the agility which a distributed force can bring to the fight, the ability of the platforms making up a particular modular task force to operate with an ability to execute tactical decision-making at the edge is critical.

C^2 is a key element for shaping the way ahead for maritime operations. The U.S. Navy highlights the importance of distributed maritime operations as it reworks its way ahead with regard to 21st century deterrence and warfighting. As Navy Vice Adm. Phil Sawyer, Deputy CNO for Operations, Plans and Strategy, has put it: "Distributed Maritime Operations (DMO) is a combination of distributed forces, integration of effects, and maneuver. DMO will enhance battle space awareness and influence; it will generate opportunities for naval forces to achieve surprise, to neutralize threats and to overwhelm the adversary; and it will impose operational dilemmas on the adversary."[66]

---

65 Our colleague Murielle Delaporte has done extensive work on the standup and operation of ACT and her assessments can be found on *Breaking Defense* and *Second Line of Defense*. The command has been led by a French Air Force officer since it was created in 2003.

66 Edward Lundquist, "DMO is Navy's Operational Approach to Winning the High-End Fight at Sea," *Seapower* (February 2, 2021), https://seapowermagazine.org/dmo-is-navys-operational-approach-to-winning-the-high-end-fight-at-sea/.

From the beginning, the standup of the Second Fleet has been built around C² to enable DMO. In many ways, the standing up of Second Fleet in 2018, with Vice Admiral Lewis and his seed corn staff, focused from the outset on C², notably mission command: how to work tailored distributed task forces across the U.S. and allied fleets to get the kind of crisis management and combat effects crucial to North Atlantic defense.

From this point of view, the standup of Second Fleet can be looked at as a "startup firm" within the U.S. Navy as it is the newest fleet in the force, and one birthed precisely as new concept of operations and technologies were being prioritized by the leadership of the U.S. Navy. Mission command is as old as Lord Nelson, as a British Rear Admiral recently reminded us. But the challenge is that for the past 20 years, such command has been overshadowed by the OODLA loop. Observe, Orient, Decide, hand over to the lawyers and then Act. Obviously, such an approach when one needs to fight at the speed of light is a war loser.

This is how Vice. Adm. Lewis put it: "An operational headquarters or a high-end tactical headquarters is a weapons system. Normally, when warfighters discuss weapon systems, they refer to their platforms. But the operational or tactical headquarters should be looked at as being a key weapons system, the glue that pulls a multitude of different weapons systems together in a coherent manner—both kinetic and non-kinetic. They can mass fire, mass effect, and maneuver in a coordinated fashion at the fleet level. That's what operational and tactical headquarters do."

For the Second Fleet, a key part of shaping a way ahead with regard to C² for a distributed maritime force is to enhance the capabilities for mobile command posts and to ensure that the right kind of command connectivity is generated. This has been a key focus for exercises from the outset of standing up C2F and working with Allied Joint Forces Command. It started with BALTOPS 19, moved to commanding the force from Camp Lejeune, to operating from Iceland, to operating from Tampa, Florida, to working off a command ship for the NATO exercise Steadfast Defender. Put in other words, exercises are being used by the command as a key way to find out what works and what does not with the technology available right now.

Rear Adm. Waddell drove home the point throughout our discussion with him that they were building an agile command structure, one that can work through mission command and with expeditionary operations centers. As he explained it, "For us, a Maritime Operations Center (MOC) is not a room with equipment. It is a capability, based on technology, process and people. We distribute it all the time, whether it's been afloat or ashore. Previously, we were in Iceland. Right now, they're down in Tampa for an exercise. I'll be joining them in a couple of days."

We followed up on how that Tampa exercise at MacDill AFB was being worked in March 2021. We discussed the expeditionary MOC with a key participant in the Tampa exercise, Captain Craig Bangor. Captain Bangor was one of the very first members of the new C2F and was tasked by VADM Lewis from the outset to work the kind of C^2 innovation he was looking for in the fleet.

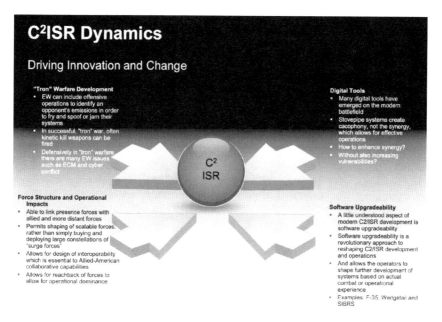

Graphic highlights dynamic C^2/ISR development which is a key part of shaping the integrated distributed force envisaged by the Navy in DMO.

As Capt. Bangor put it: "C² has become a bureaucracy unto itself. We focused on the outset on ways to unify the fleet in the Atlantic that could be distributed, work closely with allies, and be very integratable given the demands or the tasks." He argued that "expeditionary C² is a key tool we need in the toolbox; it is not just sitting back somewhere and watching the show. We need to have intimate feedback from the commanders who are actually doing the work and expeditionary C² allows me to have a much more effective force."

For the C2F team, then doing the C² piece from the beginning is really a key effort. As Captain Bangor noted: "We need to have the ability to have C² deployed to where it needs to go; and be able to be well positioned to take advantage of adversary actions because the commanders that are doing the fighting can be enabled by the most effective C² the fleet can provide. Interactive mission command is a key part of working effective distributed C²."

Because the focus is on the ability to fight tonight, this effort is not about waiting for the optimal 2030 technology solution, which almost certainly will not come in any case. C2F from the beginning of its new life has been focused on how to do distributed C² with the technology at hand. VADM Lewis has asked a simple but direct question: What can we do now with the technology which exists to deliver enhanced capability for an integrated distributed force?

As Vice. Adm. Lewis underscored to us, it is both about leveraging what we have now and to shape templates that can empower an integrated distributed force, but it is also shaping the templates for operations to incorporate new ways of enhancing the survivability and lethality of the fleet as well through opening the aperture of innovation. But the shift in templates is a key element of being able to open an aperture of innovation that drives real world enhancements in the fighting force,

Vice Admiral Lewis argued that "I've become somewhat jaded with technology because technology is just a means to an end. Said another way, it's just a tool. You have to ask what are we trying to get out of it? What's the objective? And then, how are we going to use that technology? The key point is that our processes need to be agile enough to absorb new technology without missing a beat. That's where I think we need to focus our efforts. But we need to get better at being able to craft, shape, and leverage operational or tactical headquarters as a weapon system. We have to get a lot better at doing so, and new technologies can be helpful here, which is one of my objectives for working with the Mid-Atlantic Tech Bridge."

The relationship which has been set up between C2F and Mid-Atlantic Tech Bridge is a very good example of combing a reshaped template for operations with an open aperture towards technical innovation. The U.S. Navy has set up several Tech Bridges to foster greater collaboration with the private sector in a way that does not rely on the traditional acquisition process. In addition, the Mid-Atlantic Tech Bridge is different from the others in that it is the only Tech Bridge with a formal tie to the operational Navy via its support of Second Fleet.

In our discussion with Cmdr. Bobby Hanvey, Executive Director of the Mid-Atlantic Tech Bridge, he stated: "Second Fleet is focused on a distributed C^2 network, not just a unitary and centralized capability. We're going to use DJC2. We're going to potentially use NETC2 and that's great. Well, there's a lot of commercial technology out there that can do this on a smaller and more agile scale. There's a lot of technology already in the government, the Secret Service, and the Special Operations user base, which does exactly what Admiral Lewis wants to be able to do. We can be disaggregated and distributed and work through a coalition network, or a commercial network, and still securely connect, consume, and participate. We look to adapt such technologies and bring them to Second Fleet."

"We are not here to replace existing innovation efforts, or avenues to solve complex problems. The goal of the Tech Bridge is to enable finding solutions faster, better and which are less expensive. If the Tech Bridge can't do it faster, better, or for less cost than the existing avenues we have through the Navy or the Marines, then we shouldn't be doing it. But if I can make it happen faster, give you a much better result, and/or significantly less cost, that is our sweet spot."

Obviously, the reworking of C² is a work in progress and as the quote from CDR Bobby Hanvey suggests it will indeed be ongoing, as technology evolves. And challenges to be met like the division between Second and Sixth fleets in the Atlantic or how C2F will work going forward with II MEF are examples of the work in progress. As Vice. Adm. Lewis commented on these challenges: "We are working hard on this challenge. My main effort as the Commander of two NATO commands and a U.S. Fleet command is to ensure there are no seams in the Atlantic, seams that our adversaries can exploit.[67] By communicating and working closely with our counterparts on the other side of the Atlantic, we can ensure we are working to close any perceived gaps. As an example, we recently conducted staff talks with Second Fleet, Sixth Fleet and II MEF. We are making progress thanks to the relationships we have spent time developing.

"In terms of C², we can always be better about how we exercise command and control. My focus has been on the principles of mission command in which you emphasize trust with your commanders to lead distributed forces. You must first understand the environment, and then you must give clear intent. Once you have given this guidance, you let the distributed forces operate in a way that allows them to self-organize to meet the objectives of the mission. This doesn't involve a whole lot of detailed control from various headquarters, rather it only provides enabling guidance that allows them to take initiative at the right level and to manage risk at the right level."

---

67 On the Russian approach to seam warfare, see Robbin Laird, "Seam Warfare, Exercises and Deterrence,: *Second Line of Defense* (September 15, 2021), https://sldinfo. com/2021/09/seam-warfare-exercises-and-deterrence/.

Working the Allied Integration Challenge for North Atlantic Defense

Working Command and Control is a key element for shaping an effective integrated but distributed force. But simply doing this at the fleet level is hardly sufficient. This must be done with the relevant joint force—and in the North Atlantic airpower is a very crucial element to integrate whether it is provided on the joint level by the USAF or the USMC or certainly in the case of the U.S. Army with regard to missile defense—and with the engagement of the capabilities, efforts, and interests of our allies. And this requires that the U.S. Navy does a much better job of integrating with allied navies and forces, something which has been prioritized from the standup of C2F.

Vice. Adm. Lewis put this clearly in his speech to DSI's Annual Joint Networks summit cited earlier. According to Vice. Adm. Lewis: "No one nation can face today's security challenges alone. The Joint service, allies and partners are force multipliers. Serving together, studying together, and participating in exercises together only increases our combined operational readiness.

"However, these relationships require time, effort, and we cannot assume that because they exist today, they will exist tomorrow. We value these relationships, and it takes concerted effort to build and maintain them—a critical advantage we hold over our competitors…. Maintaining security and stability in the Atlantic is a responsibility shared amongst many in order to ensure the international waters where we all operate remain free and open. Rather, it is a shared responsibility to ensure we are making changes to the way we operate TODAY, versus waiting until after hostilities start. We cannot afford to learn those lessons the hard way."

This approach ties in directly to the focus on the command as a warfighting weapon. Its value is driven by how the fleet can integrate across the combined air-maritime-land forces operated by NATO nations across the domain of the Atlantic. And this is about 360-degree defense operations, inclusive of undersea assets as well as space assets. It really is a kill web approach built around a comprehensive focus on C^2, mission command, and an open aperture to encompass the best of new C^2 technologies and leaving the rest.

By forging C2F as the command element working with Allied JFC, the real-world interaction between national fleets and C^2 integration can be worked to ensure the capability to fight tonite as well as evolving the template for incorporating new technologies and capabilities into the evolving force. As Cmdr. Guy, the head of CJOS COE put it in our discussions with him, they were supporting the Second Fleet's mission of being able to fight tonight more effectively. To do so means finding ways for the U.S. and the allies to integrate the current capabilities more effectively. And this, in many cases, requires relatively low-level technology solutions, but requires ensuring that NATO C^2 systems are compatible with U.S. ships and for U.S. Navy training exercises to encompass C^2 with European NATO navies.

As Cmdr. Guy put it: "In Second Fleet terms, we are very focused on the practical C^2 aspects, notably making sure that U.S. Carrier Strike Groups and Expeditionary Strike Groups are familiar with NATO tactics. We are focused, for example, on working with CSG-4 to ensure that NATO familiarity is built into their training approach. And we work on the reverse as well with European NATO navies ensuring familiarity with U.S. Navy procedures."

He added: "We are far from being alliance navies being completely integrated, and we are focused on the low hanging fruit. Some of this is about technology; some of it is about different operational cultures. Vice Admiral Lewis has been focused on having NATO C^2 installed on U.S. Navy ships and upon shaping exercises and training whereby the operational cultural differences are attenuated. We must ensure that Second Fleet has what it needs to be the most effective multinational maritime component command it can be, on Day Zero."

The importance of the co-location of Allied JFC Norfolk with C2F is crucial to shaping new ways to integrate the U.S. Navy with the "relevant nations." In a discussion with Capt. Paul Russell, the Assistant Chief of Staff for Operations at the Allied JFC Norfolk command, he highlighted the practical working relationships central to shaping an effective way ahead. As Captain Russell put it during the interview: "We provide a portal into NATO for the Second Fleet. The Second Fleet is the tactical maneuver headquarters, but as a NATO command, we are focused on our role as an operational headquarters on protecting and defending the strategic lines of communication between Europe and America."

Capt. Russell argued that NATO European navies, in part because of their size, work closely together. He sees the co-location with C2F as an opportunity to bring that experience to be able to work more closely with the U.S. Navy. And as Vice. Adm. Lewis has sought to put NATO C^2 on U.S. Navy ships, this effort will become more widespread and effective as well. According to Capt. Russell, one focus area on working with the U.S. fleet is to ensure that it works to NATO standards, and not just U.S. Navy standards. He noted: "NATO procedures are well-founded and need to be incorporated on the U.S. Navy side more effectively as well." Obviously, doing so will allow for a more effective integrated distributed force.

Changes in NATO policies are allowing for more flexible national engagements with other NATO nations' navies, he underscored. Rather than a more rigid process of committing national platforms to a particular joint command, more flexibility is being generated whereby national deployments for national purposes can provide capabilities for task forces for a specific duration to achieve a particular policy or combat effect. This is a clear statement as well of how shaping and operating modular task forces is a key way ahead for force distribution and integration.

Capt. Russell argued that "When one discusses the kill web, I would argue that the most gains in being able to do so will come for changes in policy, not simply technology."

The kind of policy changes crucial to progress in better integratability revolve around shaping more effective security management systems, such as foreign disclosure agreements, better use of software gateways to allow for more effective sharing of information, and the key element of shared training and warfare integration.

Capt. Russell noted that with regard to the Royal Navy and the United States, the common aircraft, the common training and common operations being shared between the USMC and the Royal Navy onboard HMS Queen Elizabeth is a key element of the kill web. "That engagement demonstrates an element of trust and information sharing beyond anything that has been shown before."

And the kill web template allows for significant innovation as well, across the allied, joint forces and fleet operations chessboard. For example, the USAF operating their F-35s from Lakenheath can work fleet integration up to and including integration with the Nordic air and sea forces, for Nordics have F-35s and are working air-sea integration. The B-1 bombers which showed up in Norway for an exercise, can be part of fleet operations as well by providing significantly expanded payloads to be leveraged by the fleet in kill web enabled operations. We have seen in the Black Widow exercise the use of the USS Wasp in an anti-submarine role, which certainly fits into our notion of "re-imagining the amphibious fleet" and its potential roles.

Indeed, the Undersea Warfare (USW) mission set as exercised by C2F in Black Widow highlights the inherent kill web approach to its operations. In our discussion with Rear Adm. Jim Waters, Commander Submarine Group Two (SUBGRU2), he emphasized that ASW has become a team sport. The Rear Adm. underscored that for Vice. Adm. Lewis, many Navy platforms maybe considered an USW platform since they all have the ability to see, to communicate, and as necessary provide weapons as contributors to what is now known as the USW Team Sport.

Clearly, the submarine remains the number one sub killer with weapons deployed for this purpose. But with the expanded capability of surface and air-borne assets to find, track and kill submarines, the role of the underwater U.S. Navy force changes as well. It can be the cutting-edge stalker or killer or work through the kill web force to get the desired result.

In fact, having a wider range of options for prosecution and destruction of adversary submarines than in the past is a key element for 21st century maritime operations and warfare.

Rethinking how to use platforms is an essential part of the process because the U.S. Navy can practice like Black Widow demonstrated, employing amphibious platforms as part of sea control and sea denial. In Black Widow 2020, they did so in the form of the USS WASP. The WASP was used as an USW helo platform, and the Rear Adm. underscored that the seaworthiness of the WASP and its deck space allowed for the team to use the Romeos operating off the WASP to provide a key capability for the integrated fight.

An MH-60R Seahawk Helicopter, attached to Helicopter Marine Strike Squadron (HSM) 46, prepares to lower a dipping sonar transducer during anti-submarine warfare (ASW) training with the amphibious assault ship USS Wasp (LHD 1) in support of Exercise Black Widow 2020. U.S. Navy photo taken by Mass Communication Specialist 2nd Class Eric Shorter, September 13, 2020.

Another driver for change in USW operations in the Atlantic is clearly new capabilities being operated by our allies, whether they be new diesel submarines or nuclear attack submarines in the case of the French and British, or new USW frigates, or new maritime patrol aircraft capabilities, whether they be the new P-8s as in the case of Britain or Norway, or new capabilities on older aircraft, as in the case of Canada.

Rear Adm. Waters certainly reinforced this point, as in the Atlantic, we have several key partners who work USW and anti-surface warfare as a core competence for their national navies, and their domain knowledge is a key part of the equation in shaping enhanced warfighting capabilities and re-enforcing deterrence. According to Rear Adm. Waters: "Because of the complexity of the underwater domain, it is necessarily a team sport. There are people that would love to say, 'It's the submarines.' And they do ASW and that's what they do. And certainly, it's a major mission for the submarine force. But the threat is so complex, and the environment is so challenging, that you can't rely on one particular platform to do this mission.

"We as a navy have evolved a very robust structure of training and assessing and preparing and innovating. We're really good at carrier-centric integration. But our ability to integrate a non-carrier-centric force, like a theater undersea warfare task force, needs to be enhanced. And that was what Black Widow represented. We operated as a fleet or a task force to deliver the desired combat effect."

In short, the kind of kill web "matesmanship" discussed in the last chapter is a key element of how the U.S. Navy is reworking its approach to North Atlantic Defense. And the transition of C2F and Allied Joint Force Command Norfolk from startup commands to operational commands is a key part of this effort.

As VADM Lewis noted in an interview we did with him after his retirement and in the context of the 2022 Ukrainian crisis: "The kind of integration which Allied Joint Force Command is working among the allies is crucial and is clearly important for enhanced warfighting deterrent capabilities necessary for crisis such as we are seeing in Europe currently.

"We cannot forget how challenging both Europe and the Mediterranean remain as we refocus on the Pacific. The kind of integration which we have put together and is evolving in the Norfolk commands is crucial to have the kind of integratability crucial to a way ahead for European defense."

CHAPTER NINE:

SHAPING A WAY AHEAD

There is a saying impressed from the beginning of the military journey at the U.S. Naval Academy on Midshipman: Ship, Shipmates, Self. It has a bedrock truth that at whatever rank in the U.S. Sea Services, Navy, or Marine: the individual has become part of something greater than just themselves.

To fight and win as a finely trained team means the difference between victory and defeat. Empowering the U.S. and Allied military forces with the absolutely best technology, training, and leadership for the deadly serious occupation of defending their fellow citizens as combat warriors putting their life on the line is everything. It is no good to talk about future technologies without starting from the nature of warfare and of the human engagement factor in that warfare.

Often looking at battles from the earliest recorded days, the forces engaged had a simple guiding rule: kill the enemy in greater numbers. There is no hard and fast rule from history of what tips a battle one way or another except one core principle: the will and means to continue to degrade one's opponent enhances winning.

For example, in very up close and personal ground combat, the combat utility of the basic Marine infantry rifle platoon member is to acquire the target and then accurately engage to kill the enemy. That type of engagement is at a very basic level but in principle is no different than senior Admirals having the same dynamic with their fighting fleet in which all hands acquire and engage targets using the different mixed and matched payloads that have evolved over time.

This universal way of war is correctly referred to as combined arms, in which layer after layer of direct and indirect fires, kinetic and non-kinetic, weapons are engaged to defeat the enemy. In fighting against a reactive enemy in a larger battle, the aggregation and disaggregation of sensor and shooter platforms with no platform fighting alone is the commander's goal. Making it all come together effectively is the challenge.

A unifying focus to identify and utilize the most effective "weapons on" can make the difference between victory or defeat in a battle. For example, at the most basic level of sea service combat, the Marine infantry squad leader directs his combat force by pre-briefing, briefing, and then direct voice commands to maneuver his fire team elements during the very confusing heat of combat, often accurately called the "fog" of war.

Using voice commands since biblical days is essentially fighting at the speed of sound and it is up close and personal. However, with early electronic devices, for example the Civil War telegraph, the fighting forces were reaching electronically up and down the chain-of-command to be part of a greater focused unity of purpose combat force.

Nothing has changed with today's modernization in terms of the importance of the need to communicate quickly and accurately as the technology of weapons, platforms, and communication systems change. Commanders at the highest level must keep cohesion of the combat engagement mission by effective communications, while concurrently relying on all to engage intelligently relying on their individual initiative to fight to the best of their ability.

Often when direct coms fail, it is the commander's guidance that carries the day. Admiral Nelson had perhaps one of the best succinct commanders' guidance in Navy history: "No captain can do very wrong if he places his ship alongside that of the enemy."

Taking a page of command guidance from Admiral Arleigh Burke and his command of U.S. destroyers in WWII, his standing order in all cases was: "Destroyers to attack on enemy contact WITHOUT ORDERS from the task force commander." Fittingly, the best class of destroyers ever built have been named for "31 Knot" Burke.

Communicated information and warfighter initiative is essential for the empowerment of the force. The key is to ensure a maximum capability for combat operations to be able to operate both synergistically and independently with accurate real time dynamic intelligence at the right level at the right time to make their combat function superior to the enemy.

Very little is different from the deck of Navy strike force or air battle or ground commander building a battle plan from a Marine platoon commander up the chain of command except the complexity of all the "moving parts" to be managed and employed to fight that often are also spread out over very great distance.

Since all military technology is relative against a reactive enemy, a war-winning critical factor is both the capabilities of weapon platforms combined with the intangible expressed by Admiral Nimitz to his WWII Pacific forces of "train, train, train." A perfect nautical example of the dynamic of ever improvement of weapons payload effectiveness and training is captured by the seminal work of Elting E. Morison.[68] This case involves the improvement in the accuracy of Naval gunners. Between 1899 to 1905 because of the introduction of naval continuous gunnery aim firing advances and improved optical sighting (telescope), British and American Navy gunners improved their accuracy by 3000% in six years. Such accuracy could be measured on gunnery ranges and working out new ways to take advantage of the new technologies was a key focus of the training regimes as well.

In this journey to effective gun-fighting at sea much credit is given to Admiral Sims, USNA class of 1880, who is known as "the father of naval gunnery" and who served twice as President of the U.S. Naval War College. He also received the Pulitzer Prize for his book *The Victory at Sea* about his experience commanding U.S. Naval Forces in Europe. In addition to

---

68 Elting E. Morison, *Men, Machines and Modern Times* (MIT Press, 50th Anniversary Edition), 2016.

reshaping the approach to enhanced naval gun effectiveness, he was also extremely successful in addressing the German U-Boat threat in World War I against Atlantic freighters.

To bring the proven demonstrated technological performance of a U.S. Navy payload accuracy in focus in modern 21st century war at sea two brilliant examples come to mind. The first was Operation Burnt Frost in which the USS Lake Erie CG-70 firing a Standard Missile 3 (SM-3) successfully shot down a satellite. The Aegis ballistic missile ship was used because that technology had had a 13 out of 15 success rates against missiles.

Petty Officer 2nd Class Robert W. Polt, fire controlman, radar system controller for the Pearl Harbor based guided-missile cruiser USS Lake Erie, is awarded the Joint Service Commendation Medal by Adm. Timothy J. Keating, commander of U.S. Pacific Command, during an awards ceremony on board Lake Erie at Naval Station Pearl Harbor. Polt received the award for his participation in Operation Burnt Frost, Feb. 2 to 22. During the operation, Lake Erie Sailors orchestrated an unprecedented intercept of a malfunctioning satellite by utilizing a modified Standard Missile-3 and the AEGIS weapons system, which resulted in the destruction of the satellite. Photo by Petty Officer 1st Class James Foehl. March 24, 2008.

The second was the successful barrage fire from USS Porter DDG-78 and USS Ross DDG-71 Burke destroyers successfully firing 59 out of 60 Tomahawk missiles against the Syrian air base at Shayrat. Sixty-nine Burkes are in the fleet with 20 more on contract.

The performance of the leadership and crew of Lake Erie, Porter, and Ross again personifies the fleet guidance from a legendary combat Naval Officer Arleigh Burke who captured the essence of combat winning in the U.S. Navy with a direct challenge: "This ship is built to fight. You better know how." Admiral Burke's CNO command guidance "Knowing how" challenges all levels of command to understand and successfully implement a payload utility function. Be it a single ship or a combined fleet believing that no platform needs fight alone, if possible, effective payload "weapons on" can mean the difference between victory or defeat.

Weapons and the Payload/Utility Function

In both an offensive and defensive combat engagement moment, successfully getting "weapons on" is essential. Using the famous OODA loop equation can bring a clear understanding of the complex dynamics in building a scalable combined fleet kill web payload utility (PU) function. Observe/Orient (O/O) is target acquisition (TA) and Decide Act (DA) is target engagement.[69]

Both TA and TE can be expressed in a very simple formula. The conceptual formula is TA and TE with more effective employment of all payloads available to the battle commander. It is the process of understanding and applying in combat the huge complexities of such a formula that is the challenge.

The quality of uniformed military personnel is critical, and the ability to mobilize rapidly and effectively is crucial. The tactical skills of combat leaders at all ranks are essential, and the correct focus on constant appropriate training makes it all come together. U.S. military doctrine must always be dynamic enough to empower all the crucial intangible components of a payload utility function when war breaks out.

---

69 For a comprehensive look at the payload-utility concept see Ed Timperlake, "Shaping a Way Ahead to Prepare for 21st Century Conflicts: Payload-Utility Capabilities and the Kill Web," *Second Line of Defense* (September 14, 2017), https://sldinfo.com/2017/09/shaping-a-way-ahead-to-prepare-for-21st-century-conflicts-payload-utility-capabilities-and-the-kill-web/.

Late in the last century Andrew Marshall Director of Net Assessment in the Department of Defense, for whom we both worked, pointed out a coming revolution in military affairs (RMA). RMA was his insight that emerging combat will have two very interesting components: precision guided munitions, with remote sensors and information war.

Being able to merge precision guided munitions with remote sensing while striving for the timeliest information available is the responsibility of a nation's fighting force, and to always focus on command and control. If the C^2 function at any level has a breakdown the ugly, very true cliché, comes in play: the enemy always gets a vote. The value of accurate secure information for target acquisition and then target engagement transmitted at the speed of light is everything, especially now with the emerging threat of hypersonic precision guided munitions. The challenge is to "fight at the speed of light," communicating the threat vectors of emerging all aspect hypersonic threats, from submarine launched High-Speed Cruise Missiles to ships and planes, to stratospheric incoming maneuvering hypersonic warheads.

Given competent skilled commanders, there are two qualities of a fighting force that are needed for the force to derive the full capabilities of its weapons systems. Both are essential to crafting successful kill webs. The first is motivation or dedication, or call it will, heart, ambition, or competitiveness. It is the quality that makes fighting personnel appear enthusiastic rather than lackadaisical or dispirited. The second is a force's technological capability: the ability at the appropriate level to have the capacity to understand and operate the rather sophisticated equipment associated with modern war.

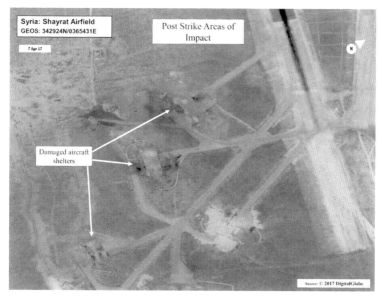

Battle damage assessment image of Shayrat Airfield, Syria, following U.S. Tomahawk Land Attack Missile strikes April 7, 2017, from the USS Ross (DDG 71) and USS Porter (DDG 78), Arleigh Burke-class guided-missile destroyers. The United States fired Tomahawk missiles into Syria in retaliation for the regime of Bashar Assad using nerve agents to attack his own people. Credit: U.S. Department of Defense, April 7, 2017.

Marrying force motivation with technological capability allows a superior force to achieve combat performance over the enemy. It is a combination of appropriate combat equipment at all levels of any engagement operated by trained individuals. Inventory of weapons systems and platforms, including sufficient munitions at the start of a war, can also make all the difference.

Over the course of a campaign significant other demanding factors come to bear: the time factor of both battle damage repair along with any possible industrial surge combined with sufficient logistical supply/resupply. Concurrently, ensuring a pipeline of well-trained individuals from E-1, basic enlisted rank to 0-10, Admiral or General is all again simple to identify but a huge challenge to get it so right at the time of initial conflict. Trained humans matched up to technology are an obvious statement and makes all the difference as a combat campaign progresses.

Twenty-first century warfare technologies concepts of operations and tactics and training are in evolution and revolution. The biggest challenge in the rapidly exploding human/electronic delivered information dynamic in this twenty-first century challenge of modern war because it is all about the ability to have the combat team make accurate decisions using information sensor/shooter light speed communication technology.

The Big Blue "Tron" Blanket

As mentioned earlier in the book, the U.S. Navy built a "big blue" blanket of ships to fight the Second World War in the Pacific. The great historian Max Hastings in his seminal book about the fighting forces of World War II said that after some very nasty setbacks early in the war, the U.S. and Royal Navies emerged as the most effective fighting forces in the war.[70] The U.S. Navy's goal in WWII was to create a "Big Blue Blanket" over the Pacific. Taking from that artful phrase in this century, the goal now is to create an electronic "Big Blue 'Tron' Blanket" which can empower an integrated distributed force.

The American military and those of our allies have fielded and tested communications, networking sensors and shooters that can fight at the speed of light right now. From the depths of the ocean to the heavens, the success of creating a technologically integrated navy fighting force is available right now. From today on, building out on an impressive partnership of the sea services with defense industry ever improving Internal Research and Development (IR&D) and Research and Development (R&D) all leading to tested fielded combat systems heralding the emergence of a digital warfare "Big Blue Tron Blanket" is the proven art of the possible. From today to the next five years forward, it will only get better.

Tron warfare is a shorthand for all things Electronic War (EW). Building out on the progression of EW it becomes not the speed of the incoming threat that is the paramount issue, it is the detection and

---

70 Max Hastings, Inferno: *The World at War, 1939-1945* (Knopf, 2011).

successful reaction communicating accurately at the speed of light to kill the threat that is the war dominating capability.

EW is a complex subject with many discrete but also connected elements. Over time all things electronic in the military took on many dimensions. Electronic Countermeasures (ECM) begat Electronic Counter-Counter (ECCM) measures, Command and Control (C²) has grown to ^C5ISR. Information war in certain applications created a multi-billion-dollar domain called "cyber," and now cloud computing, artificial intelligence (AI) and advances in encryption are all entering the battle space.

With respect to emerging U.S. Navy, "cyber" initiatives, in preparing the U.S. Navy for 21st century warfare, the Navy has stood up the 10th Fleet. According to the 10th Fleet Mission statement: "Since its establishment on Jan. 29, 2010, U.S. Fleet Cyber Command (FCC)/U.S. TENTH Fleet (C10F) has grown into an operational force composed of more than 14,000 Active and Reserve Sailors and civilians organized into 28 active commands, 40 Cyber Mission Force units, and 27 reserve commands around the globe."

"U.S. Fleet Cyber Command reports directly to the Chief of Naval Operations as an Echelon II command and is responsible for Navy information network operations, offensive and defensive cyberspace operations, space operations and signals intelligence. As such, U.S. Fleet Cyber Command serves as the Navy component command to U.S. Cyber Command, the Navy space component to U.S. Strategic Command, and the Navy's Service Cryptologic Component Commander under the National Security Agency/Central Security Service. U.S. Tenth Fleet is the operational arm of Fleet Cyber Command and executes its mission through a task force structure similar to other warfare commanders. In this role, Tenth Fleet provides operational direction through the command's Maritime Operations Center located at Fort George Meade, Md."[71]

Cyber is one of the key domains of warfare, which a modern sea service must master to be successful in a wide spectrum of operations.

---

71 "U.S. Fleet Cyber Command/U.S. TENTH Fleet," https://www.fcc.navy.mil.

The modern warships and systems already deployed with the USN and USMC as well as those coming online and anticipated in the future all rely on digital content, communications, and effective C^2 capabilities to ensure mission success.

The former Chief of Naval Operations. Admiral Greenert, prioritized the importance of cyber and even compared it to the importance that he placed on nuclear deterrence. "The level of investment that we put into cyber in the department is as protected or as focused as it would be in strategic nuclear."[72]

Cyber is often confused with computer and information security. But it is really about information operations within the context of rapidly evolving concepts of operations, as digital systems become dominant players in the evolution of war fighting capabilities. Earlier, we highlighted that indeed such an approach is built into the new generation aircraft carrier, the USS Gerald R. Ford.

Tron warfare is a key part of the evolving payload considerations for the modern fleet in 21st century combat. EW physical attacks can be generated so there always have to be considerations of actual physical protection against Electro Magnetic Pulse concerns (EMP). The necessary counter measures of 'hardening" of electronic components is essential. There are also a lot of other EW issues in a tron warfare, such as Infer-Red Sensing (IR) and always protecting "signals in space" which drives the need for ever improving encryption technology. In a tron warfare engagement, the goal is simply accurate information being successfully transmitted while concurrently trying to jam the bad guys "signals in space."

Tactically, it has been said on the modern battlefield, if not done correctly, "you emit and you die." Consequently, EW can include offensive operations to identify an opponent's emissions to target them in order to fry, spoof, or jam their systems. In a successful tron warfare, often-kinetic

72 John O'Callaghan, "Interview: Top U.S. Admiral Puts Cyber Security on the Navy's Radar," *Reuters* (May 13, 2013), https://www.reuters.com/article/usa-defence-cyber/interview-top-u-s-admiral-puts-cyber-security-on-the-navys-radar-idINDEE94C0E220130513.

kill weapons can be fired. The kinetic kill shot is usually a high-speed missile designed to HOJ (home on jam). There is also the ability to emit electronic "kill" and/or spoofing signals to emit targeted signals to an enemy's incoming weapon sensors.

In our interview with Capt. Brett Stevenson, the senior electronic warfare officer at NAWDC, he highlighted the changing nature of EW in a kill web context. The shift is from platform-specific EW delivery to working networks of sensors, to shape the kind of combat effect one would want. According to Captain Stevenson: "We envision networks of sensors that will be contributing to the common operating picture. That means quicker, more accurate geo locations with sensors contributing to the picture."

To do so, means significant training challenge as well. As Stevenson added: "We need to be able to predict how systems will respond to our capabilities and countermeasures; and we need to shape cognitive EW systems that enable us to look at how a signal behaves in response to certain stimuli and then be able to adapt and have an effective response." How do you train to this? And even more significantly, as one trains, one is also guiding the question of the further development of the systems in the EW offensive and defensive combat force as well.

How to Fight and Win with a Kill Web Enabled Force

But what is necessary to succeed to fight and win with a kill web enabled force? In taking a lesson from history, pre-WWII AT&T long lines research found that in order to build and keep operational a U.S. phone system, the key to success was the need for "robust and redundant" systems. With the growing impact of the "tron" element of warfare, this conclusion is clearly very relevant to force evolution. It is crucial to protect one's ability to operate in a shared communications space and to deny your adversary the ability to do so.

We have argued throughout the book that as one reworks the current force to fight with much greater effectiveness, one also builds a way ahead as new technology can be integrated into the evolving force. This means making much more effective use of advanced technology already resident in the force. A key example is the opportunity to leverage the U.S. and allied F-35s already operational and coming to the large deck carriers in the U.S. Naval fleet.

The F-35 has been labelled a fifth-generation aircraft. However, it is not an in and of itself platform; it is about what an integrated fleet of F-35s can deliver to transform operations. The global fleet of F-35s is a foundation for a fundamental change in the way air power operates and with it concept of operations for the U.S. and allied insertion forces.

The F-35 has a revolutionary sensor fusion cockpit that makes it effective in Air-to-Air, Air-to-Ground and Electronic Warfare aircraft. The U.S. and Allied combat pilots are already developing and sharing new tactics and training, and over time this will drive changes that leaders must make for effective command and control to fight future battles.

As discussed earlier, the wolfpack capabilities of the F-35 can be leveraged as a key integrated sensor and C^2 combat cluster. EW was designed inherently into the F-35 airframe and fusion cockpit. The revolutionary design of a Fusion Cockpit will, as time goes by, give the air battle commanders of the U.S., and allies an emerging new strategic command and control way to fight and win.

Dealing With the Hypersonic Cruise Missile Threat

Force distribution across the combat chessboard, an ability to leverage the basing architecture discussed in an earlier chapter, and the capability to deliver effective offensive strikes to support mobile offense and defense are key elements for reshaping the force to cope with peer competitor missile strike capabilities. A distributed fleet able to operate with interactive kill webs is crucial for both the fleet to be more lethal and survivable.

A notable element of the evolving threat and strike environment are hypersonic cruise missiles. Indeed, the earlier introduction of cruise missiles posed a significant challenge to the U.S. and allied forces, and the hypersonic threat will pose similar challenges but at a higher speed. The United States and its allies are evolving defensive capabilities as well to attenuate the hypersonic cruise missile threat.

And this will be done in the near to the mid-term with a force which operates as a kill web. The mobility of the seabase coupled with the capability to shape new tools to provide for hypersonic defense as a "team sport" will be at the heart of shaping a response to the defense side of the equation. We have provided a report on how this might be done for which we are taking one element from that report to provide insights with how this "team sport" might work.[73]

A hypersonic high speed cruise missile (HSCM) must travel between Mach 5 and Mach 10, or 3,840–7,680 miles per hour, to be considered hypersonic. One should think a mile a second. By comparison, a current missile AA missile operates at Mach 4 and 3.045 miles per hour. Thus, there is a speed differential of between 1 and 6 Mach and as the HSCMs are also in flight, the intercept missiles are at a standing start.

The first look at intercepting a HSCM inbound against the fleet is one of the first verbal math problem we all had in Algebra 1: "A train leaves a station going 50 mph. Another train leaves its station going 80 mph… The logic of that example is that both HSCM and intercept missile are on the "same track" and a parallel track for a perfect "face-shot."

However, the crossing angle to intercept may be much more significant, say for example an F-35 flying on a heading of 090 and the pilot's cockpit's fusion display picks up a High-Speed Cruise Missile (HSCM) coming at the Fleet heading 180 and the closest point of approach for the physical passing of the F-35 on station and HSCM for intercept is offset by, say, 30 miles and at a different altitude. The F-35 sensor shooter for an example could be 90 degrees off the nose for an intercept vector and

---

73 Ed Timperlake, The Kill Web and Hypersonic Cruise Missiles: The Future is Now (*Defense.info*, March 29, 2019), https://defense.info/special-reports/2019/03/the-kill-web-and-hypersonic-cruise-missiles-the-future-is-now/.

also offset by some miles and altitude from the physical close point of approach—this is a very hard shot.

The challenge is that at some point in space and time, the kill missile must get in front of the HSCM. It is not necessary to hit a bullet with a bullet. With the current significant Mach differential highlighted earlier, a conventional missile cannot run down a HSCM. With focused R&D perhaps a future hypersonic-interceptor missile is possible but, in this example, we are focusing on the current art of the possible and assuming a +6 Mach advantage given to the HSCM, and it is already in flight while the interceptor missile is on the rail at the start.

Therefore, detection and reaction time for launch and missile light-off the intercept angle for the missile altitude differential makes time and distance of flight against HSCM everything. At around 88 miles per minute incoming, depending on altitude it is a very hard problem. The first issue is simply just getting a missile off an F-35 in the time of calculation for sensing something approaching at a high rate of speed.

An F-35 can see something moving very fast at a distance. How far away is one key metric BUT not a showstopper. Because if the F-35 can sense at a whatever distance it is reacting electronically at the speed of light and there is the possibility of doing something about it. Slaving an immediate launch fire-control solution from the F-35 fusion cockpit sensed HSCM route of flight vector to an interceptor missile loaded on the aircraft hardpoints is one way. But just as significant is the fact that the F-35 sensor can offload the kill shot to another F-35 or kill web shooter with a better chance of success.

To have any chance of success the launching F-35 has to have a certain head on aspect—if the HSCM is beyond the wing-line the engagement is lost at first detection. The kill-shot game for that one F-35 in launching a counter-missile would already be over.

But now think of a 21st century "chainsaw" as a solution set and a way ahead. The legacy chainsaw approach was highlighted by Commander Watson as follows: "Between the 1980s and '90s, much of the fighter/air wing antiair warfare training focused on fighting the "outer-air" battle against a Soviet Union threat. The strategy was to have F-14 Tomcats armed with Phoenix and Sparrow missiles sitting on the threat's weapon release line, thus forcing enemy units to fight through our F-14s to reach a launch point—i.e., "It's easier to shoot the archer than his arrows." This meant keeping long-range fighters armed with long-range missiles fueled and on station for relatively long periods. Toward this objective, vector logic and chainsaw tactics were developed to optimize employment of U.S. air-to-air missiles, superior in both range and lethality."[74] Now let us image the 21st century version of this effort.

The USN strike commander is currently using F/A-18s to refuel F/A-18s. Since stealth in not an issue against an HSCM swarming missile attack, a mix of F-35s with F/A-18 tanking assets can put as many F-35s on a combat air patrol station as far away from the surface fleet as possible for early detection. Coming soon to the large deck carrier is the unmanned tanker, the MQ-25, which will have enhanced duration and range which will have a positive impact on shaping the 21st century version of the chainsaw. That effort can then feed-back for defense in depth combat engagements.

---

74 Commander Jerry "KarateJoe" Watson, U.S. Navy (Retired), Resurrect the 'Outer-air" Battle," *Proceedings* (September 2020), https://www.usni.org/magazines/proceedings/2020/september/resurrect-outer-air-battle.

A Boeing unmanned MQ-25 aircraft is given operating directions on the flight deck aboard the aircraft carrier USS George H.W. Bush (CVN 77). The MQ-25 will be the world's first operational, carrier-based unmanned aircraft and is integral to the Air Wing of the Future Family of Systems (AWotF FoS). Photo: Petty Officer 3rd Class Brandon Roberson, December 13, 2021.

Against even a Mach 10 threat the F-35 data linked information dominance sensor can offload at the speed of light the incoming track of swarming inbound HSCM threats to other F-35s standing CAP right over the Fleet. Additionally, all USN combat platforms can also light up; Aegis ships, Growlers, E-2 Hawkeyes, and other close in defensive combat weapon systems.

Also, the Ford CVN-78 has been specifically designed with an area on the flight deck to configure the air wing aircraft quickly and efficiently with the appropriate ordnance for the appropriate mission. In alternating between offensive strikes, using active or passive stealth with weapons in a weapons bay or non-stealth with a significant weapons load, the combat ordnance on an F-35 can be configured quickly.

As the combat situation dictates the defensive requirements of loading anti-HSCM missiles as stated above can also be done quickly. USN ship design teams working on the CVN-78 figured this all out—switching ordnance and/or reloading. It is no small issue; the Japanese carriers were sunk at the Battle of Midway because they were caught in an arming, de-arming, arming cycle. From that moment forward they were going to lose the war.

The challenge for the R&D community is to immediately give a lot of thought to and research on what type of ordinance, missiles, and warheads are best to defeat a HSCM. It is not just about getting better intelligence through space-based systems to have an historical record of what killed you. It is about the kill web operating force executing the kill function. That is why shaping a maritime kill web force is crucial for the way ahead for the fleet.

The ability to defeat hypersonic cruise missiles is enhanced as the U.S. and its allies learn how to leverage F-35 wolfpacks and their ability to share high speed sensor data. The Navy is always improving of fighting at the speed of light with a command-and-control focus in their target acquisition (TA) systems and target engagement (TE) capabilities to prioritize incoming threats to get "weapons on" using electronically communicated accurate information at the speed of light.

Warfighting in the coming age of hypersonic missile threats should have two targeting elements necessary to defend against such weapon platforms. First, it is crucial to reach back to the point of origin launch pads on land or the airfields or subs and ships or to kill the archer. It is often correctly said if go up against the U.S. military and "if you emit you die." And for many decades the quote "kill the archer not just the arrows" drove successful weapon development and long-range sensor programs. The AIM-54 long range Phoenix missiles on Navy F-14s illustrated such an approach.

The second targeting element is the arrow itself. It is up to the fleet commanders aided by industry and R&D focus to develop a means to kill incoming hypersonics in flight. The future of the fleet rests on success in solving what is often known as such a "wicked problem."

Space systems can assist in this process in terms of TA. But so far what space systems can only provide is more and more accurate monitoring of the threat until it kills you. Space systems are most helpful in TA for targeting the archers. But an F-35 enabled kill web provides distributed sensors and shooters throughout the extended battlespace. The ability to detect, pass on that sensor detection to shooters to kill the hypersonic cruise missile in its descent is one key focus of attention for currently adaptable capabilities. It is about combing TA with TE in the air-enabled force, where the integration of fifth generation aircraft with fourth generation aircraft provide a significant fighting capability for the fleet. The fourth-generation aircraft can be the shooters involved in close in defense while the deployed U.S. and allied F-35 fleet can be a key player in TE with rapid relay targeting capabilities.

To understand the challenge, it must be disaggregated to focus of the key elements of a successful defense. Each surface ship CO, from the carrier to the cruiser and destroyers must seamlessly fit together in mutual defense against incoming hypersonic cruise missile to save both the fleet and their ship. There is a need to fight at the speed of light. This requires that a fighting force at all levels must take advantages of ever-increasing technological advances to make decisions leveraging sensors able to operate at the speed of light.

With advances in all forms of "tron" war, from directed energy weapons, to cloud computing to artificial intelligence to robust encryption, many building block mathematical algorithms are now assisting the process of generating accurate and timely information in making the step from being theoretical to applied.

It must be recognized that "fighting at the speed of light" means networking information flowing at the speed of light throughout kill webs that operate a payload utility function. The ability to acquire and designate threats while engaging the best payload for a successful outcome is the payload utility function.

Command and control are always being worked against a reactive enemy, a time dependent factor that is critical to force level combat. If a commander can count on having the initiative of successful combat ops tempo over the enemy, then his forces can be dynamically optimized as a coherent combat directed fighting force.

S³: Sensors, Stealth, Speed

As the integrated distributed force evolves, the emerging "Big Three" of 21st century tron warfare will play key roles in enhancing and developing capabilities for the fleet. These are cloud computing, artificial intelligence and ever advancing encryption technology. Cloud computing and computing at the tactical edge, allows for more rapid delivery of key information at the point of attack or defense. Artificial intelligence properly introduced into the force provides decision aids to process data and allow for more rapid decision making. The challenge is to ensure that the data is not corrupted by an enemy force, which means that AI is certainly part of the overall tron warfare dynamic emphasized in this chapter.[75] Encryption technology is about providing for data and communications security within a distributed force and in shaping capabilities of integrating modular task forces and for the strategic decision-makers to be able to make effective crisis management and warfighting decisions with the distributed force.[76]

Cloud computing, artificial intelligence, and secure encryption are very appropriate research areas unto themselves. There is also the need to be ever technological vigilant for a counterpunch combat challenge initiated by a reactive enemy that is always working to deny their enemies, the

---

75 For our report on AI and autonomous systems based on an April 2021 seminar held by the Williams Foundation, see the following: Robbin Laird, *Next Generation Autonomous Systems: A Williams Foundation Special Report* (June 9, 2021), https://sldinfo.com/2021/06/next-generation-autonomous-systems-a-williams-foundation-special-report/.

76 For a look at the encryption technology issue, see Ed Timperlake, "Fighting at the Speed of Light: Making it All Work," *Second Line of Defense* (May 20, 2019), https://sldinfo.com/2019/05/fighting-at-the-speed-of-light-making-it-all-work/.

U.S., and allied forces, successful employment of those big three research areas while protecting the development and employment of their own.

The potential of secure data being interactive at all levels of command is an intriguing concept and one which a distributed integrated kill web enabled force highlights as a key warfighting capability. The theory and execution of kill webs by the U.S. sea services shows great promise. A global information network also capable of being disaggregated into scalable forces can provide useful war-fighting intelligence shared concurrently in and out of each combat theater.

This potential real time combat dynamic can be seen as learning at all levels of command including assisting machine learning to recognize threats. This will allow directed combat action delegated down to all and thus can be very significant at all levels of force engagements. In other words, successful cloud and AI research is tailor made to support scalable forces operating around the globe using validated components from a joint data base and has great promise. AI is rapidly approaching fleet wide empowerment to make truly actual speed of light decisions. It is not necessary to try and integrate AI into diverse military utility functions because it will most definitely find its own way in.

Another way of looking at the technological dynamics with shaping a way ahead with the kill web infrastructure is to think in terms of S^3 or the interaction among sensors, stealth, and speed. Each of these is a separate variable which interacts with one another.

The value of stealth, which is simply a survivability enhancement, is ultimately finite. As the military technology action reaction cycle progresses a moment of clarity and caution was expressed by a former CNO. "You know that stealth may be over-rated," Admiral Greenert, when he was Chief of Naval Operations, noted during a speech at the Office of Naval Research Naval Future Force Science and Technology Expo, in Washington, DC, in 2015. "I don't want to necessarily say that it's over but let's face it, if something moves fast through the air and disrupts molecules in the air and puts out heat—I don't care how cool the engine can be—it's going to be detectable."[77]

The CNO was exactly right. Independent of stealth, for the first time in history, the F-35 will have extensive 360-cockpit situational awareness for the air-to-air, air-to-ground and EW mission. The F-35 can load out externally significant weapons load out, which still is informed by its 360-degree situational awareness systems. Stealth currently provides an ability to operate much deeper into an adversary's air space than can legacy aircraft, which is a survivability issue inside that operational space.

Each F-35 pilot will move from having situational awareness in the cockpit to enhanced situational decision-making. This is revolutionary and instead of the current "hub-spoke" air battle management combat engagement it will become a networked distributed system. Each F-35 is a combat "node" in a distributed system of nodes that no longer will need fused data coming top down from the command center to update threats. Rather, each F-35 can generate real time threat intelligence up and out from the cockpit.

Admiral Jonathan Greenert, a nuclear trained Navy submarine officer, and General Mike Hostage, the retired Commander of the USAF Air Combat Command and an F-22 pilot were in agreement on the dynamic nature of stealth. In an interview we did with Hostage shortly before his retirement in 2014 he highlighted how he saw fifth-generation aircraft. "People focus on stealth as the determining factor or delineator of the fifth generation. It isn't—it's fusion. Fusion is what makes that platform so fundamentally different than anything else. And that's why if anybody tries to tell you hey, I got a 4.5 airplane, a 4.8 airplane, don't believe them.

"All that they're talking about is RCS (Radar Cross Section). Fusion is the fundamental delineator. And you're not going to put fusion into a

---

77 Kris Osborn, "CNO: Next Generation Navy Fighter Might Not Need Stealth," *Defensetech* (February 5, 2015), http://www.defensetech.org/2015/02/05/cno-next-generation-navy-fighter-might-not-need-stealth/#ixzz3RuYUUIG1%C2%A0Defe nse.org.

fourth-gen airplane because their avionic suites are not set up to be a fused platform. And fusion changes how you use the platform."

Just like in Admiral Greenert's initial war-fighting community, the U.S. Navy's submarine "silent service," airpower commanders have the same type of relative technology dynamic against a reactive enemy but in a different medium. Both communities, air, and sub, must be ready to fight in a very dangerous three-dimensional maneuvering environment where active and passive sensing and weapons and countermeasures to those weapons mean the difference between life and death.

S-cubed, sensors-stealth-speed, with regard to payloads, notably of weapons, can provide a new paradigm for shaping a combat force necessary for the U.S. military to fight and win in 21st century engagements. The emphasis is on sensors first because stealth or no stealth, the F-35 fits perfectly into the S^3 revolution in modern war. A point implicit in Admiral Greenert's discussions of stealth vulnerability is that the order of the words is very important. Starting with sensors, then stealth and speed (again of weapons) they can be combined in one stealth platform or as appropriate stealth and speed can be traded off against one another using separate platforms.

As Admiral Greenert correctly pointed out, improved radars and sensors continue to chip away at stealth. Military advances in technology are not absolute. Stealth is simply an airframe survivability design feature. Stealth is everything until it is nothing. How fast an erosion of stealth design features is a critical question as well as the meaning of detecting stealth within a fluid and rapidly evolving battlespace. Stealth was a clean sheet design for F-22 and F-35 and is embedded in the total airframe and it is a very sensitive multiplicative factor; one does not add stealth. Stealth is simply a survivability term that impacts the entire airframe and will eventually decline as better sensors are developed.

This is also why passive sensing is also a real revolution. Passive sensing can attenuate the problem of generating active "signals in space" which often can give away a platform's position either maneuvering or an absolute fixed location for a counterattack. Stealth dynamically over time will become more vulnerable as enemies' sensors improve. How long and against what enemy, and where in the world will the anti-stealth sensors and successful weapons be employed is unknown, but it will occur. Modern air combat, just like sonar and silent running in submarine warfare, is essentially an ever-evolving contest of "blind man's bluff."

It is an information dominance fusion platform that can be favorably compared to the equivalent of being a 21st century version of USN destroyers standing on very dangerous and heroic radar picket duty protecting the amphibious invasion force and carrier fleet against kamikazes off Okinawa.

The U.S. and its allies are the only airpower thinkers and practitioners that can learn training tactics and procedures today for example when F-35, F-22 and legacy aircraft mix it all up at a Red Flag. This is an example of the importance of leveraging the technology we already possess to make our force more lethal and survivable. As we noted earlier, Secretary Wynne noted that we already have 80% of the future force today. We need to make that force more effective, more integrated, and more capable of operating in flexible distributed modular task forces.

CONCLUSION

Rather than focusing on some long-term force design or 30-year shipbuilding plan, our book has focused upon forging the future force for today's operational challenges. The operational U.S. Navy, working with its joint and coalition partners, is building out a new approach to delivering crisis management and combat power.

This template provides a foundation for the ability to leverage new technologies and new platforms when these become available, rather than waiting until the "next big thing" comes along. It is about driving innovation regarding how to work a distributed force across the extended battlespace to deliver the kind of decisive combat or crisis management effect desired.

With a focus on peer competitors, four key challenges are evident. The first is the quantity of force. The United States faces a numerical disadvantage and as the oft-quoted phrase underscores, quantity has a quality of its own. To deal with this challenge, greater integratability across the joint in coalition force is not a nice-to-have capability, but a foundational one. And as we have pointed out earlier with core allies like Australia and the UK, the means to do so are at hand, if the policy and security frameworks are in place.

The second challenge is the question of the key role nuclear weapons play in warfare with peer competitors. There is no point in crafting a conventional force design which ignores the nuclear dimension and effect. The peer competitors who are the focus of attention are all nuclear powers. This means as conflict moves from relatively lower-level crisis conflict to higher end conflict, nuclear weapons come into play in shaping both a warfighting and deterrent concept of operations.

This is about escalation management, and one of the key challenges is that the last generation of warfighters confronting the Soviet Union lived in a world, which this generation of land-focused warriors have not. When working with strategists like Andy Marshall, Herman Kahn or Zbig Brzezinski, as we have done, there was little question that the nuclear dimension was a central piece of dealing with a potential war with the Soviet Union or in building a credible deterrent strategy.

But it is clear neither politicians nor many of today's warfighters simply do not live in this world, nor wish to. But facts really do not care about feelings. And the fact is that a second nuclear age is upon us, as well articulated by our colleague Dr. Paul Bracken.[78] In an interview we did with Dr. Bracken in 2020, we discussed the China issue from the nuclear standpoint. He noted that "China is a major nuclear power. And they are one which has missiles of various ranges within the Pacific region. What they have done far exceeds what the Soviet Union had against NATO Europe during the Cold War."

But this nuclear aspect tends to be put aside when shaping conventional warfighting strategies in the Pacific. As Bracken put it: "Nuclear war as a subject has been put into a small, separate box from conventional war. It is treated as a problem of two missile farms attacking each other. This perspective overlooks most of the important nuclear issues of our day, and how nuclear arms were really used in the Cold War."

The nuclear dimension is a key part of understanding how to address escalation management as the fundamental reality of peer competitive conflict. As Bracken put it: "When discussing defense strategies, it is crucial to understand the nature of escalation. One of the fundamental distinctions long since forgotten by today's military leaders and in academic studies is the zone of the interior, or ZI. As soon as you hit a target inside the sovereign territory of another country, you are in a different world. From an escalation point of view striking the ZI of an

---

78 Paul Bracken, *The Second Nuclear Age: Strategy, Danger and the New Power Politics* (New York: St. Martine's Griffin, 2013).

adversary who is a nuclear, crosses a major escalation threshold. And there is the broader question of how we are going to manage escalation in a world in which we are pushing forward a greater role for autonomous systems with AI, deep learning, etc. Will clashes among platforms being driven by autonomous systems lead to crises which can get out of control? We need a military strategy that includes thinking through how to go on alert safely in the various danger zones."[79]

A key reason why force needs to be distributed and integrable across the joint and coalition force is precisely to enhance the viability and capability for the force to deliver escalation management capabilities to national decision makers. And it also provides flexibility for dealing with the challenge of nuclear weapons certainly at what used to be called the tactical nuclear threshold.[80]

The third is leveraging force capabilities across the joint and coalition force to operate across the spectrum of crisis. There are a number of terms which have been created over the past few years when dealing with the authoritarian powers which have become subjects unto themselves, such as hybrid warfare and gray zone operations. But these should not be considered as subjects in and of themselves, for they are part of the full spectrum crisis management continuum and learning curve for the authoritarian powers.

For the West, the tendency is to think that there is peace and there is war with nothing much in between. For a Leninist regime, there is a broad area in between peace and war in which they believe one can aggressively contest the West and engage in political warfare and use their militaries to enhance their influence. Put in other terms, a much broader gray zone has been created within which the authoritarian regimes are contesting the liberal democracies with little fear of direct retaliation.

---

79 Robbin Laird, "Reshaping China Strategy: Reconsidering the Role and Place of the Military Dimension," *Second Line of Defense* (April 14, 2020).

80 We have dealt extensively with nuclear issues in the past and have published several essays on nuclear issues on *Second Line of Defense*. There are several books published as well, notably dealing with the nuclear competition of the 1980s with the Soviet Union.

As Dr. Ross Babbage, the noted Australian strategist has put it: "And both regimes, have got great political stories to tell domestically to support their foreign policy actions. For Russia it is about restoring Russian influence and power status and rebuilding a buffer zone. And doing so enhances the Russia's abilities to act elsewhere. For Beijing, it is about restoring the Chinese civilization's globally dominant position to it's their rightful place. Recently Xi Jinping has emphasized that they will spill blood if required to achieve their rightful place in the world. They're waging political warfare using a very wide spectrum of instruments right now; whereas the liberal democracies continue to think of warfare as a radical shift from the normal condition, which is peace. Since the Cold War the West has paid little serious attention to operations in the gray zone."[81]

With a distributed but integratable force inclusive of allied and American capabilities, global presence at a crisis point is much more likely than simply relying on U.S. or allied forces by themselves, operating even with traditional alliance working arrangements. And a key foundational capability which makes kill webs work is proactive ISR and C^2 integratability and done so in a secure environment. The tool sets which are required to do so from a force structure point of view enable the digital native warriors of today to operate much more effectively in the gray zone or hybrid warfare than their predecessors who were focused on the traditional kinetic fight.

The fourth is to shape new ways for full-spectrum crisis management dominance, or if one prefers, escalation dominance across the conflict chessboard involving peer competitors. Our focus over the past few years has been upon the shift from the Middle Eastern land wars to the refocus on peer competitors. The preparation for the high-end fight is a key part of this refocus, but not as the sole focus of attention; rather it is upon an

---

81 Robbin Laird, "The Changing of the Threat Envelope for Australia," *Second Line of Defense* (March 31, 2018).

ability to shape effective crisis management capabilities to be able to deliver escalation control.[82]

The peers we are talking about are nuclear powers. Any high-end fight will be shaped by the presence of nuclear weapons in such an engagement. Clearly, there is a desire on the United States side to protect its interests short of nuclear engagement, but the United States is not the only player in such calculations.

This means that building out conventional warfighting capabilities entails thinking through from the outset how packages of conventional forces can be clustered for crisis management events in ways that provide for effective escalation management. This requires civilians to prepare for escalation management, rather than when facing an event which can spin out of control, either ignoring or capitulating to the peer competitor. It is about doing more than verbal admonishment through zoom meetings or being reduced to invoking economic sanctions, or otherwise limited use tasks, which often have little real effect on deterring an authoritarian peer competitor.

The mindset of the peer competitor is a key part of preparing for crisis management as well. In the lead up to the Ukraine crisis of 2022, our Danish colleague, Hans Tino Hansen highlighted the challenge of a disconnect with regard to understanding the mindset of a peer competitor as follows: "It is as if the two sides are playing the well-known strategic game, Risk. But the two sides are using different playbooks."[83]

This means understanding what might allow for successful crisis management when dealing with such different cultural manifestations of global authoritarians such as Russia or China. This has a clear effect on the forces which might be tasked to perform crisis management tasks.

---

82 For an overview on the key elements of the warfighting shift from the land wars to higher end peer competitor conflict, see chapter one in Robbin Laird, *The USMC Transformation Path: Preparing for the High-End Fight* (2022).

83 Robbin Laird, "A Nordic Perspective on the Ukraine Crisis: A Discussion with Hans Tino Hansen," *Second Line of Defense* (February 13, 2022), https://sldinfo.com/2022/02/a-nordic-perspective-on-the-2022-ukraine-crisis-a-discussion-with-hans-tino-hansen/.

But this means having insertion force packages at the point of critical impact in events which can grow up the escalation ladder. As Paul Bracken put it in a 2018 piece: "The key point for today is that there are many levels of intensity above counterinsurgency and counter terrorism, yet well short of total war. In terms of escalation intensity, this is about one-third up the escalation ladder.

"Here, there are issues of war termination, disengagement, maneuvering for advantage and signaling—and yes, further escalation—in a war that is quite limited compared to World War II, but far above the intensity of combat in Iraq and Afghanistan...A particular area of focus should be exemplary attacks. Examples include select attack of U.S. ships, Chinese or Russian bases, and command and control. These are above crisis management as it is usually conceived in the West. But they are well below total war. Each side had better think through the dynamics of scenarios in this space. Deep strike for exemplary attacks, precise targeting, option packages for limited war, and command and control in a degraded environment need to be thought through beforehand.

"The Russians have done this, with their escalate to deescalate strategy. I recently played a war game where Russian exemplary attacks were a turning point, and they were used quite effectively to terminate a conflict on favorable terms. In East Asia, exemplary attacks are also important as the ability to track U.S. ships increases. Great power rivalry has returned. A wider range of possibilities has opened up. But binary thinking—that strategy is either low intensity or all-out war—has not."[84]

To deal with a world in the throes of disruptive change, shaping an agile, flexible military force is a key element to allow American policymakers to deal with relevant threats in a timely manner. When it comes to Russia and China though the challenge is even greater. It is understanding the global chessboard, how adversaries make moves on that chessboard

---

84 Paul Bracken, "Escalation and Great Power Conflict in the New Strategic Context," *Defense.info* (April 28, 2018), https://defense.info/global-dynamics/2018/04/escalation-and-great-power-conflict-in-the-new-strategic-context/.

and how to not only respond but to find ways to shape a way ahead which makes the world safer for democracy and not the authoritarian powers.

As the late Brendan Sargeant, the noted Australian strategist, put it in an interview with us in 2021: "The work of policy, an art of desire, is to say what the world might be. The work of strategy is to create the path towards that world, responding to all the known and unknown impediments that are likely to emerge. Policy lives mostly in the world of imagination; strategy lives mostly in the world of experience. The art of the policy maker and the strategist is to bring imagination into the world of experience and through this to create strategy that can change the world. In times of great change, the challenge is to imagination, for continuity in strategy is likely to lead to failure."[85]

In short, shaping a distributed integrated force, able to operate with interactive kill webs, provides significant means for crisis management. But without the strategic imagination to use these innovations effectively, the West will simply not get the full deterrent benefit which such capabilities can provide. It is about warfighting and deterrence in a period of serious strategic change. The challenges we face are as profound as those that faced the "greatest generation."

85 Robbin Laird, "Events, Policy-Making and Strategic Imagination," *Defense. info* (May 28, 2021), https://defense.info/re-thinking-strategy/2021/05/ events-policy-making-and-strategic-imagination/.

AFTERWORD: PERSPECTIVES FROM
THE MICHELSON LECTURES

Preparing the U.S. Navy for 21st Century Warfare

By Ed Timperlake and Robbin Laird

February 23, 2015

The Naval Academy Motto is Ex Scientia Tridens –Through Knowledge Sea Power, and that captures the vision for a 21st century Cyber Operations Major being developed at the U.S. Naval Academy. In preparing the U.S. Navy for 21st Century Warfare, the U.S. Naval Academy is in the formative stages of beginning to train Midshipman for Cyber Operations.

The USNA Cyber Center, the catalyst for dynamic innovative course development, is temporally housed in Leahy Hall on the Academy Yard. The building is named for Fleet Admiral William Leahy who was the most senior US Navy Admiral in World War II. The Hall is across the street from the actual path of light that allowed USNA Professor Albert Michelson Class of 1873 to experiment in measuring the speed of light.

The scientific and engineering tradition at Navy is moving ahead at flank speed in embracing all things "cyber." The effort is building on a distinguished lineage of scientific and engineering history. Midshipman Albert Michelson, Class of 1873, and then USNA Professor Michelson, in the late 19th Century pushed the theoretical boundaries of physics at the Naval Academy for the 20th Century Navy. Now on the banks of the Severn River the beginning of a dedicated Cyber Center is preparing midshipman to enter today and tomorrow's fleet.

Every year Nobel Laureate Professor Michelson is honored at the Michelson Memorial Lecture Series in which many distinguished Nobel Laureates and other prominent world-class scientists provide their insights on critical issues. The Michelson Memorial Lecture Series commemorates the achievements of Albert A. Michelson, whose experiments on the measurement of the speed of light were initiated while he was a military instructor at the U. S. Naval Academy. These studies not only advanced the science of physics, but also resulted in his selection as the first Nobel Laureate in science from the United States.

For example, in 2009, Professor Christos Papadimitriou Hogan Professor of Computer Science at University of California Berkeley presented a paper entitled: "The Algorithmic Lens: How the Computational Perspective is Transforming the Sciences." In the questions, which followed the presentation, Professor Papadimitriou was asked for his view on which country is advancing computer science the most.

His answer was very direct in stating that with all due respect to his colleagues around the world, he believed that the United States was in a leading position for two simple reasons. America has freedom of expression, which generated a framework for the development of innovative approaches, and the financial support was significant for innovative research and applications as well.

Cyber science is a new academic discipline for advancing military combat operations and it clearly is intellectually exciting to be a Midshipman at the Naval Academy during this significant moment in time. The Midshipmen are "plank holders" in a new field of study.

And it is a field of study, which is foundational for 21st century warfare. Cyber is one of the key domains of warfare, which a modern sea service must master to be successful in a wide spectrum of operations. The modern warships and systems already deployed with the USN and USMC as well as those coming online and anticipated in the future all rely on digital content, communications and effective C^2 capabilities to ensure mission success.

The U.S. Naval Academy is at the cutting edge of "breaking out of our training techniques." To understand the role, which the Academy is playing, and the approach the USN is taking to shaping new approaches we visited the U.S. Naval Academy in February 2015. We had a chance to discuss the evolving approach with Captain Paul Tortora, Director of the USNA Center for Cyber Security Studies, and with four second class midshipman (college juniors) who are part of the first class of majors in Cyber Operations. Captain Tortora is a 1989 graduate of the Academy as a math major, who then became a Navy Nuclear trained officer serving on a fast attack submarine and then mid-career switching over to become an intelligence officer aboard the USS Eisenhower.

Captain Tortora and four students in the cyber major after our interview. Credit: *Second Line of Defense.*

Because the field is in flux, the challenges are in flux, the approaches to deal with the challenges being shaped, and the mix of skill sets being defined to operate as cyber warriors, Captain Tortora is pursuing an open-ended approach to shaping the Center.

First, it is a center not an academic department. Academic departments tend to become very close ended and rigid in defining subject areas, an approach which would lead to failure to dealing with the emerging subject of cyber operations. An academic department is being set up in order to have tenured faculty, with a goal of approximately 6 departmental members, 3 military and 3 civilians, but the Center-led effort will remain crucial to the continual process of engaging with and shaping the field of endeavor. And as the first classes go into the field and experience feed back to the Academy the subject itself will be redefined, reworked, and taught differently as fleet experience folds into the teaching process.

Captain Tortora explained that there are two different but intersecting processes in play at the Academy. The first is the requirement to teach ALL Midshipmen cyber awareness and cyber security fundamentals. And the expectation is that this beginning effort will be revitalized over time as the graduates lead the way in shaping the 21st century USN and USMC. There are two mandatory cyber courses all Midshipmen take, one as Plebes (freshmen) and another as Juniors, both of which cover basic cyber awareness, security and electronic warfare.

The all-things digital approach is being laid down and built upon in shaping cyber engagement.

The second is standing up a dedicated Cyber Operations major, which is really more about how to effectively operate across the breadth of the cyber domain, similar to more of a con-ops rather than a narrowly technical cyber security curriculum.

Here the goal is to combine the technical fundamentals of this domain, with the non-technical policy and legal aspects to understand the social dynamics within which cyber-attack and defense is an operational reality. As Captain Tortora said in discussing the cyber-attack/defense enterprise, "we have no problem saying 'attack', we are, after all, educating future Naval Officers."

The interaction among the students and faculty is crucial to shaping what should be included in shaping the curriculum and what is necessary for an appropriate education. Captain Tortora repeatedly emphasized the key role, which the students were playing in shaping the major and how to forge an effective curriculum. "They are the ones crucial to helping us build out an effective curriculum; sometimes they refer to themselves as intellectual guinea pigs."

The three-year track followed by majors at the Academy (and remember the 2nd Class '16 are first ever Cyber Operations majors at the Academy) involves technical issues, policy issues, legal issues, social issues and then in the third year seminars and papers. The curriculum already has a number of courses dealing with the non-technical aspects of cyber operations, to shape a more comprehensive understanding of the operational dynamic.

The interactive nature of shaping the field is reflected in the fact that the students in the field are engaging in various outside organizations and attending external conferences and sessions, such as attending the Cy-Con Conference in Estonia.

Internships are crucial as well at places like NSA, and with various Centers located in industry and government which are engaged in shaping approaches to dealing with cyber operations.

The initial launch class of Cyber Operations majors has 28 students and the sophomore class behind them has 55. The goal is to have 40-60 students per each level, with three sections, which can be managed by two instructors per cyber course.

Midshipmen take 140-150 total credit hours of classes while at the Naval Academy with 15 dedicated courses, or 50 credit hours, in a major as part of those total hours.

Only four of the majors could potentially go directly into Information Warfare openings, with another two potentially into the Information Professional community, while the rest will proliferate into all possible fleet positions, and some could go to fields like Marine Corps Aviation or Navy SEALs. This means that in addition to the basic course work taken by everyone at the Academy, the Navy is looking to proliferate officers with a cyber major throughout the fleet.

And as Captain Tortora put it: "It won't be long before fleet admirals will want to have with them an experienced cyber officer and team to help them deal with and generate cyber effects as part of cyber operations."

The four midshipmen who participated in the roundtable had a wide variety of interests and backgrounds and illustrated that the approach being taken to prepare for cyber operations was not narrowly technical.

Sitting in during our interview with Capt. Tortora were four members of the Class of 2016.

All are 2/C and will be among the first to graduate with a major in Cyber Operations. The Midshipman were, Zachary Dannelly, Erin Devivies, William Young, and Max Goldwasser.

Because all Midshipman participate in athletics one was a competitive swimmer another played Squash a third was the Brigade Heavy Weight Boxing Champion, and Midshipman Devivies throws the Javelin for the woman's track team. She is the proud daughter of two career enlisted Marines. Additionally, all four qualified as shooting "expert" on the range with both the pistol and rifle. As one midshipman put it: "IT builds the car; Cyber Operators drive the car. I want to drive the car."

Obviously, there needs to be technical proficiency and competence, but one Midshipman was thinking about becoming a history major, another a Chinese major, and they felt that these interests could be met by dealing with the social, policy and legal dynamics of cyber operations.

These are not folks headed down the path of firewall technicians; but rather participating in military operations, which will subsume cyber operations. And the graduates from the Naval Academy as cyber operations majors will form, in the words of Captain Tortora, "a bow wave of young officers coming into the force that will force change more broadly in the Navy."

We proposed that the process is similar to the ground forces coming out of World War I with the coming of the tank, and that the tank had huge impact on concepts of operations. Captain Tortora commented:

"The concept of change is good, but it is more like the combustion engine changing warfare rather than the tank. The Navy did not stand up an Aviation Department at the Academy until AFTER World War II. What we are doing here is trying to get ahead of the curve."

The course is so new, that the process of accreditation by ABET can only happen after the first class graduates, but the staff is working to try to ensure accreditation by ABET.

ABET is a non-profit and non-governmental accrediting agency for academic programs in the disciplines of applied science, computing, engineering, and engineering technology. ABET is a recognized accreditor in the United States (U.S.) by the Council for Higher Education Accreditation.

A key challenge in shaping a Center on Cyber Operations is to be able to attract staff and to try to keep graduates in the Navy after their obligatory period will be over. Of 60 or so PhDs who received their degrees last year in cyber related fields only a handful went into academics. This means that the Academy will take flexible approaches to appropriate staffing, drawing upon visiting professors, and other ways to bring in the kind of practitioners who would both contribute to and benefit from the dynamic and highly interactive environment Captain Tortora and his team have put in place.

In short, it is not surprising then that the U.S. service academies are standing up cyber learning approaches in their curriculums and setting in motion and educational revolution for the digital warriors coming to the force. But the U.S. Naval Academy is certainly at the cutting edge of these efforts and has set in motion an approach designed to prepare the future Marines and Naval officers who are trained at the Academy for both sensitivity to and understanding of cyber operations.

The Michelson Lecture 2021

By Ed Timperlake, USNA, Class of 1969

May 14, 2021

Dr. Marcia McNutt, President of the National Academy of Science recently gave the latest Michelson Lecture at the Naval Academy. The Michelson Memorial Lecture Series brings to the Naval Academy world leading scientists to share their perspectives and knowledge with the Midshipmen.

The lecture is sponsored by my class at the Naval Academy, 1969, and "commemorates the achievements of Albert A. Michelson, whose experiments on the measurement of the speed of light were initiated while he was a military instructor at the U. S. Naval Academy. These studies not only advanced the science of physics but resulted in his selection as the first Nobel Laureate in science from the United States.

"Each year since 1981, a distinguished scientist has come to the Naval Academy to present the Michelson Lecture. These scientists have represented a variety of scientific disciplines, including chemistry, physics, mathematics, oceanography, and computer science."

This year's presentation was especially notable on many levels. The speaker was the President of the National Academy of Sciences, Dr. Marcia McNutt. Her presentation was truly outstanding, but her personal engagement with the Midshipmen demonstrated what a true scientist is all about – working with the younger generation to ensure that scientific progress continues.

Her lecture was entitled: Applications of Science and Technology for Strategic Advantage. This was how the lecture was described prior to its delivery: "Science and technology have always been essential to the war fighting and peace-keeping advantage of the US Navy and Marine Corps. To realize a critical operational edge, officers must know how, where, and when to apply an increasingly large and complex arsenal of innovations. At the same time, a strategic view to identify "just over the horizon" challenges helps Naval officers build mission resilience in the face of an uncertain future. The most successful officers will competently utilize the right blend of credibility, science and technology literacy, devotion to continual learning, courage to know when to take risks, and foresight to mitigate potential bad outcomes. This lecture will illustrate these skill sets and more the examples taken from a longer career of working with the Navy and Coast Guard on science and technology in the marine environment."

She provided a sweeping historical look at how science and technology intersected with the art of warfare to shape capabilities crucial for the United States to stay ahead of its adversaries. She noted that after the battle of the Monitor and the Merrimack, President Lincoln called for the country to harness science to gain a strategic advantage. That call resounds down to today with adversaries like China and Russia focused on shaping ways to leverage their own science and technology to dominate the liberal democratic world.

In peace and war, the National Academy of Science has risen to the challenge of focusing on cutting edge science and technology trying to always keep America as the preeminent scientific research country known and respected throughout the world. From her direct focus on the cost benefit of ever improving technology such as 21s Century underwater autonomous systems to her direct on scene leadership in abating the horrific environmental effects of the Deepwater Horizon disaster. she presented to today's Midshipman a role model for all to always quest to achieve to the best of their ability and in doing so make a real difference.

I think what really captured the attention of many of the Midshipman was when Dr. Marcia McNutt explained how she learned to set shape charges working with Navy SEALs on San Clemente Island in order to support her own work both conceptually and practically. She demonstrated that working directly with warriors was a key part in working science and technology to support an innovative and effective way ahead to gain strategic advantage.

She then participated in the 2021 USNA Oceanography Department Virtual Capstone Day after her lecture. Having the President of the National Academy of Science who is a truly brilliant and highly accomplished geophysicist discuss research performed by Midshipman in the Naval Academy Oceanography program is a unique moment in Academy learning.

Her presence and presentation provided the Midshipman with a chance to see what a leader in science all is about. How they think, how they work, and how the engage in the right kind of teamwork. She also emphasized the ethical side of the equation and warned the Midshipman that protecting one's reputation was part of surviving and thriving in the social media age. In short, Dr. Marcia McNutt added a significant chapter to the learning which Midshipman have received as a result of the Michelson Memorial Lecture Series.

The Michelson Lecture 2022

By Ed Timperlake

March 31, 2022

"Trustworthy AI" was the research topic which was the focus of the presentation by Dr. Jeannette Wing, at the 2022 Michelson Lecture. She is Executive Vice President for Research at Columbia University. Formerly, she was Corporate Vice President of Research at Microsoft Corporation.

Dr. Wing presented her research focusing on the trustworthiness of artificial intelligence (AI). She discussed the recent growth in deployment of AI systems in critical domains that directly impact human lives and focused on the increasing concerns about whether AI decisions can be trusted to be correct, reliable, fair and safe, especially under adversarial attack.

The evening program announcing the lecture, highlighted the approach: "Recent years have seen an astounding growth in deployment of AI systems in critical domains such as autonomous vehicles, criminal justice, healthcare, hiring, housing, human resource management, law enforcement, and public safety, where decisions taken by AI agents directly impact human lives.

"Consequently, there is an increasing concern if these decisions can be trusted to be correct, reliable, fair, and safe, especially under adversarial attacks. How then can we deliver on the promise of the benefits of AI but address these scenarios that have life-critical consequences for people and society? In short, how can we achieve trustworthy AI?"

Her talk posed a new research agenda, from a formal-methods perspective, to foster increased trust in AI systems. By so doing, Dr. Wing demonstrated both her brilliance and humility, in that she presented her research as essentially a very important open ended "work in progress." In doing so, she recognized that the Midshipman present will continue building from her foundational mathematical work.

Dr. Wing framed the current challenge for the United States Navy inside the ever-advancing information revolution in order to fight and win any combat engagement. She underscored that "Computer science is not computer programming. Thinking like a computer scientist means more than being able to program a computer. It requires thinking at multiple levels of abstraction."

However, tragically it was also not lost on those present in this early spring day that for the first time since WW II, a vicious war has broken out in Europe. The outcome of Russia vs. Ukraine is yet to be determined. But this war highlights that the danger for strategic miscalculation is significant for the nation and our allies. It should be remembered how important the Navy's tactical and strategic role was in abating the Cuban Missile crisis which also had the potential to spin out of control between at the time, the Soviet Union and the United States.

Taking the world as it is on defending America now and in the future, the 2022 Michelson Lecture personifies a mix of what makes the U.S. Navy the most advanced fighting force at sea in the world. It is an ability to combine cutting edge technologies with competent combat experience and leadership.

Dr. Wing's talk brings into focus the most important question on the value and accuracy of information in a fast-moving combat environment. Adding the power of AI must be filtered through a win or lose speed of light function of command and control which is simply stated: Is the information presented accurate, timely and useful?

Concurrently, with Dr Wing's research, four Navy officers, two currently serving and two who just relinquished command are perfect examples of combat officers achieving very influential roles, and in a very significant way contributed to today's fighting Navy, and all are Academy grads. Former "Supe" Vice Admiral Ted Carter, (retired) and Rear Admiral Mike Manazir (retired) former N9, along with current "Supe" Vice Admiral Sean Buck and USN Captain Ben Shupp Dean of the Academy's Math and Science Department, all bridge the practical with the possible. And the Brigade of Midshipman who are the future are the reason the Michelson Lecture series was generated and continues.

Right now, with a hot war in Europe, two Russian military announcements highlight why the fighting Navy has to be ever ready while developing useful war fighting combat systems and con-ops to fight and win around the globe against any adversary:

In a March 14, 2019 article, I asked a very direct question: "Is President Putin diabolically smart or simply a psychopath? Perhaps he is both, because by his direct action, the world is now a much more dangerous place as the former KGB officer creates a nuclear doomsday scenario backed by real Russian naval capabilities: Russia is said to have built a new 100-megaton underwater nuclear doomsday device, and it has threatened the U.S. with it and the device goes beyond traditional ideas of nuclear war fighting and poses a direct threat to the future of humanity or life on Earth."

Then in less than a week before the Michelson Lecture Russian military forces announced they fired a hypersonic sub-atmospheric missile against a target in Ukraine. Both are strategic threats, essentially a stealth fired nuclear armed torpedo, no launch plume seen by satellite sensors, and a hypersonic nuclear armed missile are right now, today, deadly serious strategic game changing weapons.

Fortunately, the U.S. Navy leadership team of the four officers mentioned earlier understood from the time they graduated into the Fleet why the USNA motto is so important; "Ex Scientia Tridens" which is translated, "From Knowledge, Sea power."

Back-to-back Superintendents highlight how this works for the U.S. Navy. Vice-Admiral Ted Carpenter was an F-14 combat radar intercept officer and Vice-Admiral Sean Buck was a former aviation crew member of the Navy patrol reconnaissance community and both are perfect examples of the right person at the right time along with the Dean of the Mathematics and Science Department Captain Ben Shupp, who earlier in his career, commanded the Gold Crew of the USS West Virginia

Fighting at the speed of light with information flowing accurately inside a dynamic payload utility function for target acquisition and then successful target engagement connected to the appropriate payload is the key to solving how to defend against evolving strategic weapons.

A nuclear warhead end of life torpedo is a very significant ASW challenge. Additional challenges such as the threat of hypersonic missiles from a sub-atmosphere shot or dealing with the complexities of IRBM/ICBM missiles with re-entry atmospheric hypersonic glide characteristics must be met as well.

As an F-14 RIO Lt "Slapshot" Carter had to direct and engage multiple bogies using then current state of the art radar and sensors to direct a missile payload appropriate to kill, while flying faster than the speed of sound. The pilot's name on the F-14 at Annapolis is Mike Manazir "Nasty" who finished his Naval career as DCNO Warfare Systems (N9.) says it all also.

The lesson learned from the names painted on the Tomcat fuselage personifies the ever-increasing combat readiness of Navy TACAIR. From the F-14 to eventual Midshipman in the audience some soon to fly the F-35, each generation is tasked to bring world class combat aviation to the fight.

Superintendent Carter should also be acknowledged as the father of the Naval Academy state-of-the art "Cyber" academic discipline. Cyber is emerging as one of the key domains of warfare, which a modern sea service must master to be successful in a wide spectrum of operations. Modern warships and systems already deployed with the USN and USMC as well as those coming on line all rely on digital content and communications moving at the speed of light to empower effective C^2 capabilities to ensure mission success.

The current Superintendent flew in the anti-submarine and maritime patrol P-3 community. That community is essential for defending both the Fleet and United States. With the transition to the P-8 and Triton, the Navy is shaping a common culture guiding the transformation of the ASW and ISR side of Naval Air. The acquisition term for the effort is a 21st Century "family of systems" whereby the P-3 is being "replaced" by the P-8 and the Triton Remotely Piloted Aircraft.

Clearly the combined capability is a replacement of the P-3 in only one sense – executing the anti-submarine warfare function. But the additional ISR and C^2 enterprise being put in place to operate the combined P-8 and Triton capability is a much broader capability than the classic P-3.

The P-8/Triton capability is part of 21st century air combat systems: software upgradeable, soon empowered by AI, fleet deployed, with a multi-national coalition peer partnership.

Software upgradeability can eventually include AI computational systems and will provide for a lifetime of combat learning to be reflected in the rewriting of the software code while adding new capabilities over the operational life of the aircraft.

Hence the essential challenge has been perfectly captured by Dr. Wing with her focus on the trustworthiness of AI. Over time, fleet knowledge will allow the U.S. Navy and its partners to understand how best to maintain, support and dynamically grow the aircraft combat systems while operating in support of global operations.

Since the only human initiated catastrophic event that could totally destroy America as a cohesive nation is the unleashing of global thermo-nuclear war, deterring such an event is the highest calling for our national security forces.

This book opened with a dedication to the United States Navy's early contribution to our "Triad" of strategic nuclear strike forces, the Polaris submarine USS Henry Clay SSBN-625. USAF Strategic bombers and ICBM silos make up the other two war fighting components.

Thankfully, since the very early days of Polaris, ever improving ICBM "Boomers" have been on silent vigilant strategic war patrols protecting us. Our "Triad" deterrence has held.

A well said motto of nuclear deterrence stated by the USS Henry Clay comes from a one of his speeches, "Preservation of the Nation, "and it has worked.

It is now fitting in today's 21st Century American national security defense posture to celebrate the great motto of the USN 'Boomer" the USS West Virginia SSBN-736. That sub was skippered by Commander Shupp who is now in charge of Math and Science at Navy.

The West Virginia's motto represents but one state but can easily personify the quest for eternal freedom for all citizens of the United States: "Montani Semper Liberi," which is translated as "Mountaineers are Always Free."

All enemies of America who wish us catastrophic harm know it would be fatal to argue with the West Virginia and all of our boomers on station. Our enemies should never forget that the men and women of the United States Navy who go down to the sea in ships are serving in the best Navy in the world, and one that is the personification of an ever-improving combat work in progress. All enemies of America who wish us harm should never forget that all our combat forces are an ever-improving work in progress.

THE AUTHORS

Dr. Robbin F Laird

A long-time analyst of global defense issues, he has worked in the U.S. government and several think tanks, including the Center for Naval Analysis and the Institute for Defense Analysis. He is a Columbia University alumnus, where he taught and worked for several years at the Research Institute of International Change, a think tank founded by Dr. Brzezinski.

He is a frequent op-ed contributor to the defense press, and he has written several books on international security issues. Dr. Laird has taught at Columbia University, Queens College, Princeton University, and Johns Hopkins University. He has received various academic research grants from various foundations, including the Fritz Thyssen Foundation, and the United States Institute for Peace. He has been associated with a research institute at Princeton University, at Arizona State University, and at the American Institute for German Studies. He also has taught part time at the U.S. Naval Academy.

He is the editor of two websites, *Second Line of Defense* and *Defense. info*. He is a member of the Board of Contributors of Breaking Defense and publishes there on a regular basis. He is a regular contributor to the Canadian defense magazine *FrontLine Defence* as well.

He is a frequent visitor to Australia where he is a Research Fellow with The Williams Foundation in supporting their seminars on the transformation of the Australian Defence Force (ADF). Recently, he has become a Research Fellow with The Institute for Integrated Economic Research-Australia. The Institute is focused on a number of key macro social/defense issues which revolve around establishing trusted supply chains and resiliency in dealing with the challenges posed by the 21st century authoritarian powers.

He is also based in Paris, France, and he regularly travels throughout Europe and conducts interviews and talks with leading policymakers in the region.

The Honorable Edward Timperlake

The Honorable Edward Timperlake is the former Director Technology Assessment, International Technology Security, Office of the Secretary of Defense, and served on the Board of The Vietnam Children's Fund, a pro-bono project that has built 48 elementary schools in Vietnam.

Previous positions he has held include serving on the Professional Staff, House Committee on Rules focusing on illegal foreign campaign donations to the American political process. As an Assistant Secretary, Department of Veterans Affairs, he was a member of The White House Desert Shield/Desert Storm Communications Task Force. He created the "TASCFORM" analytical methodology for measuring the modernization rate of military aircraft worldwide for both the Director Net Assessment and Central Intelligence Agency and was Principal Director Mobilization Planning and Requirements/OSD in President Reagan's first term.

His Bachelor of Science is from the US Naval Academy, and MBA from Cornell University.

He is a carrier qualified U.S. Marine Corps Fighter Pilot finishing his tour as Commanding Officer VMFA-321.

He co-authored *the New York Times* Best Seller, *Year of the Rat*, along with co-authoring *Red Dragon Rising* and *Showdown*.

Most recently, he coauthored with Robbin Laird and Richard Weitz, *Rebuilding American Military Power in the Pacific: A 21st Century Strategy*.

SECOND LINE OF DEFENSE
STRATEGIC BOOK SERIES

The Return of Direct Defense in Europe (2020)

The Return of Direct Defense in Europe: Meeting the 21st Century Authoritarian Challenge focuses on how the liberal democracies are addressing the challenges of the 21st century authoritarian powers, in terms of their evolving approaches and capabilities to deal with their direct defense in Europe.

As General (Rtd..) Jean-Paul Paloméros, former NATO Commander and head of the Allied Transformation Command put it with regard to the book: "One of the many great values of The Return of Direct Defense in Europe is that (it directly addresses the need) to meet the challenge of XXIst century authoritarian powers. Because the great risks that lie in front of our democracies deserve to be named: national selfishness, divergence of strategic and economic interests, trampling on fundamental and commonly agreed values."

As Professor Kenneth Maxwell underscored: "This is a fascinating and very timely account of the major shifts and challenges which have transformed post–Cold War Europe and outlines in troubling detail the formidable challenges which lie ahead in the post-COVID-19 pandemic world. It is essential reading for all those who forget that history must inform the present."

Joint by Design: The Evolution of Australian Defense Strategy (2021)

In the midst of the COVID-19 crisis, the prime minister of Australia, Scott Morrison, launched a new defense and security strategy for Australia. This strategy reset puts Australia on the path of enhanced defense capabilities. The change represents a serious shift in its policies towards China, and in reworking alliance relationships going forward.

As one reviewer commented: "It is obvious that Laird is not a simple military and security analyst. By reading his book, it turns out that thanks to his editorial work, he is also an experienced narrator with the necessary skillset to tell a complex story in an exciting way. Therefore, overall, it is important to note that *Joint by Design: the Evolution of the Australian Defence Strategy* is not just an academic book that develops the context and the making of the new defence and security strategy of Australia, but because of the wealth of reports about seminars and quotes from key actors, it is also a very credible source for historians. This is particularly valuable when its main topic is one into which it is very rare to gain such deep and detailed insight."

Training for the High-end Fight: The Strategic Shift of the 2020s (2021)

Training for the High-end Fight highlights the essential strategic shift for the US and allied militaries from land wars in the Middle East to the return of great power competition. The primary challenge of this strategic shift will be the need to operate a full spectrum crisis management force. That means training a force capable of delivering the desired combat and crisis management effect in dealing with 21st century authoritarian powers. The book looks at how the U.S. forces are reshaping training to compete effectively with peer competitors.

As Air Marshal (Retired) Geoff Brown commented: "Robbin Laird uses his significant research over the last seven years and his unprecedented access to USN, USAF and USMC senior warfighters to detail the major shift in thinking that is underway as the U.S. works through the training requirements of Allied Air Power when all the domains are contested by a capable adversary."

2020: A Pivotal Year? Navigating Strategic Change at a Time of COVID-19 Disruption (2021)

This book addresses the impacts of the COVID-19 disruption on global politics and provides assessments of the ripple effects felt throughout Europe and Asia. We are looking at the significant changes we see in building out post-pandemic societies and how the conflict between 21st century authoritarian states with the liberal democracies is reshaped. Authors based in Europe, the United States, and Australia have all contributed to this timely and unique assessment. It is the precursor to the current book and provides readers covering 2020, on the one hand and 2021, on the other hand, with regard to major defense and security issues during each of those years.

The book focuses on the significant changes in building out post-pandemic societies and how the conflict between 21st century authoritarian states with the liberal democracies is beingreshaped. Authors based in Europe, the United States, and Australia have all contributed to this timely and unique assessment.

As one reviewer commented: "The post- COVID-19 world will be different. What will it be like? Laird's *2020: A Pivotal Year?* points out the factors that will shape the post-COVID-19 world – a highly recommended read!"

The USMC Transformation Path: Preparing for the High-end Fight (2022)

This book focuses on the USMC in the strategic shift from the Middle Eastern land wars to the return to great power competition and the high-end fight. The path whereby the Marines have generated their capabilities to engage in full spectrum crisis management began with the introduction of the Osprey in 2007, and then entered a new phase with the introduction of the F-35 and now has entered another phase whereby the Marines are working ways to more effectively distributed the force through enhanced mobile and expeditionary basing.

As George J. Trautman III LtGen, USMC (Ret) Former USMC Deputy Commandant for Aviation underscored in the forward to the book: "Only time will tell how the Marine Corps navigates this treacherous transformation journey, but it's not the equipment that will make the Corps successful on the future battlefield – it's the Marines. Their imaginations, ideas and creativity will lead to innovative employment of the tools they are given. That's true of every piece of equipment in use today and it will remain that way in the future. *The USMC Transformation Path: Preparing for the High-End Fight* makes a valuable contribution to the professional dialogue that must occur by giving voice to those who are charged with managing the change."

And in the afterword to the book, LtGen Brian Beaudreault, USMC (Ret), and former II MEF Commander noted: "Robbin Laird has masterfully woven the transformation story of the Marine Corps that began well before 2019 with the 2007 fielding of the revolutionary, long-range, assault-support, tiltrotor MV-22 Osprey, followed by the fielding of the Fifth Generation F-35 stealth jet fighter and the future fielding of the CH-53K heavy lift helicopter.

"Robbin has exhaustively interviewed current high-level commanders and consequential leaders across the Navy and Marine Corps enterprise and has pieced together a fantastic body of work that guides the reader towards a comprehensive understanding of the current challenges as well as the opportunities to be exploited by U.S., allied, and coalition forces within the Indo-Pacific and European theaters.

"Robbin has crafted fresh ideas and makes solid recommendations throughout this work that can help the Commandant and Chief of Naval Operations reduce near and mid-term risk while enhancing the sensing, striking and sustainment power of naval expeditionary forces through more innovative employment of existing capabilities."

Defence XXI: Shaping a Way Ahead for the U.S. and Its Allies (2022)

This compendium of articles published in 2021 and early 2022 provides an overview of several key trends and themes regarding the evolution of U.S. and allied defense. We have focused on several key developments during the year in the defense domain which will have longer term impacts in the years ahead. During 2021, we visited several U.S. Naval and Marine Corps bases, as well as France and Poland as well as "virtually" Denmark and the United Kingdom. During those visits, we interviewed many senior commanders about how they are focused on shaping a more effective military to deal with the evolving challenges from the authoritarian powers.

As former Secretary of the USAF, Michael Wynne commented: "The articles in the book, organized as they are by natural topics, will undoubtedly enhance the reader's understanding as to just how weapons and information technology and the distribution and relationship knowledge have affected and impacted the age old concept that military action is simply an extension of diplomacy by other means."